Rethinking Constantine

History, Theology, and Legacy

Edited by

Edward L. Smither

James Clarke & Co

James Clarke & Co
P.O. Box 60
Cambridge
CB1 2NT
United Kingdom

www.jamesclarke.co
publishing@jamesclarke.co

ISBN: 978 0 227 17462 3

British Library Cataloguing in Publication Data
A record is available from the British Library

First published by James Clarke & Co, 2014

Published by arrangement
with Pickwick Publications

Contents

Abbreviations

ANF	*Ante-Nicene Fathers*
Anthol. Gr.	*Anthologia Graeca* (Greek Anthology)
App.	Optatus, *Appendices to De Schismate Donastistarum (Against the Donatists)*
Brev. Coll.	Augustine, *Breviculus conlationis cum Donatistis (Summary of the meeting with the Donatists)*
CCGTP	*Corpus Christianorum Thesaurus Patrum Graecorum*
CCSG	*Corpus Christianorum Series Graeca*
CCSL	*Corpus Christianorum Series Latina*
CSEL	*Corpus Scriptorum Ecclesiasticorum Latinorum*
CTh	*Codex Theodosianus*
Comm. in Is.	Eusebius, *Commentarius in Isaiam (Commentary on Isaiah)*
Cresc.	Augustine, *Contra Cresconium Donatistam (Against Cresconius the Donastist)*
DI	Lactantius, *Divinae institutiones (Divine Institutes)*
Ep.	*Epistulae (letters)* from various authors
FC	*Fathers of the Church*
GCS	*Die Griechischen Christlichen Schriftsteller*
HE	*Historia ecclesiastica (Ecclesiastical History)* from various authors (Eusebius, Philostorgius, Rufinus, Sozomenus, Theodoret, and Socrates)
HE gent. Angl	Bede, *Historiam ecclesiasticam gentis Anglorum (Ecclesiastical History of the English People)*
ID	Lactantius, *De Ira Dei (On the Anger of God)*
JECS	*Journal of Early Christian Studies*
JEH	*Journal of Ecclesiastical History*

Abbreviations

JTS	*Journal of Theological Studies*
LCL	*Loeb Classical Library*
MP	Lactantius, *De Mortibus persecutorum (On the Manner in which the Persecutors Died)*
NPNF	*Nicene Post-Nicene Fathers*
OD	Lactantius, *De Opificio Dei (On the Workmanship of God)*
Optatus	Optatus, *De Schismate Donastistarum (Against the Donatists)*
PG	*Patrologia Graeca*
PL	*Patrologiae Latinae*
Paneg. lat.	*Panegyric latini*
SC	*Sources Chrétiennes*
TDNT	*Theological Dictionary of the New Testament*
TU	*Texte und Untersuchungen*
VC	Eusebius, *Vita Constantini (The Life of Constantine)*
VCol.	Admomnan, *Vita Columbae (The Life of Columba)*
Vir. ill.	Jerome, *De Viris illustribus (Illustrious Men)*

Contributors

DAVID C. ALEXANDER (PhD, University of Edinburgh) is Assistant Professor of Church History at Liberty University and is the author of *Augustine's Early Theology of the Church.*

JONATHAN J. ARMSTRONG (PhD, Fordham University) is Assistant Professor of Bible and Theology at Moody Bible Institute (Spokane, WA). He is the translator of Eusebius' *Commentary on Isaiah* in the *Ancient Christian Texts* series.

PAUL A. HARTOG (PhD, Loyola University Chicago) is Associate Professor of New Testament and Early Christian Studies at Faith Baptist Theological Seminary and his works include *The Contemporary Church and the Early Church, Polycarp and the New Testament,* and a commentary on *Polycarp's Epistle to the Philippians and the Martyrdom of Polycarp.*

BRYAN M. LITFIN (PhD, University of Virginia) is Professor of Theology at Moody Bible Institute. His previous books include *Getting to Know the Church Fathers: An Evangelical Introduction* and the *Chiveis Trilogy.*

W. BRIAN SHELTON (PhD, Saint Louis University) is Professor of Theology and Church History and Vice President for Academic Affairs at Toccoa Falls College. He is the author of *Martyrdom from Exegesis in Hippolytus: An Early Church Presbyter's Commentary on Daniel.*

EDWARD L. SMITHER (PhD, University of Wales-Trinity St. David; PhD, University of Pretoria) is Professor of Intercultural Studies at Columbia International University and the author of *Augustine as Mentor: A Model for Preparing Spiritual Leaders, Brazilian Evangelical Missions in the Arab World,* and translator of François Decret's *Early Christianity in North Africa.*

Contributors

GLEN L. THOMPSON (PhD, Columbia University) is currently Academic Dean and Professor of New Testament and Historical Theology at Asia Lutheran Seminary (Hong Kong) and author of *The Augsburg Confession: A New Translation with Historical Notes* and *The Correspondence of Pope Julius I.*

Introduction

Edward L. Smither

ON THE EVE OF his battle against Maxentius at Milvian Bridge in 312, Flavius Valerius Constantinus (ca. 273/74–337) reportedly saw a symbol in the sky, which played a role in his conversion to faith in the Christian God. Victorious at Milvian Bridge, Constantine took control of the western empire and then, after victory over his rival Licinius in 324, he emerged as the sole Roman emperor ruling until his death in 337. Mark Noll, in his introductory work on Christian history *Turning Points*, correctly notes that "In the long view, Constantine's victory at Milvian Bridge was much more important for the history of Christianity than for the history of Rome." He adds that Constantine's vision on the eve of battle "changed the course of his life as well as the course of the Christian church."[1] Indeed, during his lifetime, Constantine gave peace and preference to the church and set into motion a relationship between church and state that has never been the same.

What happens to the church when the emperor becomes a Christian? Should such a triumph be perceived as God's will and the fulfillment of prophecy? Or, was it the beginning of compromise and worldly captivity for a pilgrim people? Constantine's life—his career, faith, and relationship to the church—raises questions for Christians and for historians of the church that cannot be ignored. Scholars continue to be intrigued with Constantine the man, his motivations for Christian faith, the influence he wielded over the church, and the paradigm that he introduced for church-state relations. While some have approached the study of Constantine as

---

1. Noll, *Turning Points*, 42.

Roman historians with little interest in religion, others have endeavored to make sense of Constantine through the lenses of theology. The amount of scholarship on Constantine in recent years, 1700 years after Milvian Bridge, continues to bear witness to the seismic paradigm shift that his life and reign initiated.[2]

The aim of the present work is to reassess our picture of Constantine through careful historical inquiry largely within the scope of the early Christian period. Our approach is threefold: to re-examine the history surrounding Constantine's life, to consider his connection to the development of Christian theology, and to then assess his legacy regarding the church. In the opening chapter, Glen Thompson begins by summarizing the most important recent literature on the emperor. Next, through a careful look at the sources, he engages the important question of Constantine's conversion and Christian faith. Though approaching the issue historically, Thompson interprets Constantine's story within the Lutheran framework of *simul iustus et peccator*—that followers of Christ (even monarchs) are righteous sinners. In chapter 2, Brian Shelton examines Constantine's story through the eyes of Lactantius (d. 320)—the African rhetor who had served in Diocletian's court and tutored at least one of Constantine's sons. As far more scholarly energy has gone into exploring Eusebius of Caesarea's take on the events, Shelton's article—framed by the motif of architecture—offers a timely look at Lactantius, a source who was closer to the emperor than Eusebius and who wrote in an earlier period. In a very thorough third chapter, David Alexander re-examines the Donatist issue—the first church controversy in which the emperor chose to get involved. Alexander carefully reviews recent scholarship on the African movement and the narrative of the emperor's response. In short, the author shows not only how Constantine's engagement with the Donatists would shape his intervention on other church matters (such as Arianism), but he also lays the groundwork for an early Christian understanding of church and state that would continue through the first millennium.

Moving from history to theology, in chapter 4, Jonathan Armstrong re-examines Constantine's involvement at the Council of Nicaea of 325 and especially explores the trinitarian theology of Eusebius of Caesarea (263–339). With fresh insights on Eusebius' thought from his recent translation

---

2. See Glen Thompson's article for a helpful review of recent historical works on Constantine.

of Eusebius' *Commentary on Isaiah*,[3] Armstrong argues for a rather Nicene-minded bishop who probably influenced Constantine towards a more Nicene way of thinking.

The final chapters deal with Constantine's legacy and impact on the church. In chapter 5, Paul Hartog challenges the popular notion that Christians worship on Sunday because Constantine changed the Sabbath from Saturday to the "day of the sun." Hartog further evaluates a variety of perspectives on the Sabbath—Seventh-Day Adventist, Reformed, Lutheran, and free church—before returning to the Patristic sources to resolve this question. In chapter 6, I ask the question, did the rise of Constantine signal the end of authentic Christian mission as understood in the Scriptures? While acknowledging that the motives for conversion and the means of Christianity's spread indeed became confusing, there is still evidence for mission following the advent of Christendom. In a brief epilogue, Bryan Litfin offers some summary arguments for rethinking Constantine.

This volume of essays is the result of a number of conversations from 2012 on Constantine. A summary of each chapter was read in an invited session on Constantine at the annual meeting of the Evangelical Theological Society in Milwaukee in November. We were joined by Bryan Litfin who read a summary of his article, "Eusebius on Constantine: Truth and Hagiography at the Milvian Bridge," which has since been published in the *Journal of the Evangelical Theological Society*.[4] Some of these conversations were held elsewhere as Paul Hartog read his chapter as a paper at the Patristic, Medieval, and Renaissance Conference at Villanova University in October. Finally, part of my chapter was developed from the response I gave to Peter Leithart's lectures on Constantine at the Eastern Regional Evangelical Theological Society meeting in Lancaster, Pennsylvania, in March.

The intended audience for this book includes specialists in Constantinian and early Christian studies as well as students of theology, and church and missions history. In light of that, the primary sources consulted have been listed in the bibliography in both their critical editions and English translations. In order to make the book accessible to all, the primary sources cited in individual chapters have been made available in translation in most cases.

3. Eusebius, *Commentary on Isaiah*.

4. Liftin, "Eusebius on Constantine: Truth and Hagiography at the Milvian Bridge," 773–92.

The editor and authors wish to thank the Evangelical Theological Society and the other noted forums for a place to reflect on Constantine during the 1700th anniversary year of the victory at Milvian Bridge. Finally, we are grateful for the editorial team at Wipf & Stock and their willingness to publish this work.

1

From Sinner to Saint?

Seeking a Consistent Constantine

Glen L. Thompson

SEVENTEEN HUNDRED YEARS AFTER gaining control of the western Roman world, Constantine remains one of only a handful of Roman emperors whose name is still widely recognizable. This is due primarily to the new relationship that he formed between himself, the Christian church, and the empire and its legal system. Yet even some of the most basic aspects of that relationship are still hotly debated by scholars. This chapter presents a brief overview of the past several decades of Constantinian scholarship and then addresses several areas where history and theology converge and where consensus is still lacking. In particular, an Augustinian approach is used to examine the motives for and timing of Constantine's conversion and to evaluate his Christian "walk." The final section examines how both Christians and pagans[1] viewed the emperor in the years following his reign, and this serves as a further check on the earlier sections.

---

1. On the legitimacy of using *pagan* as a non-pejorative term for non-Christians in this period, see the recent masterly discussion of Cameron, *Last Pagans of Rome*, 14–32.

"Out of the Mist": The Current State of Constantinian Studies

In a typically trenchant overview of the state of Constantinian studies, Timothy Barnes writes that it was only with the publication of Lactantius in the late seventeenth century that "the historical Constantine . . . began to emerge from the mists of the emperor's own propaganda, of fourth-century polemic, of distortion by ecclesiastical historians and of sheer myth-making."[2] However, as Barnes himself shows in the pages that follow that statement, misreadings and misunderstandings in most of those areas have continued to prevent us from gaining an accurate picture of the so-called "first Christian emperor" right to the present. Yet, in the past several decades much solid groundwork has been laid for a more nuanced and accurate study of Constantine, even though a great divergence of interpretation remains on many key points.

Eusebius and Lactantius remain fundamental to our knowledge of Constantine and his relationship to the church, yet in the first half of the twentieth century it became almost axiomatic that due to their Christian partisanship, both played very loose with the facts. While it is still recognized that they, as all authors, at times slant or omit facts to fit their purpose, the charges of radical manipulation of their sources have now been shown to be totally unjustified. For Lactantius, Barnes notes that the 1958 article of Christian Habicht, following upon the commentary of Jacques Moreau and the numismatic studies of Patrick Bruuns, removed any final doubts as to the basic accuracy of *De Mortibus (On the Manner in which the Persecutors Died)*, written in 314/315.[3] The rehabilitation of Eusebius began at almost the same time with the 1954 publication of a papyrus letter of Constantine that confirmed the accuracy of that same letter as Eusebius had entered it into his *Vita Constantini (Life of Constantine)*.[4] In 1962, two works by F. Winkelmann dismantled the remaining objections to Eusebius' reliability.[5] As a result, the introduction and notes accompanying Cameron

2. Barnes, *Constantine: Dynasty*, 6–7; his entire review of the development of Constantinian studies (ibid., 6–26) is the best single introduction to the subject that I have seen, and the paragraphs that follow owe much to it.

3. Habicht, "Zur Geschichte"; Moreau, *Lactance*; and Bruun, *Constantinian Coinage*. See also Bruun's more extensive *Roman Imperial Coinage*.

4. Jones and Skeat, "Notes on the Genuineness of the Constantinian Documents."

5. Winkelmann, *Die Textbezeugung der Vita Constantini*; and Winkelmann, "Zur Geschichte."

and Hall's 1999 translation of Eusebius' *Vita Constantini* make it clear that, even if it was not written totally as a history but is also part encomium and part sympathetic biography (*bios*), the content must be taken seriously.[6] More thorough and nuanced research into the numismatic, legal, and epigraphic record for the period, together with Wilkinson's recent re-dating of Palladas' epigrams to the first half of the fourth century, have all refined our ability to use the rest of the extant source material more accurately.[7]

Barnes himself must be given pride of place in the narrative study of the Constantinian period. For the past forty years, he has churned out a constant stream of articles and books on the period, cataloging the movements of the emperors, pointing out faulty dates in the legal codes, and distinguishing different editions and revisions within the ancient literary texts—and castigating those with other views. Although it was only in 2011 that he produced a volume resembling a biography of Constantine, his previous articles, and especially his volumes on *Constantine and Eusebius* (1981) and *The New Empire of Diocletian and Constantine* (1982), have become essential reference tools for the period.[8]

Numerous other monographs and biographical studies have swollen the literature on the period during the past several decades. In 1972, Norman Baynes penned an influential biography of the emperor from a Byzantinist's point of view, and seven years later Ramsay MacMullen added a Roman historian's perspective. Five years later in 1984, the latter published *Christianizing the Roman Empire AD* 100–400, re-opening the debate on the rate and depth of Christianization before and during the fourth century.[9]

But it was with the turn of the millennium that monographs on the period became a growth industry. In 2000 alone, three important monographs appeared: Elizabeth DePalma Digeser used the rehabilitated Lactantius to argue that his program of tolerance was a strong influence on Constantine and his policies; Harold Drake's study emphasized how

---

6. Cameron and Hall, *Eusebius, Life of Constantine*, 30.

7. Wilkinson, "Palladas and the Age of Constantine." On Constantine's literary, legal, and epigraphic corpora, see respectively Silli, *Testi Costantiniani*; Dörries. *Das Selbstzeugnis Kaiser Konstantins*; and Gruenewald. *Constantinus Maximus Augustus*.

8. Barnes, *Constantine: Dynasty*. Many of his early articles have been collected in *From Eusebius to Augustine: Selected Papers 1982–1993*. He and Peter Brown must be given credit more than any others for the appearance in the past half century of Late Antiquity as a recognized period of academic study.

9. Baynes, *Constantine the Great and the Christian Church*; MacMullen, *Constantine* and *Christianizing the Roman Empire*.

Constantine developed a nuanced working relationship with the hierarchy of Christian bishops that allowed them both to flourish; and John Curran's work traced how Constantine and his family were integral to the physical changes that turned the capital of the empire from a pagan to a Christian city.[10] Two additional studies in mid-decade re-examined Constantine's relationship to his new faith. R. Ross Holloway gleaned insights from his study of the memorial arches, basilicas and tombs in the capital, while Johannes Roldanus attempted to evaluate the ethical and theological implications of the emperor's conversion and its impact on church and empire.[11] Hans Polsander's 1996 biography came out in a second edition in 2004, while the following year, Charles Odahl's work on the emperor appeared.[12] Raymond Van Dam sought to take a more political approach in his 2007 monograph, *The Roman Revolution of Constantine*, downplaying Christianity as the central theme of his reign and seeing him rather, like his predecessors, focusing on legitimizing his rise to power, solidifying his rule internally and against the barbarians, and his dynastic preparations for his sons.[13]

As scholars approached the 1700th anniversary of the Milvian Bridge, attention refocused on Constantine's dream, conversion, and its aftermath. Charles Freeman sought to explain how the Roman Empire of the fourth century developed into a monotheistic state. Peter Leithart attempted to defend Constantine and the Christian state from modern theological attacks that view a Christian state as a fundamentally flawed concept, while the French historian Paul Veyne argued that only a fundamental religious experience could have caused Constantine to adopt the Christian cause and stay with it. Meanwhile, Van Dam sought to examine the Milvian Bridge incident itself and how its interpretation has been used throughout history, while Jonathan Bardill exhaustively studied iconographic issues in order to "achieve a better understanding of the emperor's philosophy and propaganda of rulership and its relationship to his changing public and private faith."[14]

10. Digeser, *Making of a Christian Empire*; Drake, *Constantine and the Bishops*; Curran, *Pagan City and Christian Capital*.

11. Holloway, *Constantine and Rome*; Roldanus, *Church in the Age of Constantine*.

12. Pohlsander, *The Emperor Constantine*; Odahl, *Constantine and the Christian Empire*.

13. Van Dam, *Roman Revolution*. For Barnes's critique, see "Was There a Constantinian Revolution?"

14. Freeman, *A.D. 381*; Leithart, *Defending Constantine*; Veyne, *When Our World*

These and other full-length monographs on Constantine and his period have been buttressed by hundreds of articles and shorter studies. The bottom line? Constantine's Christianity is now rarely questioned, and his relationship with the church is seen as more complicated and symbiotic than earlier. However, there is still no agreement as to when, why and how he became a Christian, or how his Christianity and his attitude towards the non-Christian segment of the empire changed or remained the same throughout his reign.

THE MOTIVATION AND TIMING OF CONSTANTINE'S CONVERSION

The discussions over Constantine's conversion have been muddied by a lack of clarity on what is meant by Constantine becoming a Christian. Secular historians have often assumed that it simply meant that the god of the Christians either had been added to or had risen to the top of the emperor's personal pantheon, or that, as the result of astute political calculation, he began publicly siding with the Christians. However, such definitions would not have been acceptable to the Christian church with which he now identified, or to its leadership—a church that clearly now accepted him as in some way one of themselves, or at least their most elevated supporter. Thus, it would be more useful to look at the church's own definitions of conversion and membership.

Then as now, conversion to Christianity presupposed an acquaintance with its most basic teachings and worldview. The more formal conversion process included three parts: 1) a spiritual and mental "turning away" from other gods and exclusive attachment to the creator God and his incarnate Son Jesus Christ as the one true God; 2) formal instruction in the new faith; and 3) public acceptance of the rule of faith, or creed, together with baptism. As with the case of Augustine, the turning away could be a process of months or years and was normally achieved through some type of repeated or on-going contact with Christians and their message. This was

---

Became Christian; Van Dam, *Remembering Constantine*; Bardill, *Constantine, Divine Emperor*, 1–2. Since Leithart wrote as an evangelical, his work has received much attention in evangelical circles. He is certainly right in seeking a more balanced approach to Constantine and many of his conclusions are correct; yet his analysis is not grounded in a direct and nuanced use of the primary source material, and his pre-conceived conclusions about Constantine and the Christian state will keep his work from having much impact in the more general field of late antique history.

then followed by a formal catechetical period that by this time lasted several weeks or months. The final stage, public confession of faith and baptism, took only hours and these two steps often occurred within minutes of each another. Such a pattern, however, does not seem to fit Constantine well at all.

There is some evidence that Constantine was exposed to Christian beliefs within his own family environment while growing up. Despite his later claims, however, it appears that his father was not a Christian (although he may have had sympathies for the faith and its adherents).[15] Constantine's serious commitment to the new faith did not begin until sometime after the time in 310 when he was said to have seen the god Apollo while performing sacrifices at a temple in southern Gaul.[16] Yet by the end of October 312, when he defeated the army of Maxentius under the banner of Christ, he was willing to publicly identify with this exclusivist minority religion. While the discussions over his continued use of solar imagery will continue, his personal and total commitment to the new faith was seen already at this juncture in both his snubbing of the traditional victory sacrifice to Jupiter Optimus Maximus on the Capitoline and in his immediate patronage of the local church of Rome and the wider church and its clergy. While he would leave the city of Rome within a few months to return only on the rarest of occasions, he never again left his new religion.

Paul Veyne, writing openly as a non-believer, has noted that Constantine's actions in late 312 have to be taken at face value. First, he cites J. B. Bury's classic statement: "It must never be forgotten that Constantine's revolution was perhaps the most audacious act ever committed by an autocrat in disregard and defiance of the vast majority of his subjects." Then he adds that Constantine's conversion "made it possible for him to take part in what he regarded as a supernatural epic, indeed to direct it himself and thus ensure the salvation of humanity." Shortly afterward he adds that "the major decisions that he took . . . were designed to prepare a Christian future

15. Alföldi (*Conversion of Constantine*, 6-7) notes that one of Constantius Chlorus's daughters was named Anastasia, showing Christianity had entered the family by then and that Constantine later said (Eusebius, *VC* 2.49 and 1.27) his father had called on the Redeemer for aid for much of his life.

16. *Paneg. lat.* 6(7).21.4–5; cf. the reconstruction of events by Woolf, "Seeing Apollo." Also, by re-evaluating Jerome's *Vir. ill.* 80, Digeser (*Making of a Christian Empire*, 135) and Barnes (*Constantine: Dynasty*, 177–78) argue that Lactantius began his tutorship of Crispus in 309/310 at Constantine's court in Trier. If so, he may have been a new source of Christian information and influence on the emperor as well at this very same time.

for the Roman world." Thus Veyne sees clearly that these are not the actions of a man who regards Christianity as "an 'ideology' to be inculcated in his subjects for political purposes."[17] His consistent support of Christianity and its organized church must be interpreted as the actions of a "true believer." Of this Constantine himself was sure, even if others may have yet doubted.

On this point, Christian interpreters should heartily agree with Veyne and they could use Augustine to add further substance to the argument. Too much ink has been spilt on Constantine's religious preferences and political motives. The discussion needs to be turned on its head. This would have been done for us if the author of *The Confessions* rather than Eusebius had written the emperor's *Vita*. We would then have an account of the emperor's early brushes with the Christian faith and teaching, his dalliances with Apollo, Sol, and Hercules, and, in particular, we would know more about how God had gradually reeled the emperor into his church. As it is, we do not know the details, but we can guess the process for Constantine may have been almost as lengthy as that for Augustine. And we do know the result. As the late French historian Yves Modéran put it, "It is clear that, from the Christian point of view, as of 312 Christ had chosen the Emperor."[18]

An interpretation that stresses the divine assault on Constantine and his eventual succumbing to it may be less historically satisfying, even if it is more accurate. But it is more theologically valid and it is the best explanation for the emperor's unwavering allegiance to his faith and his personal vocation within it. He knew that he had been sought and found, and, like St. Paul, he had then been given a purpose that even a young ambitious emperor could hardly have imagined earlier—not merely to re-unite and strengthen a fragmented empire, but to change the world forever. This is what gives his frequent allusions to his calling its unshakable foundation despite the setbacks he experienced in leading the church and empire towards its divinely-ordained future glory. It was his lack of theological depth and insight, not any lack of genuine commitment that led to any future failings as a Christian emperor. From a theological perspective then, Van Dam has set up a false dichotomy when he says "before Constantine was

---

17. Veyne, *When Our World Became Christian*, 2, 7–8.

18. "Il est clair que, du point de vue chrétien, le Christ avait choisi l'empereur dès 312." He continues: "Et on imagine mal, étant donné l'excellence des relations de l'Eglise avec Constantin dès ce moment, qu'elle ait répandu cette interprétation sans l'accord du pouvoir" (Modéran, *La conversion de Constantin*, 8).

a Christian emperor, he was a typical emperor."[19] Instead he was a Christian emperor faced with the same problems as previous emperors but now seeking to deal with them from a worldview that saw the advance of the Christian faith as essential to Rome's glorious future, and himself as the key player in God's plan.

An Emperor Living as a Christian

Already while lecturing on Romans in 1514–15, Martin Luther came to understand that while the Christian, despite his best intentions, continued to sin outwardly, through faith God still viewed him as righteous. From this he then concluded, "God is wonderful among his saints, for they are at the same time both just and unjust for him (*cui simul sunt iusti et iniusti*)."[20] Here is yet another place where Luther was indebted to his monastic order's illustrious namesake, the great bishop of Hippo. Augustine and Luther agreed that, if the Christian is truly *simul iustus et peccator* (*at the same time righteous and a sinner*, as this teaching came to be phrased)—a constant fight between the new man and the old—then the life of a Christian will not always look Christian. Even more so the life of a Christian emperor.

From the time of the Milvian Bridge, we see the emperor supporting the church and trying to live like a Christian, although he may well have been unsure what that meant in many practical aspects of his life, especially in his imperial duties. As mentioned earlier, he seemed to understand that as a Christian he could not lead his victory parade to the Temple of Jupiter for sacrifice.[21] He may not even have addressed the Senate in the Curia, since that would have involved offering incense to Victory on the altar found there. Instead, we find him within days donating a parcel of land to the Roman church on which a magnificent basilica would be erected

---

19. Van Dam, *Roman Revolution*, 11.

20. The Luther citations can be found in *Der Brief an die Römer*, WA 56:268-269.

21. Straub comments rightly "At the very moment of his conversion he was compelled to realize that from then on he was forced to respect the *lex propria Christianorum*, defined by Tertullian; he had to renounce, at least for his own person, pagan sacrifices if he really intended to remain sure of the protection of the powerful God who had rendered him his miraculous aid, or—in other words—if he was seriously interested in appearing to the Christians as worshipping their God. To make a sacrifice or to refuse to make it had been, of course, the official test of religious faith in the time of persecution" (Straub, "Constantine as ΚΟΙΝΟΣ ΕΠΙΣΚΟΠΟΣ," 41). See also Straub, "Konstantins Verzicht Auf Den Gang Zum Kapitol," 297-99.

at his own expense to serve the church in the city.[22] He also ordered the completion of the magnificent basilica in the Forum Romanum begun by Maxentius. But it is not a gigantic statue of a god that fills the apse, but rather a statue of himself, holding his new military standard equipped with a Christogram.[23] Thus his commitment to his new religion was put in plain sight for all to see, even while he portrayed himself as a larger-than-life emperor.

It is on these and other such actions that we should first and foremost judge his commitment to the new religion, not on what he did or did not do to the structure or practice of traditional Roman religion.[24] On that latter subject, he had to feel his way forward. As a new adherent to the faith, he would have sought the advice of Christian leaders or Christian confidents within the imperial entourage. The Roman bishop or his representatives would have been consulted in determining his benefactions and other activities in the capital in the last months of 312. It appears that by that time the Spanish bishop Ossius was already a member of his entourage, giving him advice on his dealings with the larger Christian church.[25] Perhaps he had already begun private instruction in the faith. But certainly from this time on, Ossius and others were used in this capacity wherever the emperor's travels took him. A more thorough chronological examination of his writings might well reveal traces of his theological development in the decade after 312. For instance, Alföldi has pointed out that as early as the Synod of Arles (314) he referred to himself as the *famulus Dei* (servant of God), a phrase used of Moses in the Septuagint (2 Chr. 1:3), and one that became a favorite of his.[26]

On the other hand, even his Christian advisors may at times have been unable to provide clear advice for him in practical matters. For never before had there been a Christian emperor. So the church as well as the emperor had to improvise in this new reality. As Straub put it, "*The Church was not prepared for a Christian emperor of the kind represented by Constantine.*

22. On the procedures involved, see Krautheimer, *Ecclesiastical Building Policy*, 520–25.

23. On the question of whether he was holding a cross, a Christogram, or some other Christian symbol (as Eusebius claimed in *HE* 9.9.11), see Curran, *Pagan City*, 78–79.

24. Already in late 312 or early 313, a mass of denarii and a few large medallions were minted in Trier showing Constantine with the new Christian monogram on his helmet (Alföldi, *Conversion of Constantine*, 41).

25. Eusebius, *HE* 10.6.2.

26. Alföldi, *Conversion of Constantine*, 33.

. . . Constantine, therefore, could not expect any special advice from the Church in regard to his imperial duty. Even when he wished to obtain the guarantee of the Christian God for the prosperity of the Roman Empire, he had to make use of the well-tried methods of traditional Roman policy."[27] While perhaps somewhat overstated, Straub must surely be correct that the emperor's own Christian advisors would have struggled to give the emperor advice in matters of state policy that involved religion. Yet his actions, benefactions, and decrees all indicate that he was attempting to show the church, and reassure its God, that he was a pious and committed believer. While we don't know God's opinion, all evidence from the church is that they accepted him as a "friend" of the church, an imperial "God-fearer" or proselyte of the gate, although probably not a formal catechumen. The Donatists also approached the emperor for a hearing, expecting that they would find a fair if not a sympathetic ear for their brand of Christian practice.

This brings up the question of his delayed baptism. Already a century earlier, Tertullian's writings clearly indicated that baptism was viewed by many as an initiation rite that cleansed a person from past sins, but not future ones. In fact, it made future sins even more difficult to erase! This made for a very real dilemma for a Christian emperor who knew that in the coming years his official duties would include taking part in battle, ordering executions, and overseeing justly a predominantly pagan population and governmental system.[28] It is perhaps this above all that led Constantine to delay his own baptism for twenty-five years. He must have felt the unnaturalness of this situation, for he clearly saw himself in some way as God's earthly representative over the secular Roman world in the same way as bishops were his spiritual representatives. This is the best way to understand his famous statement that he was κοινὸς ἐπίσκοπος, "a bishop common to all."[29] The description by Eusebius in the *Vita Constantini* is

27. Straub, "Constantine as ΚΟΙΝΟΣ ΕΠΙΣΚΟΠΟΣ," 46; emphasis his. Pagans must have been just as confused about how to interact with the new convert. Nixon and Rodgers (*In Praise*, 293), when discussing the imperial orator who was charged with delivering a panegyric for Constantine in 313, comment that he was "apparently a pagan who does not quite understand what Christianity requires, or perhaps does not quite approve." Van Dam (*Roman Revolution*, 10) comments that "the greatest challenge that the reign of Constantine posed, for both Christians and non-Christians, was simply imagining a Christian emperor."

28. In 313, for example, he had many prisoners executed after his victory over the Franks (cf. *Paneg. lat.* 12[9].23.3–4).

29. Eusebius uses the term κοινὸς ἐπίσκοπος ἐκ θεοῦ καθεσταμένος (*VC* 1.44.1) when

accurate when it says, "Just as if he were one sharing in the holy mysteries (οἷά τις μέταχος ἱερῶνν ὀργίων) of our religion, he would seclude himself daily at a certain hour in the innermost chambers of his palace, and there in solitary communion with his God, he would kneel in humble supplication and entreat the blessings of which he stood in need" (*VC* 4.22). Note well the "just as if." The unbaptized were not allowed to share in or even view the celebration of the sacrament, or to take full part in the worship of the Christian community. Eusebius is not solely serving as hagiographer when he points out that Constantine did still regularly kneel in prayer and worship within the imperial quarters. Straub misses the most important point when he interprets this passage as indicating that the emperor was making the palace into a new church. What Eusebius was most interested in communicating was that Constantine was being as Christian as possible in his devotional life, even though he had decided, due to his circumstances, to forego baptism and the public participation in church life that his baptism would have allowed.[30]

But, if he was trying so hard to be a good Christian, how could he have done some of the things he did. The acts most commonly cited are the execution in 326 of his firstborn son Crispus and the emperor's second wife Fausta. Crispus, born most likely about the turn of the century, was raised in close proximity to his father, and was tutored by the Christian Lactantius, perhaps as early as 310. In 324, Crispus distinguished himself with both an important naval victory and a leading role in the land battle of Chrysopolis, helping to seal the fate of Licinius and making his father sole emperor. However, within a score of months he was tried, condemned, and executed upon his father's orders. Soon after, Constantine's second wife Fausta was also put to death. The precise reasons for his actions have

---

describing how the emperor called church councils to deal with issues that were transregional, thus playing the part that the Roman bishop would later seek to fill as ἐπίσποπος τῶν ἐπισκόπων. Elsewhere, when speaking to bishops he calls himself ὁ συνθεράπων ὑμῶν (their "co-servant"). Dagron argues (*Emperor and Priest*, 135) that Eusebius stressed the "conception of the emperor as *quasi-bishop*" in order to exclude the "more radical conception . . . of the emperor as *bishop of bishops.*"

30. On his deathbed, after deciding to be baptized, Constantine acknowledges that God could still restore him to health, if he so wished. If that would happen, he says, he could then finally be numbered among God's people and meet and join in their prayers (Eusebius, *VC* 4.63.3). Whether this reflects Constantine's actual words or thoughts, or just Eusebius' reconstruction of events, in either case it illustrates clearly that the church had not publicly made any imperial exceptions to their normal policy of membership or worship life.

been long debated without a satisfactory explanation. It really matters little whether it was caused by an incestuous relationship or a plot against the kingdom. For our purposes we need only note the parallel with King David. Supreme rulers who are also sincere men of faith at times succumb to impetuous and self-serving actions that belie their religious convictions. Does this invalidate their faith? Not if repentance follows. And Augustine and Luther would not even be surprised by such actions; after all, even a Christian emperor is *simul iustus et peccator*.

Eusebius does not attempt to whitewash the deeds in any way, but simply omits reference to them, although stories must have abounded among the populace—especially the pagan community. Nor do we have evidence that the Christian hierarchy either reprimanded or excused his actions. This is an area where one would welcome some additional scholarly musing. Perhaps this silence indicates that contemporary church leaders were just as baffled about what had happened as we are, but also were not quick to rush to judgment. Since the emperor had otherwise been acting in such a pious way, there must have been some good reason for these actions as well.[31]

Constantine's involvement at the Council of Nicaea should also not be over-interpreted. First of all, much is often made of the fact that he took the initiative to call together the council and set its agenda, at least in part. It is unlikely that he did this on his own initiative, but rather it would have been after consultation with, or even at the instigation of, his Christian advisors. The use of a council had already become the time-honored and formal method for addressing problems within the wider church. Since the days of Paul, Christians had been encouraged to settle their own disputes in-house, *not* in public by use of the Roman court system. However, what was to be done when such local arbitration failed? The natural solution was for an appeal to leaders in the regional church. When even that failed, the North African Donatists in 313 appealed their case directly to Constantine. While accepting their right to do so, the emperor decided against a governmental review of this religious case and instead directed the appeal trial to be conducted before well-known Christian leaders from outside the province—first at Rome, then at Arles.[32] In other words, he was merely

---

31. Stephenson (*Constantine*, 272) suggests the executions may have caused Ossius to leave court and return to Spain, but there is no evidence to support this beyond the chronology.

32. Straub notes that the proceedings were the equivalent of the Roman *cognitio* with the examining bishops serving as *iudices dati* ("Constantine as ΚΟΙΝΟΣ ΕΠΙΣΚΟΠΟΣ,"

following traditional Roman judicial procedure with a twist. A decade later problems in the Egyptian church had spread throughout the eastern Mediterranean, so Constantine used the same procedure, commanding the bishops from across the empire to gather and settle the issues through a sort of episcopal "senate."

The change of the original venue from Ancyra to Nicaea (site of an imperial summer residence) was surely so that the emperor could be present. He did give an opening speech. But since our knowledge of the actual proceedings is so sparse, we do not know for certain how much he spoke in the official sessions or whether he instead met with individual delegates to do some arm-twisting.[33] What does seem clear is that he did not have a vote. This was similar to his position in the Roman senate, where he could offer his own *relatio* on a subject and listen to individual responses, but it was the Senate, cowed as it surely was, which officially enacted all legislation.[34] So while he certainly made his presence felt, and while it was an innovation to have a non-clergyman addressing the group and present at its sessions, he probably viewed it as part of his duty as God's appointed κοινὸς ἐπίσκοπος, and we have no record that the bishops present found his presence offensive.

When the council had made its decisions, the emperor then saw it as his duty to use his position and authority to confirm and enforce them. They were, after all, legal rulings from the point of view that the emperor had called for this procedure and had overseen the judicial fairness of it. Thus, he enforced the exile of heretics. But note that he never of his own accord removed a bishop from office. When a few years later the Synod of Tyre removed Athanasius from office, Constantine was inclined to agree that this would help quiet things in the East. However, when Athanasius personally appealed, the emperor merely ordered him to Trier for further consultations without confirming or rejecting his dismissal. That was a

---

47). I am unconvinced that Roldanus is correct that Constantine wanted Miltiades of Rome to discuss this with a "small arbitration committee" and that the bishop "thwarted" his plan when he invited fifteen Italian bishops to participate and thus made it into a council (*Church in the Age of Constantine*, 39).

33. Eusebius exaggerates when saying that Constantine responded to each speaker (*VC* 3.13), although it is possible that the emperor took part in some of the formal sessions. As an example of what appears to be a more private conversation with a bishop at Nicaea, cf. the story preserved by Socrates (*HE* 2.17) of Constantine's conversation with Acesius where, after hearing of his separatist theology, the emperor retorted, "Place a ladder and climb alone into heaven!" (cited in Drake, "Constantine and Consensus," 1).

34. Straub, "Constantine as ΚΟΙΝΟΣ ΕΠΙΣΚΟΠΟΣ," 48–49, citing F. Dvornik.

matter for the church to work out, and he could only assist in their deliberations or confirm their decisions. Again, we see an emperor who is consistently seeking to carry out his office in accord with what he saw as proper Christian teaching and practice.

Thus, it seems clear that Constantine saw himself as a devout Christian from 312 to the end of his life. Yet, despite constant access to Christian advisors, some more competent and orthodox than others, he (as is normal for converts) only slowly absorbed a Christian worldview and the implications of that for his own life and vocation. He was certain that the Christian God had chosen him to rule and reunite the empire, as well as to further the Christian religion, but exactly how each of these was to be done on a day-to-day basis was often harder to determine. Christian scholars, who still often struggle with how to live their faith in an increasingly secular academy, should perhaps be kinder in their evaluation of how well Constantine succeeded in his "walk."

Van Dam thinks that "in the end Constantine seems to have concluded that perhaps Christianity was incompatible with emperorship. After his baptism he appeared like a typical initiate dressed in white" and that then "like Diocletian, Constantine seems to have abdicated . . . he had resolved the tension between Christianity and emperorship by giving up his imperial rule. Now he was just a baptized Christian."[35] Barnes more specifically has suggested that the emperor's ultimate plan was first to imitate Christ by being baptized in the Jordan, then to abdicate, and finally as a soldier of the cross to lead his army against the Sassanids and achieve the ultimate Christian status of martyr. He may well have thought his baptism would disqualify him from serving further as commander in chief with the judicial power to order executions.[36]

Let me briefly add that such a picture of Constantine might also influence how we view his rival Maxentius. It is common to emphasize the joy with which Constantine was received after his victory over the usurper at the Milvian Bridge. This situation may not have been so black and white. Why would a predominantly pagan populace think that Constantine, in some ways just as much a usurper,[37] would be an improvement, especially when he marched into town with his army displaying strange cultic symbols that seemed to be related to the recently persecuted Christian sect?

35. Van Dam, *Roman Revolution*, 357.

36. Barnes, *Constantine: Dynasty*, 166–67.

37. Humphries shows this in detail in his "From Usurper to Emperor."

This would have caused uncertainty among the general population and significant consternation among the still mostly-pagan elites.

On this issue we must beware of an uncritical acceptance of the sources. It is true that Maxentius had become more autocratic in his last years and had started to make more enemies among the upper classes. And it was not just the Christian Eusebius who blackened the defeated leader while praising the victor; a pagan orator did the same: "Your divine valor and its companion mercy . . . revived Rome when she was downcast and completely prostrate, restored her, raised her up . . . from the very jaws of fate . . ."[38] However, such rhetoric in a panegyric is not useful for historical analysis, and the overblown description of Maxentius' excesses by Eusebius seem suspicious. Maxentius, unlike most emperors of the time (including Constantine), spent nearly his entire reign in Rome, carried out an extensive public building program there, and helped revive the city's prestige. Maxentius "promoted an ideology in which he and Rome were inseparable." The coins produced by his mints at Rome "depicted him receiving the globe that symbolized universal rule directly from the goddess Roma."[39] While he probably did alienate many in the city, the picture of him as a totally cruel despot is probably a caricature.[40] On the other side, Van Dam notes that "Constantine never was truly admired by people in Rome, and left it in 326 in disgust."[41] If we view the newly converted Constantine as *simul iustus et peccator*, we might be less inclined to accept overly hagiographical accounts of his conduct, and how others viewed it, especially at the beginning of his reign when most Romans probably adopted a wait-and-see attitude.

AN EMPEROR BECOMES A SAINT

The emperor Julian would later look back at Constantine as "a wicked innovator and tamperer with the time-hallowed laws and the sacred ethical traditions of our fathers."[42] Many within the Protestant church have

---

38. *Paneg. lat.* 4(10).3.3, from ca. 322. It is attributed to Nazarius and the translation is adapted from Nixon and Rodgers, *In Praise*, 345–46.

39. Van Dam, *Roman Revolution*, 45, 83.

40. Note David Alexander's comments in chapter 3 below on Maxentius's non-adversarial interactions with the Christian community in Rome.

41. Van Dam, *Roman Revolution*, 326.

42. "*[N]ovator turbatorque priscarum legum et moris antiquitus recepti*" (as quoted by Ammianus, 21.10.8; translation by Alföldi, *Conversion of Constantine*, 31.

basically agreed with Julian, although from their own Christian perspective. They speak of a "Constantinian fall" in which he ushered in a period of great outward growth in the church along with an equally dramatic a spiritual decline into superstition, sacramentalism, and caesaropapism. The Latin church came to have a much more positive view of the emperor, viewing him as a hero for ending the era of persecution and championing the faith. The Orthodox church goes even further, remembering him yet in their prayers as St. Constantine and referring to him in their liturgy as ἰσαπόστολος (equal to the apostles), effectively ranking him above many other fathers and doctors of the church![43] But how was he viewed by pagans and Christians in the fourth century?

As noted earlier, the church was just as surprised as the pagan world at the sudden presence of a Christian emperor in their midst. Van Dam is probably right when he says that "a Christian emperor was a seeming contradiction in terms since Christian leaders were expecting that Christ's 'heavenly and angelic empire' would succeed the Roman Empire, not replace it."[44] Yet by 325, many Christians would have agreed with Eusebius in seeing Constantine as a "heavenly angel of God," not just in appearance, but in calling.[45] According to Freeman, Eusebius developed "an ideology of Christian kingship" during Constantine's reign, seeing him as "God's vice-regent on earth, mortal perhaps but enveloped in a supernatural aura as the result of the close friendship and support of his creator."[46]

The sources make it clear that Constantine saw himself as God's gift to the church, called of God to lead the church toward its destiny as the new imperial religion. He thus saw himself in the company of a very select group of historical figures who had been given such momentous callings. He was a new Moses, or a new St. Paul, for like them, he too had received a divine vision calling him to lead God's people out of bondage and to expand his kingdom in new directions.[47] Constantinople, with its Church of the Twelve Apostles, was to be a new Jerusalem as well as a new Rome. And

---

43. Jerome also referred to Origen as equal to the Apostles (see Rufinus, *Apologia* 1.22).

44. Van Dam, *Roman Revolution*, 10.

45. Eusebius, *VC* 3.10.3.

46. Freeman, *A.D. 381*, 13–14.

47. Eusebius compares him to Moses in *HE* 9.9.10-11 and *VC* 1.39. In Heb. 3:5, Moses is called a faithful θεράπων in the house of God. For an extensive study of this theme, see Rapp, "Imperial Ideology."

there Constantine was to be interred in the midst of memorials and relics of the Twelve—physically, historically, and spiritually an ἰσαπόστολος.[48]

At the time of his death in 337, the Roman world was still overwhelmingly pagan. That section of the population wished to bestow even more extravagant honors on the man who had reunited the splintered and beleaguered empire. In his pre-Christian days as tetrarch, Constantine had briefly identified himself with Hercules, just as the other tetrarchs had identified with Jupiter or Hercules, and had even been commemorated as "begotten of the gods and creators of gods."[49] The contemporary poet Palladas referred to Constantine in one of his epigrams as the "god-beloved man" if Wilkinson is correct.[50] Late in his reign, the Italian city of Hispellum requested permission to construct a temple in honor of the Constantinian dynasty.[51] And the abridged history of Eutropius ends its discussion

48. The structure and its purpose have been highly disputed. Was it to be seen as an imperial tomb, a martyrion, a Hellenistic heroön, or a church—or some combination of these? Was the placement of the emperor's body intended to garner the prayers of the apostles, indicate that he was a thirteenth apostle, or that he was even in some way equal to Christ? Eusebius is our only contemporary source of information. He several times calls it a temple or shrine (νεώς) while describing its construction (*VC* 58–59). He then goes on to say "All these things the Emperor dedicated to perpetuate for all mankind the memory of our Savior's Apostles. But he had another object also in mind when he built, which though secret at first was towards the end surmised by everybody. He had prepared the place there for the time when it would be needed on his decease, intending with supreme eagerness of faith that his own remains should after death partake in the invocation of the Apostles, so that even after his decease he might benefit from the worship which would be conducted there in honor of the Apostles. He therefore gave instructions for services to be held there, setting up a central altar" (*VC* 60.1–2; unless otherwise noted, all translations of *VC* are from Cameron and Hall). Thus, the debate rests on how accurately this reflects the actual intentions of Constantine rather than Eusebius' own interpretation. Wortley calls it a *heroön*, giving the erroneous impression that Eusebius referred to it as such (*Sacred Remains*, 352). See also Dagron, *Emperor and Priest*, 138–43; Bardill, *Constantine, Divine Emperor*, 267–76.

49. *Paneg. lat.* 11(3).2.4.

50. *Anthol. Gr.* 10.91; Wilkinson, "Palladus," 43–44.

51. Van Dam, *Roman Revolution*, 233–34, 249. The Hispellum incident is central to Van Dam's book and his entire reconstruction of Constantine's reign, but Barnes has argued convincingly that the appeal was directed to Constans, not his father (*Constantine*, 20–23). Van Dam more appropriately cites an Italian dedication to Constantine at Saepinum that must date between 313–315: "to the restorer of public liberty, begotten of the gods, our lord emperor Caesar, Flavius Valerius Constantine, pious, fortunate, unconquered Augustus, by decree of the town councilors" (*Restitutori | p[ublicae] libertatis | di[i]s genito d[omino] n[ostro] |imp[eratori] Caes[ari] Flavio | Val[erio] Constantino | pio felici inv[icto] Aug[usto] | d[ecreto] d[ecurionum]*); Van Dam's translation, 249, citing

by telling how his death was foretold by a comet and stating that "he was deservedly enrolled among the gods."[52] With ideas of this sort emanating from their pagan neighbors, Christian leaders may well have welcomed a Constantine that was merely "equal to the apostles."

Constantine himself confused the issue. When he erected a colossal statue of himself atop a porphyry column in his new capital, he had himself depicted as an emperor holding a spear and a globe. To many of the city's pagans, this surely looked indistinguishable from statues of other deified Hellenistic kings or Roman emperors of the past. Yet by Christians the image might have been seen as the ruler who had been given power by their God to restore the glory of the empire. Still others probably regarded it merely as yet another grandiose image of their majestic and egocentric emperor.[53] This confusion would have continued after his death. Was it really Christians or also pagans who, as we are told by both Philostorgius and Theodoret, left burning lamps and candles in front of the statue, and addressed to it prayers for healing?[54] Some of Constantine's coinage was also confusing, since solar imagery continued to be used until 319 at several mints, and even until 323 at Arles.[55] Other numismatic representations seem to depict him, just like earlier emperors, becoming *divus* and being taken into heaven, although Harrison has shown that the images chosen were not those most natural for portraying the emperor as either a god or

---

L'année épigraphique 1984 (1987) 94n367. Cf. Grünewald, *Constantinus Maximus Augustus,* 222n272.

52. *atque inter divos meruit referri* / ὁ μὲν οὖν συνηριθμήθη τοῖς θεοῖς (Eutropius, 10.8).

53. Barnes shows that there is no early mention of a radiate crown, and therefore the idea that Constantine depicted himself as Helios is misguided. Citing Bassett (*Urban Image,* 201-4), Barnes shows that the statue was in the form of a Hellenistic king or Roman emperor (*Constantine,* 23–25). Bardill, unconvinced, makes the case for it being a radiate statue, but rejects the claim that the radiate statue represented Sol/Helios. Rather it was "a statue of Constantine sporting certain attributes of Sol, not a statue of Constantine as Sol"; yet "Constantine shared in the divine light and divine power (*numen*) of his protective deity" (Bardill, *Constantine, Divine Emperor,* 109).

54. Philostorgius, *HE* 2.17, and Theodoret, *HE* 1.34.3.

55. Barnes, *Constantine: Dynasty,* 18, citing Bruun, "Disappearance of Sol," 28–37. Bardill concludes that "the solar attributes of the Father and the Son familiar from the scriptures were clearly thought sufficient to justify Constantine's continued use of the long-standing iconography of Sol," and goes so far as to posit that he may have continued its use hoping "to lead others from paganism to Christianity" (*Constantine, Divine Emperor,* 398).

a saint.[56] Still, the coins described by Eusebius that show him riding in a four-horse chariot with a hand stretching down to receive him, while probably meant to show the faithful servant being taken to heaven, could easily be interpreted as the deification of the emperor. Only a skilled theologian could be expected to distinguish between his ultimate *deosis* and a traditional imperial *apotheosis*.[57]

Christian writers of the time, however, were quite circumspect in their language. In his own panegyric of Constantine, delivered in 336 as part of the celebration of the emperor's thirty years in office, Eusebius was not only clear that Constantine had served as God's sole temporal representative on earth, but he also uses the analogy of the Logos' relation to the Father.[58] Yet, as Van Dam points out, "Even as he flattered the emperor by correlating him with the Logos, Eusebius clearly stressed that both the Logos and the emperor were subordinate to God the Father."[59] In the *Vita Constantini*, Eusebius simply calls the emperor "thrice-blessed" (τρισμακάριος) for having reigned three decades and having three male heirs to succeed him. He was greater than any other emperor that could be remembered, "so God beloved and Thrice blessed, so truly pious and complete in happiness, that with utter ease he governed more nations than those before him, and kept his dominion unimpaired to the very end."[60]

Christian writers throughout the fourth century remained equally cautious in their language and attitudes. Several decades after his death, a complete rebuilding of the burial complex and church occurred under

---

56. Harrison, "Constantinian Portrait," 95–96.

57. On the coins, see Bardill, *Constantine, Divine Emperor,* 376–80. He concludes that "The title *divus* accorded to Constantine by his sons on the coins they minted to commemorate their father's ascent was, it would seem, not indicative of absolute divinity, but rather an honorary title meaning roughly 'of blessed memory'" (*Constantine, Divine Emperor,* 380). Cf. Straub, "Constantine as ΚΟΙΝΟΣ ΕΠΙΣΚΟΠΟΣ," 44–45. Is it possible that such imagery of Constantine contributed to the developing theology of *deosis* in the eastern church? The images on the coins may also have reflected the abilities of the individual mints, many still staffed by pagans, to carry out the wishes of the emperor.

58. So Van Dam, *Roman Revolution,* 291, citing Eusebius, *De laudibus Constantini*. At the end of chapter 1 Eusebius expounds on the pre-existent Logos, and then in chapter 2.2 makes the first of a number of such comparisons: "[T]hat Preserver of the universe orders these heavens and earth, and the celestial kingdom, consistently with his Father's will. Even so our emperor whom he loves, by bringing those whom he rules on earth to the only begotten Word and Savior renders them fit subjects of his kingdom."

59. Van Dam, *Roman Revolution,* 291.

60. Eusebius, *VC* 1.6.

the sponsorship of Constantius. Constantine's body was moved from its original burial site at the center of the memorials of the twelve apostles to an adjacent location where his successors were also then laid to rest. Two passages in Chrysostom describe the new situation: "In Constantinople those who wore crowns did not wish their own bodies to be buried near those of the apostles, but outside at the very threshold" and "his son thought he was bestowing great honor on Constantine the Great by burying him in the porch of the fisherman; for what gatekeepers are for kings in their palaces, that kings are at the tombs of the fishermen."[61] While Constantius indeed sponsored the rebuilding, the idea for the realignment must certainly have come from church leaders who were uncomfortable with Constantine occupying his original position. No emperor was either equal to the apostles or a thirteenth apostle; Christ alone was the central focus of the church. It was only much later that the emperor began being referred to as ἰσαπόστολος.[62]

Augustine held up Constantine as a model of a Christian emperor who loved God properly and was in turn rewarded with the gift of a long reign and sons to succeed him, but claims to sainthood are absent in his writing. In fact, the first direct references to him as "Saint Constantine" do not appear before the mid-seventh century when the Cypriot Leontius in his biography of Patriarch John of Alexandria ("the Almsgiver") speaks of Constantine as being "truly the holy one of God" (ὁ ὄντως ἅγιος τοῦ θεοῦ Κωνσταντῖνος).[63] Soon after, Anastasius of Sinai would write of "the blessed and holy Constantine" (ὁ μακάριος καὶ ἅγιος Κωνσταντῖνος).[64] At some point, May 21 became the day when the eastern church remembered the emperor and his mother—οἱ ἅγιοι Κωνσταντῖνος καὶ Ἑλένη οἱ Ἰσαπόστολοι. In the modern Orthodox liturgy, the *troparion*, the short verse chanted towards the close of the Vespers service to set the theme for the services of the

---

61. Chrysostom, *Contra Judaeos et gentiles quod Christus sit deus* 9 (CPG 4326; PG 48:825); *Homilies on I Cor.*, Homily 26 (on 1 Cor. 12:10, paragr. 5; CPG 4428; PG 61:582). Cf. Dagron, *Emperor and Priest*, 135–43.

62. Bardill (*Constantine, Divine Emperor*, 392n373), Pohlsander (*Emperor Constantine*, 92) and others say this began with Theodoret in the early fifth century, but the passage sometimes cited (*H.E.* 1.1) makes only a vague comparison, and, a search of the *TLG* would indicate that the Greek term ἰσαπόστολος was not used of Constantine for centuries to come. Its first consistent use may well have been in the liturgy.

63. Festugière and Rydén, *Léontios de Néapolis*, 389.

64. Munitiz and Richard, *Anastasii Sinaitae Questiones et Responsiones*, Append. 17.8.76.

coming day, includes the following: "He saw the image of the cross in the heavens and, like Paul, he did not receive his call from men, O Lord. Your apostle among rulers, the Emperor Constantine, was appointed by Your hand as ruler over the imperial city that he preserved in peace for many years, through the prayers of the Theotokos, O only lover of mankind." And the *kontakion*, read after the Gospels, says in part: "Today Constantine and his mother Helen reveal the precious cross, the weapon of the faithful against their enemies. For our sakes, it was shown to be a great sign and awesome in battle."

While these verses surely date to several centuries after our period, the inclusion of Helena as ἰσαπόστολος illustrates the already growing legend. Her discovery of the true cross is seen as being due to just as miraculous a heavenly vision as that which her son received. It is unclear to this writer whether the Orthodox Church came to believe that Constantine was no longer *simul iustus et peccator*, but had already become permanently *iustus* and thus *hagios* already at the time of his death. But there is no sign of this as a theological belief in the fourth or even fifth centuries. Modern historical and theological studies would benefit from viewing Constantine as those Christians did who were his near contemporaries—as *simul iustus et peccator*.

2

Lactantius as Architect of a Constantinian and Christian

"Victory over the Empire"

W. Brian Shelton

THE HISTORIC EVENTS LEADING to the accession of Constantine irrevocably rely on a crucial but obscure rhetorician who taught in Nicomedia. It was a contemporary voice from North Africa that entered this eastern city into the court and life of the emperor, a voice of erudition and of suffering. The writings of Lactantius offer both a philosophical and historical report on the pursuits of the Roman leader who came to champion Christianity in an empire that resisted the new religion. In particular, his writings shaped Constantine's understanding of the faith and influenced the later religious policies that he would enact. Scholars have established Lactantius as a contributor to the genius of a new religious empire and an inescapable historical voice of that evolution, but they are only beginning to scrutinize his exact influence. This chapter seeks to identify and disaggregate the contribution of Lactantius in his fourth-century influence and in his twenty-first-century legacy.

In particular, it depicts this influential turn-of-the-fourth-century philosopher using a paradigm of architectural narrative. This is the notion that a historian writes in a way with intentional design, employing a metanarrative that creates not the events but the blueprint of those events—the frame for understanding, the interpretation, the significance, the divine providence of the events, or, to use the language of historical interpretation of Earle Cairns, "history as the product of inquiry."[1] Yet, for Lactantius, this is not *vaticinium ex eventu* or a theological spin on events crafted by the victors, but he was himself the champion for a cause of religious freedom that he was able to affect and witness fulfilled in his lifetime. In this way, a historian like Lactantius can be seen as a "narrative architect." He designed a modified empire based on religious idealism but also records the impulses of the era in a way that history will forever view the development of this new empire. This essay, with an architectural theme, will consider his role as designer, as builder, and as narrator. After dealing with his role in the paradigmatic imperial shift, it will summarize his place in the edifice that we call history.

Lactantius the Philosophical Architect

Biographically, Lactantius was a rhetorician from North Africa called to Nicomedia to teach rhetoric there about the year 303. Jerome reports that he experienced the dream of many a professor there, that "on account of lack of students he betook himself to writing."[2] In his final years, he moved to Trier to tutor Crispus Caesar, son of the emperor, and participated in the imperial court there. This proximity to Constantine himself makes Lactantius' influence hardly surprising. Lactantius composed his *Divinae institutiones* (*Divine Institutes*) sometime between 303 and 313, at roughly the same time that he made his way from Nicomedia, where he was no longer welcome because of his reputation of writing against imperial religious policy, particularly that of Diocletian and the philosophical guild that defended it.

The contemporary history of imperial persecution against the church of the day is the indubitable context in which Lactantius' *pathos* must be interpreted. Under Gallienus (253–268), Christianity had been tolerated; yet Diocletian (284–305) and his maximus Galerius razed churches, burned Scriptures, and executed church leaders. According to Lactantius, an oracle of Apollo in 303 identified Christians as "enemies" of the state proved to be a typical, influential oracle to Diocletian that led him to issue notorious

1. Cairns, *Christianity through the Centuries*, 18.
2. Jerome, *Vir. ill.* 80. This chapter uses the translation from *NPNF* 2:3.

edicts against Christians.[3] This situation made the rhetorician/writer take up his craft to engage the empire that he saw as unjustly persecuting the church.

LACTANTIUS THE DESIGNER

We see his design for an empire that would be sympathetic to the Christian faith in two ways—an apologetic and a politically constructive approach, both of which are philosophical in nature.

Apologetic Design

The ideological foundation of a new empire characterized by religious freedom required a battle for the ideological landscape to establish the validity of building a religious-friendly empire. Here, the classical Lactantius is at home in his apologetic writings.

First, Lactantius carefully employed Greco-Roman values to justify the success of the new emperor and to promote the cause of the faith in the imperial political shift at work. His powerful rhetorical skills are his most commonly recognized attribute, immediately respectable to his Roman audience. His *Divinae institutiones* is an opus that marshals the classical tradition of literary and philosophical figures to show their principled support of Christianity. He posits that the Emperor Constantine is like the best thinkers of the Greek tradition: "We may be able to instruct the minds of men to the worship of the true majesty. For they, the [Greek] philosophers, were considered teachers of right living . . . We now commence this work under the auspices of your name, O mighty Emperor Constantine, who were the first of the Roman princes to repudiate errors, and to acknowledge and honor the majesty of the one and only true God."[4] Likewise, Christianity embodies the best virtues of the Greek tradition. "This road, which is a path of truth and wisdom and virtue and justice is the one source, the one force, the one seat of all these things. It is a single road by which we follow . . . and worship God; it is a narrow path—since virtue is given to rather

---

3. Lactantius, *MP,* 11; Digeser, "Lactantius, Eusebius, and Arnobius," 36. *De Mortibus persecutorum* was written ca. 318, and this chapter uses the translation from *ANF* 7.

4. Lactantius, *DI*, preface and 1. The *Divinae institutiones* was written between 303-313, and this chapter uses the translation from *ANF* 7.

few."[5] Karl Baus comments on his rhetorical power and its influence: "In Lactantius there is a found a Christian writing in Latin whose regard for the greatness of the past of Rome made possible a more favorable estimate of its literary achievements."[6]

Secondly, he presented Constantine as a *pater familias* with cultural household principles governing an entire empire. For example, his work *De Ira Dei (On the Wrath of God)* displays anger as an application of punishment and evenhandedness that would apply to any respectable head of a household and that similarly characterized the Emperor Constantine. The theological foundation of this quality lies in scripture's testimony of God himself.[7] In more subtle terms, his work *De Opificio Dei (The Workmanship of God)* depicts how anthropology finds its origin and its potential for great accomplishment not in the natural human rationale or in the inspiration of the Greco-Roman pantheon, but in the Christian God. The work has been described this way: "It analyzes the physical equipment of man and shows how the perfect adaptation of the parts of the body to their ends can be due to none other than the Divine Artificer."[8]

Thirdly, his essays and histories are defensive of both the emperor and the success of Christianity that targeted the negative liabilities of the culture as causes of its own demise. His writing *De Mortibus persecutorum (On the Manner in which the Persecutors Died)* chronicles the terminal violent sufferings of prior emperors who had persecuted Christianity.[9] Eloquent journalism, promotion of vindicated martyrs, and prosecution of past imperial policies collaborate for a case of divine providential conquest through the agency of Constantine. For example, describing the pattern of destruction following emperors who persecuted the church, he writes: "Thus did God subdue all those who persecuted His name, so that neither root nor branch of them remained . . . So, by the unerring and just judgment of God, all the impious received according to the deeds that they had done."[10] Frend describes how Lactantius saw the decline of the Greco-Roman culture,

---

5. Ibid. 6.7–8.

6. Baus, *Handbook of Christian History*, 315.

7. For a discussion of Lactantius' Aristotelian argumentation against Stoicism on divine wrath, see Wilken, *Spirit of Early Christian Thought*, 297–98.

8. Introduction to *OD* in *FC* 54, 3.

9. For a discussion of the events surrounding the writing that lead to the contemporary dating of the work, see Barnes, "Lactantius and Constantine," 29–46.

10. Lactantius, *MP* 50.

particularly the religious component: "He wrote as one who was disillusioned with the injustices of the time and the vanished vision of the Golden Age. The work of assimilation and absorption which he was performing in literature resembles what the unknown painters in the catacomb on the *Via Latina* were attempting in art."[11] Likewise, he offers a positive review of all powers favoring the cause of the faith, tying their constructive influence into the popular values of Roman culture. In its most obvious expression of divine handiwork, the inauguration of the Constantinian era followed the divine judgment of imperial leadership. Lactantius writes, "All the adversaries are destroyed, and tranquility having been re-established throughout the Roman Empire, the late oppressed church rises again."[12] Generations of imperial rejection of the faith paradoxically led to a united Roman Empire ruled solely by the champion of that same persecuted faith. Such indicators should indeed be an omen to the Roman Empire at the turn of the fourth century. On the other side of the same coin, Lactantius promoted an optimistic belief that divine providence would lead human history to reward principles of righteousness and justice while counterbalancing pagan and impious values. In this reasoning, he foreshadows the case of Augustine in *City of God*.

Political Design

Confronted with what he considered a biased and ineffective case for persecution of the church in the name of this piety, Lactantius in *Divinae institutiones* sought to challenge the rationale of an exclusive restoration of Greco-Roman worship. In the spirit of Justin, he argued for an illumination that lent itself to philosophical monotheism yet also advanced the cause into the political arena. Elizabeth DePalma Digeser writes, "Lactantius accorded the classical tradition and those who treasured it respect beyond that of any previous Christian author."[13] The very form and manner of his writing could garner the respect of a Greco-Roman reader, citing Roman philosophers and employing allusion to Greek ideals. His writing style and

---

11. Frend, *The Rise of Christianity*, 451; cf. *DI* 5.6 on the collapse of a Golden Age of justice. The catacomb art of the *Via Latina* outside Rome included Christian images that were iconic expressions of belief in an era inimical to Christian belief, at times similar the era of Lactantius.

12. Lactantius, *MP* 1.

13. Digeser, *Making of a Christian Empire*, 89.

classical knowledge has long impressed Latin scholars, earning him the historic title of *Cicero Christianus* ("Christian Cicero").

More importantly, his writings unmistakably call for a monotheistic state and the legitimacy of Christianity. Robert Wilken insists, "He is the first thinker in western culture to defend freedom of religion on religious grounds. Religion must be voluntary, he wrote."[14] Lactantius seemed content with a broader scope of religion inclusion: "His efforts to articulate a broadly based Christian theology that was compatible with the beliefs and practices of late Roman philosophical monotheism are important."[15] Digeser identified three qualities foundational to Lactantius' appeal: forbearance without force, free will in the realm of religion, and a policy of concord—not tolerance.[16] These values should be practiced by both Diocletian's Rome and then by a Christian Rome. Like a natural selection of ideals, such permission would eventually lead to the dissolution of ancient paganism and the triumph of the Christian faith.[17] An underlying premise for this rhetorician and tutor, Digeser says, is that "education was the tool that would craft a change in policy."[18] It is noteworthy that sometimes this cause came at the expense of the revived Roman nostalgia for her own classical heroes while permitting the highest values of the culture to continue.

LACTANTIUS THE BUILDER

The philosopher from North Africa influenced directly and indirectly the mind and heart of Constantine. Indirectly, the above writings persuaded readers, philosophers, and politicians to weigh Christianity, especially compared and contrasted with Greco-Roman ideals, that helped to shift the empire towards greater religious latitude. Constantine saw the effects of this momentum, although we cannot quantify the exact influence of Lactantius on the pagan philosophical guild or on the popular culture. Yet, for validity

14. Wilken, *Spirit of Early Christian Thought*, 297. Wilken ("In Defense of Constantine," 37) adds that Lactantius provides "the first theological rationale for religious freedom, because it is the first rationale to be rooted in the nature of God and of devotion to God."

15. Digeser, *Making of a Christian Empire*, 90.

16. Ibid., 118–19; Reimer uses the phrase, "Forbearance as distinct from toleration." Reimer, "Constantine: From Religious Pluralism to Christian Hegemony," 86.

17. Digeser, *Making of a Christian Empire*, 111; Shelton, review of Digeser, 166.

18. Digeser, *Making of a Christian Empire*, 9.

for any cause to be established, it would have to build a philosophical and rhetorical case in the culture of the day.

More directly and interpersonally, Lactantius was personal tutor to the emperor's son and held a presence at the imperial court in Trier. We have no evidence of their personal relationship, yet scholars easily suppose one. In the seminal work on the place of Lactantius in the life of Constantine, *The Making of a Christian Empire: Lactantius and Rome,* Digeser sets out to evidence the exact influence that this seasoned philosopher had on the person and policies of Constantine as he began to implement imperial laws in favor of a free Christianity.[19] Their shared religious concerns to protect the church, their exposure to one another at court in Trier, the authorship of the *Divinae institutiones,* and their shared value not to aggressively harass those practicing traditional religion seem to reflect a genuine personal affinity. She argues that Lactantius' views contributed to Constantine's own understanding of religious tolerance as early as 310.[20] Digeser asserts that by 324, "the Lactantian motifs come thick and fast" and that "Constantine incorporated all the major elements of Lactantius' notion of concord into the edicts and speeches" that year, although not with the same forbearance to traditional cults.[21] Some scholars claim that Lactantius regularly read the *Divinae institutiones* to Constantine.[22]

This leads to the greatest question of all: the exact influence of Lactantius on Constantine. Here, Digeser excels, as her interest in history focuses on the broadly inclusive new Christian order that Constantine would champion, rather than the theological examination that has been

19. As a matter of approach, Digeser claims that the historical view of the overlooked Lactantius neglects several important influences, and she claims in fact that the *DI* has not been interpreted as a scholarly source. Ibid., ix.

20. Although Drake concurs, not all classical historians have agreed with Digeser's conclusions; see Drake, *Constantine and the Bishops,* 207–12. Constantine's seemingly inconsistent religious perspectives and policies remain complex questions. See Digeser, *Making of a Christian Empire,* 115–43; Wilken, "In Defense of Constantine," 36–40; and Dörries, *Constantine and Religious Liberty.*

21. Digeser, *Making of a Christian Empire,* 136. Bowlin ("Tolerance among the Fathers," 29) declares, "His ideas were eventually set in place, not so much by the Edict of Milan, with its broad provision of religious liberty, but in the letters and legislation of Constantine's later years." Cf. Digeser, *Making of a Christian Empire,* 12–13, 122, 135.

22. Bowlin, "Tolerance among the Fathers," 29; Reimer, "Constantine: From Religious Pluralism to Christian Hegemony," 87; Wilken, "In Defense of Constantine," 37; Digeser, "Lactantius and Constantine's Letter to Arles," 51–52. Such a claim sits squarely in the debate of the dating of Lactantius's works.

more common.[23] The writings of Lactantius and his presence as a premier Christian philosopher exerted an influence on the emperor's life that cannot be denied. His writings take on an apologetic flair that is usually covert, comparing the value of the ancient Romans to the case for Christian thought for the fourth-century state. He sets up two clearly dichotomous and competing models that were used by opposing emperors to unify an empire to their advantage, and makes judgment about the inferiority of traditional Roman piety. Lactantius writes, "For the worship of God being taken away, men lost the knowledge of good and evil. Thus the common intercourse of life perished from among men, and the bond of human society was destroyed."[24] The coming of Christ brought back "justice which had been put to flight, that the human race might not be agitated by very great and perpetual errors. Therefore the appearance of that golden time returned, and justice was restored to the earth, but was assigned to a few."[25]

Maijastina Kahlos explains that Lactantius promoted the virtue of *patientia* against pagan opponents. Christians should exercise patience towards the impious as God does, then expect God to meet them "quickly" (*celeriter*) at final judgment.[26] This is the justification of the imperial suffering in *De Mortibus*—time will reveal the power of God, as it always has, not the intolerant persecution of a new way of imperial Christianity.[27] Kahlos contrasts this method to that of Firmicus Maternus, Eusebius, and Athanasius who employed a stronger "rhetoric of intolerance and policy of coercion."[28] These are just some of the influential ideas promoted by Lactantius to the culture and person of Constantine.

---

23. Shelton, review Digeser, 166.

24. Lactantius, *DI* 5.5.

25. Ibid. Bowlin ("Tolerance among the Fathers," 25) describes the intentions of Lactantius's case: "Christian's wisdom and worship can restore Rome to the piety and equity of the golden age that Cicero describes and the absence of which the poets lament. Their monotheism can return Rome to the virtues of the Principate, with its uncluttered calculus of one God and one emperor. Above all, Christians can carry the educated elite along this path, an elite whose own commitments place them just a short step away from this salvific restoration."

26. Kahlos, "The Rhetoric of Tolerance and Intolerance," 86.

27. For a thorough reflection on the effects of compulsion of religion in the early church, see Bowlin, "Tolerance among the Fathers," 3–36. For a historical and linguistic treatment of compulsion of religion in this regime, see Kahlos, "The Rhetoric of Tolerance and Intolerance," 79–95.

28. Ibid., 94.

LACTANTIUS THE NARRATOR

Finally, this ever-important figure Lactantius provides one of the key biographical episodes of the events of the empire at the beginning of the fourth century. In this way, he not only influences his own era, but through writing influences every era to follow as one of the few voices to testify to these events as Christianity's victory over the empire. For example, concerning the vision at the Battle of Milvian Bridge, Lactantius declares, "The hand of the Lord prevailed, and the forces of Maxentius were routed."[29] Likewise, against Licinius and his army, "The Supreme God did so place their necks under the sword of their foes, that they seemed to have entered the field, not as combatants, but as men devoted to death."[30]

Unlike the historian Eusebius who witnessed and recorded the reign and legacy of Constantine after his success, Lactantius saw and wrote about the emperor's rise to power before its final solidification. His subject for analysis was a nascent series of religious and military gains, an experiment in imperial Christianity of which he had not yet seen permanent success. His sympathy for the cause was no less, however, and like Eusebius, his writings must be filtered for this bias. Thus, Lactantius inevitably invades any historical judgment of "the first Christian emperor" in a way that will always deserve recognition and scrutiny. The establishment of his influence is thus uncomplicated while his exact influence remains mysterious.

The title of this chapter gets its name from the most obvious fingerprint of Lactantius: that Christianity overcame an empire inimical to the faith. R. G. Collingwood describes how Christian historical narratives have four key elements, including the notion of an "apocalyptic" dimension to their history. He writes, "A history is divided into two periods, a period of darkness and a period of light" because of a distinguishing, qualitative event between the periods.[31] This is typical of the conditions of Lactantius' writing about Constantine. Yet, the language of "victory over the empire" is underused by history but best depicts the paradigm shift. Lactantius uses it comfortably in *De Mortibus* to describe such things as the legacy of Diocletian and Maximian, enemies of the church: "The Lord has blotted them out and erased them from the earth. Let us therefore with exultation celebrate the triumphs of God, and oftentimes with praises make mention of His

29. Lactantius, *MP* 44.
30. Ibid., 47.
31. Collingwood, *The Idea of History*, 50.

victory."[32] Opening the essay, he declares, "The late oppressed church rises again."[33] Philip Schaff recognizes this feature in Lactantius, as he describes the self-destruction of the inimical past emperors in the work: "This treatise is, in fact, a most precious relic of antiquity, and a striking narrative of the events which led to the 'conversion of the Empire,' so called."[34] Colot has argued that this work was a first history of its kind, depicting the powerful culture change that had been developing for generations. However, he says it was quickly displaced in its narrative style with Eusebius' "canonical history" form expected of today's readers.[35] Nonetheless, its use of triumphal language came to characterize the empire.[36] The work has been described elsewhere, "In its burning accents, we find a passionate outcry, the chant of Christian victory, the bursting of flood gates previously held in restraint through long years of oppression."[37]

In the end, our inability to secure his exact historical narrative of influence is probably limited by our understanding of Constantine himself. This is what makes works like Digeser's so important in the present, as scholars will continue to probe the mind of a Christian emperor who showed persecution against pagan religious practice in the military, on one hand, while allowing traditional imperial cult principles to apply to himself.[38] He claims a Christian conversion and clearly advanced the church's cause, but he also syncretized the new faith with the old Roman traditions seemingly to his political advantage. The emperor's ambiguous religious position makes our identification of Lactantius' influence that much more elusive.

---

32. Lactantius, *MP* 52.

33. Ibid., 1.

34. See Schaff's note in Lactantius, *MP* 1 (*ANF* 7:301n1).

35. Colot, "Historiographie Chrétienne et Romanesque," 135.

36. Ibid., 136; Lactantius, *MP* 52. Eusebius (*HE* 10.8.19–9.1, 10.9.8) reports: "God led forth Constantine in the dense and impenetrable darkness of a gloomy night, caused a light and a deliverer to arise to all. To him, therefore, the supreme God granted from heaven above the fruits of his piety, and the trophies of victory over the wicked . . . Edicts were published and issued by the victorious emperor, full of clemency, and laws were enacted indicative of munificence and genuine religion." This chapter uses the *NPNF* translation.

37. Introduction to Lactantius, *MP*.

38. Glen Thompson's chapter has certainly raised the issue of the seemingly duplicitous behavior of Constantine as Christian emperor.

CONCLUSION

With attention given to Constantine these anniversary years, Lactantius will be a crucial figure in the literature and in scholarly dialogue. Lactantius' work should be considered inspirational and foundational to understanding the enigmatic first Christian emperor in the decade ahead. With respect to the larger enterprise of this book, Lactantius is an inevitable source for any effort to rethink Constantine. Inspiration came to the emperor from the writings and relationship of the apologist philosopher. His articulation and architectural design of religious freedom and the Christian cause seemed to win the respect of some, the ire of others, and the heart of an emperor seeking to make sense of his own faith experience and a growing Christian community changing the makeup the Roman Empire.

3

Rethinking Constantine's Interaction with the North African "Donatist" Schism

David C. Alexander

WITHIN TEN YEARS OF Constantine's accession to his father's position of emperor[1] over the western Roman provinces, the autonomous existence of a majority schismatic church in North Africa, under the leadership of one Donatus, had gained formal recognition by becoming a persecuted entity under Constantine's government in 317. This resulted from a period of dramatic change and division, understood in Africa in terms of assigning identity relative to the traditional church of the martyrs or the "catholic" church of the alleged "betrayers"—to which would be added the "state sponsored" church.[2]

---

1. Initially as Augustus, though later changed to Ceasar. See Barnes, *Constantine: Dynasty*, 89, for a chart of perceptions and claims as Augustus or Caesar between York and 311. Cf. Lenski, "Constantine," 262.

2. Tilley, *Donatist Martyr Stories*, xii–xvii. Cf. Tilley, "When Schism becomes Heresy," 16, with references to Shaw and Markus' conclusion regarding the two groups' relation to African tradition: "kept intact" or "developed it along Roman lines." As these authors indicate, the term "Donatist(s)" is a problematic one, especially during the period considered here, and that is reflected in the various terms progressively employed below.

In ten more years, the anti-Caecilianist, or "Donatist," church had achieved a virtually unassailable position in North Africa,[3] where it could appropriate as its own the benefits that Constantine had bestowed on the Caecilianist "catholic church" (e.g., buildings and *munera* exemptions).[4] In identity terms, marked division occurred, yet in all of this, relatively little altered in the manner of regular worship and religious practice for perhaps the majority of the African Christian community (save with regard to rebaptism–a crucial issue as will be seen). Contention, including some violence and property shifting, occurred early on and periodically, but for most locations differences were in identity and labels, or gradually over potential rights and privileges.[5] While this story of continuity amid empire-wide change and schism is deserving of renewed consideration in its own right, this chapter focuses on the effects that Constantine's interaction with the church in North Africa had on him and what they reveal about his theological and church political development.

The study of Constantine's engagement as Christian emperor with the North African "Donatist" schism is a study of two contentious phenomena.[6] Also, their interaction centers on periods critical for the actions, identity, and development of both during the years 312–316 and 316–321.[7] Any study of Constantine is subject to certain significant difficulties related to sources[8] and the bias and agenda latent in many of the studies of the so-called "first Christian emperor."[9] Moreover, our reconsideration takes

3. Evidenced by Constantine's response to appeals for aid from North African "catholic" bishops in 330 (Optatus, *App.* 10); cf. Barnes, *Constantine and Eusebius*, 61, and discussion below.

4. Cf. Optatus, *App.* 16; 15; Eusebius, *HE* 10.6; and *CTh.* 16.2.7.

5. Even if schism multiplied by two the churches where one could worship, many locations continued with just one church. Regardless of its choice of which side to join, it is hard to see how much immediate change happened in the local membership and their practice. If the schism began as early as 307/308, such options and choices would have become well established and there were liturgical changes, especially after 317 (see Tilley, *Donatist Martyr Stories*, xv–xvi).

6. Such as the basis, timing and nature of Constantine's conversion to the God of the Christians; or of the events in the African church following persecution that precipitated the focal point of schism over Caecilian's episcopal election.

7. Drake, *Constantine and the Bishops*, 212–13. highlights the significance of 312–325 and the place of the North African schism in this.

8. Cf. Barnes, *Constantine: Dynasty*, 1-8.

9. See Smither's discussion in chapter 6 below regarding an earlier Christian monarchy in Armenia.

place in view of a number of recent monographs on Constantine and his context,[10] treatments whose various overall pictures reaffirm Cameron's assessment: "Still today, arriving at a fair appreciation of Constantine requires extreme caution and not a little good judgment; by no means all specialists would agree."[11] The wealth of contributions does make accessible a number of convenient summaries.[12] The general starting point taken here is outlined in Cameron's chapter, "Constantine and the 'peace of the church'" with chronological details usually starting with the work of T. D. Barnes.[13]

NORTH AFRICA (UP TO THE GREAT PERSECUTION)

In North Africa, a decidedly independent regional church existed at the end of the third century. The tradition of a rigorous Latin Christianity closely identified with the Spirit through the martyrs that had appeared from the outset in the province[14] reached its most organized and autonomous form during the latter half of the third century, in significant part by the work of Cyprian, martyr bishop of Carthage (d. 258), during the Decian and Valerian persecutions of the 250s.[15] In addition, the regular practice of regional

10. *Inter alia* relevant to our consideration, Bardill, *Constantine, Divine Emperor*; Barnes, *Constantine: Dynasty*; Leithart, *Defending Constantine*; Stephenson, *Constantine*; Lenski , "The Reign of Constantine"; and various chapters in the *Cambridge Companion to the Age of Constantine*, including ch. 5, "The Impact of Constantine on Christianity" by Drake, and ch. 30, "Constantine and the 'peace of the church,'" by Cameron. Beyond this tip of the massive iceberg of scholarship on Constantine in recent years, see Glen Thompson's chapter.

11. Cameron notes "the literary sources must be supplemented by the evidence of coins, inscriptions and legal texts. Modern scholars have dealt with this wealth of contradictory and often difficult information in accordance with their own preconceptions, sometimes by attacking the reliability of sources not to their taste" ("Peace of the Church," 539).

12. For background on North Africa, see Tilley, "North Africa," esp. the final paragraph, ibid., 396; cf. Leone, "Christianity and paganism, IV: North Africa"; and Hall, "Ecclesiology forged in the wake of persecution." For controversy and results see Barnes, *Constantine and Eusebius*; Frend, *Donatist Church*, 141–68; and his entry on "Donatism" in *Encyclopedia of Early Christianity*.

13. Cameron, "Peace of the Church"; Barnes, *Constantine and Eusebius*, ch. 4–5; *New Empire*, chs. 3–4; *Constantine: Dynasty*, chs. 3–6.

14. For a summary illustrating this for early Christianity in North Africa, see Alexander and Smither, "Bauer's Forgotten Region."

15. Cf. Tilley, *Donatist Martyr Stories*, xiii; "North Africa," 389–91; and "When Schism becomes Heresy," 16 and n43. On Cyprian and relevant ecclesiological developments

councils of the growing number of churches in North Africa gave crisp reinforcement to the vibrancy and autonomy of this regional church.[16] Following Gallienus' edict of toleration in 260,[17] effectively legalizing Christianity, the growth and wealth of the North African Church is seen mostly through the window of later persecution: in the level of its adherents, the items and buildings of its possession, and the number of its bishops that gathered for councils and for significant ordinations.[18] The point is that perhaps like nowhere else in the empire (certainly in the West) was the church as organized, interconnected, passionate, traditional, and regionally autonomous as in North Africa.[19] The rising eminence of the Roman see notwithstanding, Africa remained the vibrant hub of Latin Christianity on the eve of the "Constantinian revolution." This sense of identity will have major bearing upon our discussion.[20]

---

from the 250s forward, see Burns, *Cyprian the Bishop*, esp. ch. 9; and Hall, "Ecclesiology." Despite the very real divisions within Cyprian's Christian communion, an adherence to a generally strict line of penitential discipline for the lapsed and affirmation of the true victories of the martyrs as belonging to the unified church, most manifest by her unified bishops, allowed the cohesion of a distinct North African catholic Christianity.

16. Cyprian was willing to take on the bishop of Rome (and expected support from eastern churches in so doing) over his arguments for the unity of the church that ought to respect, among other things, the African traditional practice of rebaptizing those who were first baptized outside the church in either heretical or schismatic groups.

17. Corcoran, "Diocletian," 248. For further details, see Tilley ("North Africa," 391) where she notes, "On Valerian's death, Gallienus revoked the edict of 256. While Christianity did not become a *religio licita* ("lawful religion"), its adherents were free to assemble and could regain possession of places of worship and cemeteries. Nearly four decades of relative peace ensued."

18. From the point of Cyprian's martyrdom (258) and Stephen of Rome's death shortly before (which brought the almost mutually excommunicating argument over baptism to an unresolved close) up until the events brought on by Diocletian's and Galerius' edicts of persecution against the church in 303 and 304, we lack evidence from the ongoing life of this church, save a sense of its numeric growth and extension deeper into the provinces of Africa Proconsularis, Numidia and Mauretania. In September, 256, as many as eighty-seven African bishops could meet for a council, and estimates reach as high as 200 for the possible bishoprics at that time. Decret (*Early Christianity in North Africa*, x) considers 150 as a top end.

19. Alexander and Smither, "Bauer's Forgotten Region: North African Christianity."

20. Cf. Tilley, *Donatist Martyr Stories*, xii–xiii.

CONSTANTINE (UP TO HIS ACCLAMATION AS EMPEROR IN 306)

The immediate historical background of Constantine's rise to power is well established.[21] He was the son of Constantius Chlorus[22] and his first wife Helena[23] and born ca. 273/274. Constantius divorced Helena to remarry the emperor Maximian's (step?) daughter, Theodora, ca. 389.[24] However, all indications are that Constantius accorded Constantine full rights as his eldest heir. Constantine was located to the eastern court for his early career and there served successfully in the military under both Galerius and Diocletian.[25] Around the turn of the third century, Constantine would have witnessed the steps being taken against religious groups such as Christians in the army, and against the Manichees beginning in March 302.[26] He would have heard the increasing anti-Christian arguments from figures like Porphyry at court[27] and been there when Diocletian and Galerius issued

21. Even if some details, dating and interpretation remain open for discussion. That such a statement can be made is largely due to the last few decades of scholarship that have clarified confusions created in Constantine's day by misleading propaganda (e.g., about his age, flight from Galerius, etc.) as well as confusions of scholars over evidence. This is especially related to Constantine's first war with Licinius, the proximity of Lactantius and his writings to Constantine in the years 310 and following, and the accuracy and dating of key texts like the *Origo Constatini* and several sections in Eusebius' works. See Thompson's chapter below for more details.

22. The Western Caesar and one of two junior emperors, Constantinus was responsible for the northwestern provinces of the empire (Britain, Gaul, and after 305, Spain) and served in the "Herculean" line under the Augustus Maximian. Diocletian himself was Augustus in the east and partnered by his Caesar, Galerius–the "Jovian" line (cf. Corcoran, "Diocletian," 230–31). We have clear indication of patron gods of each: Maximian with Hercules; Constantius Chlorus with Sol/Apollo; Diocletian with Jupiter, and Gallerius with Mars (Barnes, *Constantine: Dynasty*, 57; *Constantine and Eusebius*, 12).

23. On dating the marriage of Helena and Constantius and of Constantine's birth, see Barnes, *Constantine: Dynasty*, ch. 2, esp. 33–37. Helena's religious influence on Constantine's youth is unclear, but Constantius Chlorus leaned toward a general monotheism, Mithraism and the solar cult as he rose from the regular ranks of the army to emperor.

24. Both the dating and exact family relationships are complicated; see Barnes, *Constantine: Dynasty*, 38–42.

25. See Barnes, *Constantine: Dynasty*, ch. 3, esp. 51-62, for his career at court.

26. Manichaeism had some association as a Christian heresy but was primarily offensive to Diocletian in its Persian connection.

27. Lenski, "Constantine," 248; Green, *Christianity in Ancient Rome*, 210–11. Persecution started earlier with the Manichees and the army; cf. Stephenson, *Constantine*, 104–6.

four edicts against the Christians in 303–304.[28] The first edict, 23 February 303, may have been the only one applied in the West and contained numerous provisions against Christian assembly, properties, Scriptures, religious items, individual and legal status, and added requirements that sacrifice attend any legal proceeding. Since no specific penalties were apparently listed for violations (leaving the most extreme open), disparate local application resulted. In some places, such as Africa, officials ordered all Christians to sacrifice as well. Not very enforced in Constantius' regions in the West,[29] such legislation was applied aggressively under the western Augustus Maximian in Italy and Africa.[30]

The joint abdication of the Augusti Diocletian and Maximian in 305 resulted in an untested and fragile power structure.[31] Present for elevation of Maximin Daia as Caesar in the East, Constantine left Nicomedia in 305 to reach his ailing father in Gaul, well before the latter's death at York in 306.[32] His personal devotion and religious understanding were still informed by pagan perspectives, but he also had real respect for his father's beliefs.[33] Constantine's response and actions immediately follow-

28. Barnes, *Constantine and Eusebius*, 22–24. Perhaps Galerius hoped that Constantine might betray affinity for Christians there, but the future emperor eschewed involvement in these politics at the time. Still, Constantine's presence at the epicenter of this outbreak would later cause him to over exaggerate his youth at the time. Barnes, *Constantine: Dynasty*, 57.

29. It is clear that Constantius did not openly defy the edicts of his fellow emperors during this comprehensive persecution against Christians but also that he did not embrace them. To the degree possible, he apparently let their directives fall moribund in the locations under his control (naturally there were local exceptions). Constantius would also have cultivated key Christian contacts in towns along the Rhine frontier and in Gaul generally. Both Eusebius' reference to Constantine's "choice to venerate his father's God alone" (*VC* 1.27.3; unless otherwise noted, all translations of *VC* are from Hall and Cameron, *Life of Constantine*) and the Donatist appeal to his father's reputation (Optatus, *App.* 12) show awareness of Constantius' stance at that period.

30. Barnes, *Constantine and Eusebius*, 23. In the Eastern half of the empire an additional three edicts were issued over the course of about a year, ending with the universal demand to sacrifice to the gods.

31. Barnes, *Constantine: Dynasty*, ch. 3 *ad fin.* In what Barnes calls the "Dynastic Coup of 305," Galerius turned the tables on expected dynastic appointments. With Maxentius and Constantine denied as incoming Caesars, Severus took over Maximian's areas of the west (Italy, N. Africa) and Maximin Daia took over the far eastern provinces.

32. With Maxentius increasingly outspoken in Rome both were far from out of the imperial picture. Lenski, "Constantine," 258–59.

33. In which general and solar monotheism were prominent and a monotheistic tolerance for Christianity evident. Eusebius, *VC* 1.27.2–3; 1.28.1.

ing Constantius' death and his own acclamation reveal a pagan man with monotheistic leanings and some affinity for Christianity, since he immediately restored "property and freedom to Christians in Britain, Gaul, and Spain."[34] Now an emperor, Constantine was full of ambition and avidly seeking both destiny and the patronage to secure it.

BACKGROUND OF THE SCHISM: AFTERMATH OF THE GREAT PERSECUTION TO DISPUTE OVER CAECILIAN'S ELECTION

Amid such dynamic developments, politically Africa found itself one of the most commonly traded properties amongst imperial aspirants during the breakdown of Diocletian's Tetrarchy.[35] During this period of both shifting politics and relatively short but especially sharp persecution of the Christian church in Africa, the familiar hallmarks of African Christianity again emerged. First came the appearance and recognition of dedicated confessors and martyrs[36] closing with Crispina's martyrdom account at the end of 304.[37] Second, contentions multiplied regarding many who lapsed by sacrifice and, especially amongst clergy, by handing over (*traditio*) the Scriptures to be burned by the authorities.

It was within this context and its aftermath that circumstances birthed a schism centered on church politics in Carthage, provincial ecclesiastical rivalry, and rigorist versus more progressive or laxer sensitivities. How deep and old the schism was when Constantine first engaged it is a subject of debate. That it was serious, no one doubts. Due to compounding

---

34. Bardill, *Constantine, Divine Emperor,* xxv. Even if his legislative order also served at least a dual political purpose as his first move as an Augustus (only Augusti could legislate, not Caesars, cf. Barnes, *Constantine: Dynasty,* 64–66) and his identification as a liberator and bringer of peace.

35. In particular, it was variously ruled over the course of a decade by the popular Maximian who then abdicated along with Diocletian in 305; then overtaken by Maximian's usurper son Maxentius, lost to Domitius Alexander's rebellion in Africa from 308–10; regained by Maxentius again, only to be won over by Constantine's defeat of Maxentius in 312—at last finally returning to what was left of the "Tetrarchic" empire.

36. Possibly including the forty-nine Abitinian martyrs (cf. critique by Dearn, "The Abitinian Martyrs"). Clearly there were Christians who were eager to provoke persecution and martyrdom as Mensurius's complaints show (see Barnes, *Constantine and Eusebius,* 54–55, 315n120, cf. Augustine, *Brev. Coll.* 3.13.25) even if the historicity of our account of the Abitinian martyrs is suspect.

37. From this point up to Caecilian's accession as bishop of Carthage, there were no apparent martyrs in North Africa. Tilley, *Donatist Martyr Stories,* xxxi.

threads of discontent,[38] the schism quickly ran very deep and on each side laid hold to significant patrons, numbers of clergy, and traditions. The focal point was the claims of those African bishops "of the party of Majorinus" against Caecilian's election as the rightful bishop of Carthage.[39] The years in focus here are 305–311, during which fissures in the North African church spread as it dealt with the repercussions of persecution. These issues emerged in the community immediately following persecution but scholars have differed on the dating (and order) of the key events that led to formal schism. A later chronology has been more broadly assumed but the current state of the debate is more balanced. For example Kaufman,[40] Dearn,[41] and

38. These include factions at Carthage, enthusiastic confessors (and their supporters), more restrained faithful like Mensurius, individuals like Secundus who were tied to a clear traditional "party" line, hard core rigorists like Donatus, those (on all sides) in search of ecclesiastical position. These all compounded the interprovincial, class, and local church politics.

39. For these anti-Caecilianists the fundamental stance that had typified North African Christianity of the purity of the church against the world (confirmed by the blood of the martyrs) led to a situation where unity under this banner triumphed over unity to the universal churches of apostolic lineage and traditional collegiality. Tilley, "When Schism becomes Heresy," 14; cf. Tilley, "North Africa," 392–95.

40. Kaufman acknowledges both "early" and "later chronologies" as options but leans to the latter. "Perhaps as early as 305CE, although more likely in the next decade, neighboring prelates objected to the incumbent's [Caecilian's] alleged disdain for confessors, questioned the validity of his consecration, and elected Majorinus to replace him." Kaufman, "Donatism Revisited," 131–32. He continues ("Donatism Revisited," 131n1): "Timothy Barnes, 'The Beginnings of Donatism,' . . . prefers the earlier date; for other views of Donatist origins, see W. H. C. Frend (1952, repr.1985); Bernhard Kriegbaum . . . (1986); and Maureen A. Tilly . . . (1997)." Tilley reasserted her previous assignments of the disputed election to 311 in 1996 (*Donatist Martyr Stories*, xiv) and in her 2006 NAPS Presidential Address ("When Schism becomes Heresy," 14). In agreement would be Drake (*Constantine and the Bishops*, 214); and Evers ("A Fine Line?," 183 and n25) who opts towards the "end of 311 or early 312."

41. Dearn ("The Abitinian Martyrs," 1 and n1) prefers "the 'early' chronology of 307/8" but considers that "both remain arguable." He emphasizes that "it should be noted that the dating of Caecilian's consecration remains controversial . . . . I prefer the 'early' chronology of 307/8 to the more traditional date of early 312, although both remain arguable. See, in particular, T. D. Barnes . . . (1984), arguing for the early dating. For . . . response, see W. H. C. Frend and K. Clancy . . . (1977). For a summary of the pertinent issues in support of Barnes's view see . . . Birley (1987)." In this most helpful English treatment, Birley notes that "Barnes was supported by Lancel (1979), with a slight modification, putting the Cirta meeting a little later." He follows Barnes/Lancel in his chronology of Donatism, His summary of events and of Barnes' dating also highlights the lack of attention or weight given to Barnes arguments, especially on *tyrannus imperator* even by such scholars as Frend or Mandouze (see Birley, "Some Notes on the Donatist Schism,"

Birley[42] all consider the early chronology to be a perspective that deserves serious consideration. A comprehensive or decisive summary of the issues is beyond the scope of this chapter, but some comments are required. The course of the initial controversy is confused by several dating uncertainties, some of which are noted below.[43] Accordingly the breach happened either in

- 307/308 (early chronology), such that "when Constantine became master of Africa late in 312, he confronted a deeply divided church"[44] and "a situation at Carthage in which attitudes and parties had been hardening for years";[45] or

---

30–32, 37–40). Finally, Odahl (*Constantine and the Christian Empire,* 296n22) along with Decret (*Early Christianity in North Africa,* 102) also adopted the early chronology of 307, though Decret acknowledges that some scholars "have suggested 312."

42. As Dearn identifies, Birley's especially helpful treatment and appendix offers a helpful chronology of Donatism (Birley, "Some Notes on the Donatist Schism," 30–32, 37–40); Birley, of course, takes the early view.

43. The following is a select list of the core events and the corresponding dating issues and implications:

- Dating of the peace granted the church by Maxentius in 306/307 (Barnes, *Constantine and Eusebius,* 55–56; 316n129) and whether this is distinct (so Barnes) from the restoration of property to the church by Maxentius in 311 (see Frend and Clancy, "When did the Donatist schism begin?," 104–9).

- Dating the correspondence Mensurius (Bishop of Carthage and Primate of Africa Proconsularis) and Secundus (Bishop of Tigisis and Primate of Numidia) in light of the persecution, since the earliest sense of latent or building division emerges in this interchange (Barnes, *Constantine and Eusebius,* 54–55).

- Dating when Mensurius was summoned to Italy on account of his deacon, Felix, since Mensurius died before returning to Carthage (in 305 or 311). Felix wrote a circular against a *"tyrannus imperator,"* meaning either "persecuting emperor" (i.e., Maximian, which implies a date of 304) or "usurper emperor" (i.e., Maxentius, which implies a date between late 310 and 312).

- Dating of Caecilian's disputed and hurried election as bishop of Carthage (either 307/308 after the "peace" of Maxentius or between late 310 and 312 when Maxentius had reclaimed Africa from Domitius Alexander).

- The date when Secundus, the Numidian Primate, convened a council of seventy bishops at which Caecilian's election was declared invalid since (allegedly) one of his consecrators, bishop Felix of Abthungi, was a *traditor*. Majorinus was consecrated bishop of Carthage in Caecilian's place. Caecilian was not in attendance but was in his church; there was communication between the two.

44. Barnes, *Constantine and Eusebius,* 56 (also 316n129). In *Constantine: Dynasty,* 100, Barnes clearly affirms his earlier placement of the counter council in 307 or 308.

45. Frend and Clancy, "When did the Donatist schism begin?," 104.

- 311/312 (later chronology), in which case the "outbreak of the Donastist schism . . . confronted Constantine with a novel and unexpected situation."[46]

While I think priority should now be given to the early chronology of Barnes and Lancel,[47] the evidence is not strong enough to exclude the more traditional, later possibility. The significant networking of this schism by means of its occurrence and the seventy bishops in council against Caecilian meant immediate depth of division regardless of the date of his election. Still, this depth, spread and hardening of feeling would all have been greater if they had been growing for years instead of months. Either way Optatus recorded the end result of this disputed counter-election of Majorinus to replace Caecilian: "In this manner they went forth and altar was

46. Frend and Clancy, "When did the Donatist schism begin?," 109. Barnes claims the Frend and Clancy view "depends on 3 erroneous premises: the argument misrepresents *tyrannus imperator* [*Optatus* 1.17] as "usurper" (it here means "persecuting emperor," it equates *tyrannus* with Maxentius [*Optatus* 1.17–18] distinguishes the two), and finally it confuses Maxentius' grant of toleration in 306/7 with his restoration of church property in 311" (Barnes, *Constantine and Eusebius*, 316n129; cf. Barnes, *New Empire*, ch. 15).

47. Birley's Donatism Timeline up to Milvian Bridge (Partial), "Some Notes on the Donatist schism," 37–38:

23 February	303	Diocletian launches Great Persecution
	304(?)	Bp Mensurius of Carthage summoned to Italy after his deacon insults *tyrannus imperator*
1 May	305	Diocletian and Maximian abdicate
	305(?)	Mensurius dies before returning to Carthage
27 July	306	Constantine proclaimed emperor at York
28 October	306	Maxentius proclaimed emperor at Rome
November	306	Maxentius recognized in Africa and restores freedom to Christians there
13 May	307(?)	Silvanus consecrated Bp of Cirta
	307	Caecilianus consecrated Bp of Carthage; Numidian Primate Secundus Bp of Tigisis convenes Council, Caecilianus deposed and Maiorinus consecrated Bp in his place
	308	Domitius Alexander proclaimed emperor in Africa
	309	Maxentius' prefect Volusiamus defeats Alexander and regains Africa for Maxentius
28 October	312	Constantine defeats Maxentius at B. of Milvian Bridge

raised against altar."[48] The power of this image should not be overlooked. "Altar vs. altar" had already long been the case for the persecuted church against the polytheistic pagan state and this corresponded to a spiritual war.[49] As it happened, despite all the Christian wrangling, the territory of Africa itself came into Constantine's possession by peaceful transition late in the fall of 312.

CONSTANTINE'S EMERGENCE AS A CHRISTIAN EMPEROR IN THE WEST (306–312)

We have already observed Constantine's first legislation upon elevation to emperor in 306, restoring property to Christians and formally considering them free to practice their religion. Further details on the careers and various imperial actions and counter claims during the Tetrarchic crisis are readily available.[50] Our focus picks up in 310 at the court at Trier when a Gallic panegyric alleged several significant associations around Constantine, including the reputation to have seen divine visions, especially one from the god of the sun.[51] Moreover, the vision of the sun was an experience shared by his army and provided Constantine with a natural link to increasing Christian claims over the next two years.[52] Among such claims would be those of Lactantius, who also arrived at Constantine's court around 310

48. *Optatus* 1.19. Unless otherwise noted, all translations of Optatus' *De schismate Donatistarum* with Appendices are from Vassall-Phillips' translation at: http://tertullian.org/fathers/index.htm#Against_the_Donatists.

49. It is worth noting that once the counter election occurred, a clock started ticking in North Africa during which association with one of these two parties would need to be made by all the bishops in the provinces. Only so much time existed to bridge such a divide before it created an enduring chasm; an observation that Constantine, and/or his advisors, did not make until it was too late.

50. See Barnes, *Constantine and Eusebius*, ch. 3; *New Empire*, chs. 3–5; *Constantine: Dynasty*, 72–80; and Lenski, "Constantine," 255–65 for details. For his part, Galerius chose to accept Constantine's inclusion in the imperial college (though only as Caesar, to which Constantine assented).

51. Other associations were made between Constantine and the Emperor Claudius (268–270), now asserted to be Constantine's ancestor, and Apollo. In the turbulent politics surrounding Maximian, and also Galerius, a move away from Mars as patron was beneficial. The benefit of now appearing as the third in a line of emperors put Constantine in a privileged place amongst the current Tetrarchy.

52. Lenski, "The Reign of Constantine," 67, 71; see Barnes, *Constantine: Dynasty*, 72–73, 75–80, for discussion; cf. Grant, *Constantine*, 131–32.

and serves to highlight Constantine's Christian connections prior to the victory at Rome.[53] Among these connections, Lactantius and Ossius of Cordoba deserve particular attention.

Lactantius, the African professor of rhetoric at Diocletian's court ca. 295–305, would have known Constantine at Nicomedia. Following the rhetorician's resignation of his position in the face of persecution, Lactantius likely left Bithynia after May 1, 305, possibly to return to Africa in 306.[54] In any case, he reemerged at Trier in 309 or 310[55] where Constantine assigned him tutorial responsibilities for Crispus until at least ca. 313. Barnes has recently canvased the wide range of views on Lactantius' location as well as the time of tutoring.[56] One interesting possibility relevant to the schism in North Africa may result if Barnes is right both about Lactantius' travels *and* about the dating of the schism. If so, Lactantius himself may have brought some knowledge of North African Christian divisions to Constantine's court.[57] In any case, at court Lactantius' Christian voice was well and often heard.[58] As Brian Shelton's chapter discusses, Digeser has argued effectively for several significant areas of contact, commonality and influence between Lactantius and Constantine. Overall, "Lactantius' works

53. The Christian influences and surrounding advisors at court in Trier and along the path to the Milvian Bridge are tantalizing but somewhat veiled.

54. Barnes (*Constantine: Dynasty*, 178; cf. *Constantine and Eusebius*, 13, 291n96) then has Lactantius perhaps moving from North Africa to Gaul when Maxentius' forces suppressed the rebellion of the *vicarius* of Africa Domitius Alexander in 309. See also Digeser, *Making of a Christian Empire*, 133–35.

55. This is according to Barnes's reconstruction, *Constantine: Dynasty*, 176–78; cf. Stephenson, *Constantine*, 169.

56. See Barnes, *Constantine: Dynasty*, 8–9, including his appendix on 176–78 giving a "Chronology of Lactantius."

57. Curiously, Barnes now writes (*Constantine: Dynasty*, 100) that in the winter 312/313, Constantine had *"unwittingly* stepped into the middle of the controversy with three letters" (emphasis mine), which seems a step back from his prior assertion (*Constantine and Eusebius*, 56) that Constantine's "first contacts with the African church deliberately declared that he supported one party."

58. He likely read portions of the first edition of his *Divinae institutiones* to Constantine. See Digeser, "Lactantius and Constantine's Letter to Arles," 34–37, 51–52. Stephenson (*Constantine*, 169) has the first edition of *DI* being "written between 305–310" and also likely being heard at court in Trier. Stephenson also puts the writing of *De Mortibus* at Trier with "each chapter read as finished" during this period (contra Barnes). In this, "Lactantius saw Constantine as his god's tool" to punish the persecutors. Barnes (*Constantine: Dynasty*, 178) has Lactantius moving back east to Bithiniya where he would write *DM* after 314.

had profound effect upon Constantine" and, as illustrated by the *Oration to the Saints*, these concepts were "embraced by 315 and continued to be refined over the following decade."[59]

The nature of bishop Ossius' relationship with and impact upon Constantine is frustratingly opaque. Ossius is almost always listed as one of if not the "most influential" of Constantine's advisors[60] from 312/313 up to the bishop's departure from court in 326 to return to his see in Cordoba; yet, we do not know when the first point of contact between these two occurred.[61] Indeed one of the first references to Ossius in association with Constantine appears in the emperor's letter to Caecilian as our controversy breaks. Here Caecillian is to distribute 3,000 *folles* (and more if needed) "among all the above mentioned persons in accordance with the schedule sent to you by Hosius"[62] Yet, at no additional point do we see Ossius explicitly connected with the African controversy.[63]

---

59. Stephenson, *Constantine*, 171. He also notes (ibid., 170) the description by recent translators of *DI* of the "plea for religious freedom" in book five as being "the most elaborate and elegant from antiquity."

60. *Inter alia* Ricciltti (*Age of the Martyrs*, 197) writes, "Although the figure of Hosius never emerges too clearly, he was possibly the most influential of all the Christians in the imperial court."

61. Frend's (*Donatist Church*, 145n5) thoughts are typical: "After leaving Spain, Ossius evidently gained access to Constantine's court at Trier, and accompanied him on his campaign against Maxentius. By the end of 312 he was one of the Emperor's most trusted advisers . . . In any case, Hosius was considered to have influenced the Emperor against the opposition to Caecilian."

62. Eusebius, *HE* 10.6.2. Unless otherwise noted, translations of *HE* are from Oulton and Lawlor, *Eusebius: Ecclesiastical History*. The implication is that Ossius had information on particular sees or bishops in North Africa upon which he could counsel Constantine, and that Constantine's trust in Ossius' counsel was complete.

63. Still, we must recognize that Ossius's contact with Caecilian as well as the degree to which Constantine trusted him. Both suggest a networked figure with potential connections in North Africa (to Mensurius?) before and after arriving and gaining favor with Constantine as a Christian advisor at Trier. Three additional notes seem relevant to our discussion. Barnes (*Constantine and Eusebius*, 53–54) observes that Ossius was one of the eleven bishops who, prior to 303, attended the Council of Iliberris (the first such in Spain), the canons of which are very strict. One could take this to indicate signatories who would be sympathetic to some of the more rigorous North African views. Second, Ossius "was imprisoned briefly, earning the title of confessor," when persecution touched Spain. One could expect such background to foster sympathy with some of the anti-confessor allegations made in North Africa against Caecilian. Last, Ossius appears to have been an ally with Miltiades, the bishop of Rome, whose actions will loom large in the controversy. Drake, *Constantine and the Bishops*, 218; cf. Stephenson, *Constantine*, 261.

Thus, Constantine's actions from 310–312 show a man earnestly seeking clear divine patronage; a position of legitimacy and precedence relative to the Tetrarchy; and to include Christianity and leading Christians at court offering advice on personal and political concerns. However the events surrounding the fateful battle at Rome's Milvian Bridge[64] and Constantine's conversion are to be reconstructed,[65] Lenski is surely correct that "we have good evidence that its effects were real and immediate."[66] What Grant called the "wonderful ambiguity" of Constantine's public expressions (such as with the chi-rho, the labarum, his statue or arch) combined with the way Constantine moved forward without "trumpeting his own belief too openly" allowed an ongoing tipping of "the scales in favor of Christianity."[67] It was not only the kind of favor and equality Constantine immediately bestowed upon the Christian community[68] that stands out following the victory at the Milvian Bridge. The ensuing context was very full both politically and religiously; and yet Christianity was brought into the core orbit of concerns at every level.[69]

64. Of the victory there Grant (*Constantine*, 144, 145n55) wrote: "to (Constantine the message) was clear. It was the Christian God who caused him, on that morning, to win the Battle of the Milvian Bridge, and henceforward it was the Christian God whom he revered.t demonstrated to him . . . he believed, what he had to do to vanquish foes, it identified, he believed, the divine power capable of ensuring this outcome as the God of Christianity." However this God may have been variously associated as *public* patron and in *public* presentation (with the highest divinity, Sol Invictus, the Supreme, Christian symbols, or more ambiguous monotheism), Grant's verdict seems merited on the evidence.

65. Lenski ("Constantine," 260–61), has a concise, clear account and summary of Constantine's conversion (time scale) and events from 310–312. Regarding Eusebius' account and others relative to records of what "actually" happened around the Milvian Bridge, see Litfin, "Eusebius on Constantine."

66. Lenski ("Constantine," 262) observes that it was only "after his conversion and defeat of Maxentius that (Constantine) began actively displaying his favor to the church and extending his efforts on its behalf into the realm of his fellow emperors." For a broader conversion presentation and progression from 313 to 317, see Stephenson, *Constantine*, 167–73. The whole affair raises the issue of "public patron" and "private worship" that eventually Constantine held in tension.

67. Grant, *Constantine*, 143, 152–53.

68. Consider the North African example just cited.

69. In all of this, Constantine came with a background of Christian experience that was primarily Latin and western.

CONSTANTINE'S FIRST INTERACTIONS WITH THE CHURCH IN AFRICA

Constantine would stay in Rome until Epiphany on 6 January, 313. In this crucial two and a half months, he had to understand and carefully undo many but not all of Maxentius' changes and in so doing cultivate favor in Rome with the Senate, the general populace, and the Christian community. Upon entering Rome, Constantine would have made contact with its Christians and ascertained their state of affairs. Regarding Maxentius and the Christians at Rome, there are hints not only of a non-adversarial relationship but of the "tyrant" acting almost as an engaged arbiter of their leadership affairs (as part of his consolidation of support from all constituents).[70] While not something Constantine would acknowledge or emulate, it set the stage for him to be more than just a liberator, since Christians under Maxentius were already free of persecution and were even used to some cultivation of favor. In this vein, Constantine first interacted with the church in North Africa via three letters.[71] They indicate not only that the emperor was eager to support and bless the church but also that he was already aware of Christian disputes in the provinces,[72] though he does not claim to understand their nature. A survey of the letters' contents reveal why contention in Africa escalated so quickly under Constantine. *Prima facie* Constantine's communications betray straightforward traditional reasoning: as the overseer of the state's licet religions, he sought to recruit and enable Christian priests to undisturbed religious duty in order for the "greatest benefits" to become manifest upon the state (and himself).[73] Moreover, as a particular

---

70. As Bernard Green has recently noted (*Christianity in Ancient Rome*, 217–18 and n38): "[T]hough [Decker's] case might be overstated, the suggestion that Constantine resembled Maxentius far more than his propaganda could acknowledge and continued his [Maxentius'] policies is very attractive." Cf. *HE* 8.14.1 where Eusebius describes how Maxentius "counterfeited our faith . . . feigning piety."

71. These key texts as well as the others from the Donatist controversy and their dating are listed in Barnes, *New Empire*, 238–47.

72. Lenski ("Constantine," 262–63) who notes that Constantine's "efforts at healing the rifts created by persecution began in earnest, however, only after his conversion and defeat of Maxentius," whereupon "Constantine had openly displayed his allegiance to the church, not merely as its benefactor, but as an active arbiter in its disputes." Lenski recognizes that the "schism was already in full spate by the time Constantine gained control of Italy and Africa from Maxentius in 312."

73. Drake, *Constantine and the Bishops*, 216; cf. Stephenson, *Constantine*, 261–62.

patron driven by the same incentive, he desired to elevate dramatically Christian worship and status in his new provinces.

The first of these letters from early winter 312–13 was to Anullinus, the vicar of Africa, regarding the immediate return of property to the Christian church, so that "everything, whether gardens or houses, or whatever else belongs to these churches, be restored to them *as soon as may be possible.*"[74] That such return had not occurred under Maxentius is interesting.[75] Still, the return of property, though problematic when one has to ask "to which group?" was one thing; but the distribution of the emperor's largesse was another matter altogether. This emerged in the first imperial letter addressed directly to the church in North Africa, and on its behalf, to Caecilian, bishop of Carthage.

The letter to Caecilian[76] informed the bishop of the sizeable grant mentioned above, that he should use and distribute to the churches via certain "named persons according to the schedule received from by Ossius."[77]

74. From Optatus, *App.* 15, Constantine's letter reads: "Hail, Anullinus, most highly esteemed by us! After this manner is our benevolence, that we will that those things which by just title belong to others should not only remain unmolested, but also, when necessary, be restored, most esteemed Anullinus! Wherefore we decree that, so soon as you have received this letter, if any of those things which belong to the Catholic Church of the Christians, in the several cities or other places, are held by Decurions or by any others, *these you shall cause immediately to be restored to their churches.* For we have determined that whatever these same churches formerly possessed shall be restored in accordance with justice. When therefore your Fidelity to this decree of our orders is most clear, you will make haste to see that everything, whether gardens or houses, or whatever else belongs to these churches, be restored to them *as soon as may be possible*—that we may learn that you have attended to, and most carefully carried into execution, this our decree. Farewell, my most esteemed and beloved Anullinus"; emphasis mine. Cf. Eusebius, *HE* 10.6.

75. This is especially true as Maxentius seems to have delayed restorationthis for the church at Rome until they had been able to settle peaceably on clear leadership (a two-year process, that he had to goad forward). See Green, *Christianity in Ancient Rome,* 217–18. Was Maxentius also aware of similar problems in Africa that would complicate the return of items to the church in cities of other location? If so, perhaps the relative press to replace Maxentius's deputies in Africa cut off Constantine from available and useful political observations regarding the state of the North African church.

76. Coming from the same period as the first, Barnes, *New Empire,* 240–41 and n12, who also identifies "the first two letters are clearly earlier than the third." Cf. Frend, *Donatist Church,* 145.

77. Eusebius, *HE* 10.6 (Winter 312/313): "Constantine Augustus to Caecilian bishop of Carthage. Inasmuch as it has been our pleasure that in all provinces, namely, the Africa, Numidia, and Mauretania, *certain specified ministers of the lawful and most holy catholic religion should receive some contribution for expenses,* I have sent a letter to Ursus

Constantine also mentions personal conversations he had with the African vicar, proconsul, and procurator on behalf of the church in Africa, Numidia, and Mauretania "when they were here."[78] Constantine first shows awareness here of "certain persons of unstable mentality" in North Africa who are "eager to lead the laity of the church astray."[79] Accordingly, Constantine had ordered the officials to mediate correction to "any such men persisting in this *madness* (emphasis mine)" and instructed Caecilian to take advantage of this. Constantine was acting as a patron, not just generally but strategically. His aim was the most immediate elevation possible of publicly perceived worship of the Christian God in the provinces. Yet, by making provision and protection available selectively, *de facto* he made an enormous decision about the North African church and its problems. State persecution was the majority experience and perception of the African Christians who had endured it and then political upheaval. Although the coin was flipped here, the perception that churches were being bribed by the state could have caused many in North Africa to assume something ungodly in the *quid pro quo*. Ironically, the ambiguity of Constantine's Christianity designed to appeal to the largest number may have played well in many venues, but North Africa was not one of them, and here Constantine's actions dramatically chose sides in a schism he had yet to grasp.

While the first two letters took established actions of imperial oversight and patronage and brought them, albeit inequitably, to the North African churches, the third letter, in February 313, brought the inequity to

---

. . . finance officer of Africa, informing him that he should pay to your Steadfastness three thousand *folles. When you have received this sum, your task will be to arrange that it is distributed among all the persons named above according to the schedule sent to you by Ossius.* If later on you find that you lack anything to carry out my intentions in this matter in respect of them all, do not hesitate to ask our procurator Heraclides for whatever you find necessary. When he was here I gave him orders that if your Steadfastness should ask any money from him, he was to pay it over without question.

"And since *I have learned that certain people of unstable mind desire to lead astray the laity of the most holy catholic church* by some vile enticements, know that when they were here, I fully instructed Anullinus, the proconsul, and also Patricius, the vicar of the prefects, that . . . especially in this they are not to overlook such incidents. Therefore if you observe *any such men persisting in this madness*, do not hesitate to bring this matter before the aforementioned judges so that, as I instructed them when they were here, they may turn these people from their error. May the divinity of the great God keep you safe for many years"; emphasis mine.

78. Eusebius, *HE* 10.6.4. For instance, those "at Rome very shortly after 28 October 312." Barnes, *New Empire*, 82, 240n12.

79. Frend, *Donatist Church*, 145.

the personal and ongoing level. In another letter to Anullinus, Constantine ordered the exemption from public duties and taxes for the clergy in Africa. Moreover, he specified that this applied to clergy "in the catholic church, over which Caecilian presides."[80] This can be read two ways: either simply identifying the churches that are naturally connected to the Christian primate of Africa Proconsularis, the bishop of Carthage; or it may specify the churches in connection with Caecilian in contrast to known churches over that he did not preside. My interpretation is that Constantine was not yet aware that large numbers of *churches* were in schism with Caecilian even though he did know there were agitators in and amongst the laity of some churches. Either way, Constantine firmly pinned his identification of the catholic church in North Africa to the person of Caecilian. This fact alone created new and almost irreconcilable problems. While it seems prudent to avoid reading too much prejudgment into these opening communications, both Barnes and Drake are certainly correct when they note that Constantine engaged a deeply divided church in 312, "Yet his first contact deliberately declared support for one party."[81] The emperor's communication clearly aimed at generosity toward the church in the provinces: he wanted to bless, not just restore, and so make an impression favorable to the Christian God.[82] Unfortunately, Constantine made assumptions and picked

---

80. Eusebius, *HE* 10.7: "*Many facts prove that the vitiation of religious worship,* by which the highest reverence for the most holy, heavenly [Power] is preserved, *has greatly endangered public affairs and that its lawful restoration and preservation have conferred the greatest good fortune on the Roman name and extraordinary prosperity on all human-kind--blessings bestowed by divine grace.* It has therefore seemed good that those men who give their services to conduct divine worship with due holiness and observance of this law should receive the rewards of their own labors, most honored Anullinus. *So I desire that those in your province in the catholic church, over which Caecilian presides, who devote their services to this sacred worship—those whom they customarily call clergy-men—should once and for all be kept entirely free from all public duties. Then they will not be drawn away from the worship owed to the Divinity by any error or sacrilege but instead strictly serve their own law unencumbered. In so rendering total service to the Deity, they will clearly confer immense benefit on the affairs of state.* Farewell, our most honored and esteemed Anullinus"; emphasis mine.

81. Barnes, *Constantine and Eusebius,* 56–57; Drake, *Constantine and the Bishops,* 216.

82. He assumes that as clergy/priests are freed up to "serve their own law unencumbered. *In so rendering total service to the Deity, they will clearly confer immense benefit on the affairs of state*" (Optatus, *App.* 16; emphasis mine).

sides more strongly than he realized, without understanding the depth of the dispute, and the very expediency and generosity undermined his goal.[83]

PETITION OF THE ANTI-CAECILIANISTS TO CONSTANTINE AND THE SYNOD AT ROME

The significance of the clear petition to Constantine from the churches aligned with Majorinus against Caecillian (from churches that did not think much of the state instinctively) has long been recognized. Frend called the appeal of the Donatists to Constantine "one of the decisive moments in the history of the early Church."[84] In fact, the willingness on all sides to consider ecclesiastical issues as subject to the state's adjudication in the form of a Christian emperor is one of the most striking results of Constantine's ascendance to the purple and movement through the "Donatist" issue.[85] The petition, sent 15 April 313, reached Constantine attached to a letter from Anullinus that described the delivery of Constantine's letter regarding *munera* exemptions to Caecilian and his clergy and the delegation and attending large crowd that resulted a few days later claiming that "Caecilian must be opposed." This ensemble presented him with two formal documents, *libelli*, which he has forwarded to Constantine.[86] The

---

83. Based on our discussion of Ossius, and his apparent encouragement of these decisions, one wonders if the isolation caused by the rebellion of Domitius Alexander in North Africa and the following repression of it was to blame for a lack of communication by the (relatively autonomous) North African churches with the "church beyond the sea." Perhaps the lack of concerted effort to establish connections outside the provinces was reflective of the focus upon fierce competition to establish connections in the provinces themselves. If so, a simple association with the immediate successor of Mensurius was given reason to be a lightning rod for the controversy about to unfold.

84. Frend, *Donatist Church,* 148, where he continues: "Appeal had been made to the State in the person of a Christian Emperor. For the first time schism or unorthodoxy could become an offence punishable by law. The 'secular arm' stood at the disposal of whoever could prove himself orthodox. Constantine's Instruction to Anullinus was thus one of the major steps which brought about the alliance between catholic church and Roman Empire."

85. Greenslade, *Church and State,* 16–17; cf. Drake, "Impact of Constantine," 117.

86. Preserved in Augustine, *Ep.* 88.2, they read "[I sent . . .] your Majesty's heavenly letter, . . . to Caecilian and his subordinate clerics; . . . But a few days afterwards I was approached by *certain persons, followed by a great throng of the populace, who held that Caecilian must be opposed,* and presented me in my official capacity with two documents, one bound in leather and sealed, the other a *libellus* unsealed, and demanded with insistence that I should send them to the sacred and venerable Court of your Highness. This

title of the sealed document mentioned read: "The catholic church's list of the crimes of Caecillian, from the party of Majorinus." The petition itself is preserved by Optatus: "O Constantine, most excellent Emperor, since you come of a just stock, and your father (unlike other Emperors) did not persecute Christians, and Gaul was free from this wickedness, we beseech you that your Piety may command that we be granted judges from Gaul; for *between us and other Bishops in Africa disputes have arisen.* Given by Lucianus, Dignus, Nasutius, Capito, Fidentius *and the rest of the Bishops* [who adhere to Majorinus]" (emphasis mine).[87] Frend and others note that the financial advantages and especially immunities made matters pressing for the anti-Caecilianist party.[88] Even if as Stephenson notes they had little to lose and were lacking in support at court and around the rest of the Mediterranean,[89] the petition *prima facie* indicates the confidence of the petitioners in their position. Only "a few days" were required for a sizable deputation to form and act on behalf of a "great crowd" as well as numbers of distant bishops who were also in opposition to Caecilian and his "other bishops." On what would such confidence be based?[90] It may well have been based on numbers that would have shown the emperor that Caecilian was not currently representative of the majority of North African Christians

---

my littleness has been careful to do (preserving Caecilian in his position), and I have forwarded their Acts, that your Majesty may be in a position to determine everything. I have sent the two *libelli,* of which the one bound in leather has been endorsed *Libellus Ecclesiae Catholicae criminum Caeciliani traditus a parte Maiovini*" (emphasis mine). Cf Optatus 1.22.

87. Optatus 1.22. Some translations like this one read "[who adhere to Donatus]," likely due to a latter scribal emendation since Majorinus died soon after this and was replaced and represented by Donatus. The manuscript and translation tradition includes both phrases: see previous note and the translator's commentary on the matter at http://tertullian.org/fathers/optatus_01_book1.htm#188.

88. It created a radically new reason why Christians should be concerned with the emperor (and state officials). Frend (*Donatist Church*, 147) writes, "For the opponents of Caecilian the situation at once became more serious. Orthodoxy now brought with it financial privileges, and it was therefore desirable to avoid a direct sentence of unorthodoxy. Opinion rose against Caecilian and his supporters. In the words of a Donatist pamphleteer, 'the Devil rewarded the lapsed clergy not only with the restoration of ecclesiastical honours, but also with royal friendship and earthly riches.'"

89. Stephenson, *Constantine*, 260.

90. Drake (*Constantine and the Bishops*, 216–17) argues they were needing to widen the field because things were lost at Carthage. I think it more likely that they hoped the emperor did not yet realize the schism was spread well beyond Carthage nor spread in Caecilian's favor.

in Africa. The petitioners certainly would have thought the pure reputation and numbers of the martyrs/confessors was on their side, with at least seventy bishops, and numbers and patrons in Carthage. Opposed to all this stood Caecilian, some "other bishops," along with a number of (albeit influential) Christians in Carthage, a very irregular and suspect consecration, and possibly, a smaller number of churches.[91] Such a picture is even more likely if the early chronology of the dispute is assumed.[92]

Constantine's displeasure at further report of division from Africa did not prevent his care in deciding direction forward. He replied to the Majorinists in June, 313 and his response gave them hope.[93] Constantine was gone (to Milan then Trier) before the hearings occurred,[94] as was Majorinus who had died and been replaced by Donatus, but the emperor's instructions for arbitrating the appeal are clear in his letter to Miltiades of June 313:

> Whereas . . . Caecilian, Bishop of Carthage, has been *accused on many grounds by certain of his fellow-bishops in Africa . . . where there is a vast population, and the multitude (as it were divided in two) are found to be deteriorating, and the bishops, amongst others,*

91. Though perhaps in more of the major cities, especially in Africa Proconsularis.

92. Should further research confirm the probability of that chronology, I would argue that the anti-Caecilianist confidence was such that the only thing they could have fathomed that would overturn the ecclesial situation in North Africa was some unknown massive influx of external power and resources for Caecilian and those aligned with him outside Carthage. When such a case in fact occurred, it was time to ring the alarm for the clear side of the right and probable majority in the provinces. In such a case, things would have moved beyond a few signatories to a recognized party. Indeed, the confidence and vehemence in delivering the petition may itself argue for a longer term division. Tangential support may be glimpsed in the apparent confidence with which those gathered under Secundus in council against Caecilian at Carthage concluded their proceedings after ordination of Majorinus and returned to their own sees, presumably satisfied and confident that justice had been done. Still, each of these confidences could still obtain in case of a more recent (311/312) schism for reasons already set forth.

93. *Optatus*, 1.23. Constantine agreed to send three bishops from Gaul to hear the case at Rome along with its bishop, Miltiades, and one Markus. Constantine also directed officials in Carthage to have Caecilian come with ten bishops supporting him and ten of the bishops opposing him to appear before this commission (Eusebius, *HE* 10.5.21–22). The anti-Caecilianist hope was to be shattered at Rome, however, in part because Constantine's instructions to achieve resolution of the schism were not followed when the commission turned into a Synod of Rome. Barnes (*Constantine and Eusebius*, 57) notes, "in the event, however, the hearing was not an arbitration in the form prescribed by Constantine, but a Church council according to ecclesiastical precedent." Cf. Stephenson, *Constantine*, 261.

94. Drake, *Constantine and the Bishops*, 219.

are at variance––I have resolved that this Caecilian with ten of the Bishops who accuse him and ten others whom he himself may choose to aid in his defense, shall sail to Rome; that there in your presence and in the presence of Reticius, Maternus and Marinus your collaeges, whom I have ordered to hasten to Rome for this purpose, *this case may be determined in the manner which you perceive to be in agreement with the most holy Law*. Moreover . . . I have added copies of the documents sent me by Anullinus, to my letters to your above-mentioned fellow-Bishops. After you have perused these *your Gravity will carefully consider in what way this controversy may be most carefully investigated and justly decided*. Since *it will not have escaped your Carefullness* that so great is my rrespect for the most holy catholic church *that I wish you to leave no schism whatsoever nor division in any place* (emphasis mine).[95]

The instructions reflect that thought had been given to the matter, now understood to involve many in the province. A commission was to be assembled at Rome under Militiades, its bishop, with three Gallic bishops and the assistance of an unknown (bishop?) Markus. The aim for this commission is equally clear: "in agreement with the most holy Law" Miltiades should direct in whatever way would proceed most justly to the end where no schism or dissension should be left in place. As others have noted, Constantine's clear aim seems to be arbitration that would go the extra mile for the sake of securing resolution. This did not happen and was not achieved. It seems that Miltiades grasped the first underlined passage above (the means) but missed the latter two (the manner and objective). Constantine wanted a result of unity, not simply judgments. In consideration of the anti-Caecilianist petition, he had been careful to grant much they requested: a majority of judges from Gaul, in a convenient location for all with possible precedent,[96] and with the added benefit of affirming Miltiades' significance.[97] The three bishops from Gaul were ones Constantine would have known and whose decision he could trust.[98] However, this Gallic majority was supplanted as Miltiades added fifteen Italian bishops to hold a synod that met on 2–4 October 313, in the *domus Faustae* at the Lateran. Far from

95. Optatus *App.* 13; cf. Eusebius, *HE* 10.5.18–20; *Optatus*, 1.22; Augustine, *Ep.* 43.5; 93.13; *Cresc.* 1.2.61.

96. In the appeal to Aurelian over the Paul of Samasota incident (Stephenson, *Constantine*, 260, 80), which I doubt played much of a role here.

97. Perhaps important since Ossius was, according to Drake (*Constantine and the Bishops*, 219) and others, an ally of Miltiades.

98. Drake, *Constantine and the Bishops*, 218; cf. Stephenson, *Constantine*, 260.

arbitration, Militiades insisted on a full legal case presentation when the Majorinists were only ready with allegations and irregularities but not such standings of proof.[99]

In short, the synod was effectively hijacked by a past controversy between North Africa and Rome over rebaptism and by fears of accusations of *traditio* that lacked explicit proof. This shifted the focus to prejudgment of the petitioners and a formal trial structure that downplayed suspicions of *traditio*—something to which Miltiades may well have been sensitive.[100] The discussion was overtaken by the issue of rebaptism[101] and Miltiades used the synod as an opportunity to drive home the Roman position as the right one at the expense of the petitioners who were committed to the traditional African position. This was particularly true of Donatus who was condemned after affirming he had rebaptized *lapsed clergy* from the Great Persecution.[102] Effectively, rebaptism was now illegal.[103] This danger may have been foreseen in the original petition to Constantine and thus was the primary reason for the request for judges to come to Africa and from Gaul. Lacking preparation of formal proof, the synod cut short and, as Stephenson summarizes, with the petitioners "wrong-footed and ill-prepared, the council ruled in favor of Caecilian by default."[104] Caecilian was upheld as right bishop of Carthage as no charges against him had been proven.[105]

99. Stephenson, *Constantine*, 261.

100. Green, *Christianity in Ancient Rome*, 215–18.

101. We note that Caecilian and his supporters were apparently quite willing to submit to the Italian line here. There was no way for Constantine to have known the background of dispute over the practice of rebaptism, which was firmly established in Africa, but which had been refused by Italian bishops for at least sixty years. Though one wonders how Ossius would be unaware of this potential problem.

102. To recall Greenslade's comment (*Church and State*, 15): "At this stage we observe first that Miltiades' council set a precedent of the highest significance by asking Constantine to banish the ten Donatist bishops who had been before it." It is also significant that such rebaptism (of the lapsed) was not necessarily in line with Cyprian's doctrine or practice, which insisted on rebaptism of those baptized by heretics or schismatics.

103. Barnes, *Constantine and Eusebius*, 57. Rebaptism of the lapsed was explicitly so in the condemnation of Donatus, and it should be noted that his zealous application of baptism to lapsed clergy did his cause no favors and was not necessarily normative for the African view. The equation and summary dismissal of all relevant forms of rebaptism was a most tangential and unfortunate focus on the issues at hand by Miltiades.

104. Stephenson, *Constantine*, 261.

105. It is unclear whetherin whether Militiades' and Italian thinking even if the alleged *traditio* of Felix as consecrator were true this would have annulled Caecilian's consecration.

For the Majorinist party, now headed by Donatus, with any inquiry into Caecilian and his consecration having been cut short (in their mind Felix's condition was critical) and Roman preoccupation with rebaptism having been asserted in condemning them, they appealed the decision to Constantine.[106]

Before moving on to the effects of these new developments as well as the new petition, it is worth taking stock of the context for Constantine's consideration of the North African situation. Politically he had established his legitimacy via the Roman Senate as senior among the remaining *Augusti* and had appointed his delegates in the key positions in Africa, Rome's breadbasket. Heading to Milan in February 313, he was positioned to cement political peace with Licinius via marriage to Constantine's sister and was eager that their conference should result in joint commitment to Christianity being relieved of persecution in the East and brought favors already applied to it in the West. Militarily, Constantine had to make ready for results to follow the coming conflict between Licinius and Maximin Daia.[107]

To summarize the emperor's position relative to Christianity in 313, his communication to Maximin Daia (as senior emperor of the three in latter 312) insisting the far eastern *Augustus* cease his persecution of Christians, combined with the issuance of new and increased privileges for Christian clergy and churches in the West upon his defeat of Maxentius (312) and his backing for the policies of general religious freedom articulated by Licinius in 313,[108] all witness to how Constantine was now particularly favoring Christians and patronizing the Christian God and to the way that his clear, special promotion of Christianity remained quite conscious of the political realities on the (still) majority pagan ground across the empire.[109] In light of all of this, the emperor could be excused for assuming that his directives to resolve the African schism would bear fruit or at least movement toward reconciliation. So it was with obvious disappointment that he learned

106. Also consider the date and picture of this appeal presented in the letter to the *vicarious* of Africa in Optatus, *App.* 3, Spring 314.thedate and presented thein the

107. We note the monotheistic prayer Constantine passed on for Licinius to use with his army (which the latter did against Maximin) as an indication of the strategic role religion played in their discussions.

108. This joint policy of religious freedom, which is dependent on Lactantius, was prominent when such policy directives were issued by Licinius after Milan in letters to each of his provinces from at least June onwards. Barnes, *Constantine: Dynasty,* 95–96.

109. Cf. Grant, *Constantine,* 150–55.

that matters in Rome had not been resolved and indeed were worsening in Africa.

APPEAL OF THE SYNOD OF ROME'S JUDGMENT TO CONSTANTINE AND THE COUNCIL OF ARLES

The immediate responses to the Synod at Rome were not surprising: the bishops around Donatus appealed to Constantine on the basis of prejudice, procedural hamstringing, and incomplete investigation (e.g., allegations against Felix and irregularities of election protocols); Miltiades and his synod urged that the anti-Caecilianist bishops be detained or exiled; and Constantine was displeased with the overall results.[110] More important are the unforeseen repercussions these events catalyzed. It had been another situation where Constantine and his advisors, surely including Ossius, had overestimated Christian collegiality and the priorities of Miltiades. The actions of Constantine's deputy panel at Rome had put the church connected with both (and all areas under Constantine's rule) *doctrinally* at odds with the bulk of the North African church that affirmed the broader application of rebaptism—something that had nothing to do with the original petition. He probably realized the problem had become larger, but it is doubtful that he grasped the doctrine at issue. Regardless, Constantine saw he would have to take matters to do with the church and its division more directly into his hands.

Thus, despite his frustrations at the many appeals and, in person,[111] but "surely angered by Miltiades's ploy and still desirous of unity,"[112] Constantine's response was both innovative and unprecedented. In January 314, and through the spring, he called for a general council of the churches under his jurisdiction to meet at Arles on 1 August of that year, issuing invitations to the bishops in Spain, Gaul, Britain, and Italy. From Africa, however, he invited only those who were already involved in the dispute, including representatives of both sides from the Synod of Rome. It would not have taken much to assume that a regional synod could be overridden by a larger, more representative council of bishops; and this time Constantine intended to be present as a participant of some sort. It was a first for an emperor—or any Roman official—to call a general council of the church

110. Frend, *Donatist Church*, 149–50.

111. Optatus, *App.* 3, *ab init.*

112. Stephenson, *Constantine*, 261.

and on their authority as one responsible for the church within his jurisdiction.[113] As such it was to be reflective, *though not truly representative*, of the provinces under his rule with bishops and their attendants being afforded use of the imperial post services for transport.[114] Constantine remained active on other fronts between his meeting with Licinius at Milan (February 313) and the Council of Arles, which was to start on 1 August 314.[115] In North Africa, however, delay afforded divisions time to solidify and the opportunity for the partisan movements there to take on a life of their own.[116]

The Council of Arles is a study of contrasts: the significance of the council is unprecedented but the actual event was by most measures an anticlimactic flop.[117] Going in, expectations had some reason to be high. In Constantine's letter to the *vicarius* of Africa instructing him to send the relevant parties to Arles, the emperor recalled how he was made aware that "many persons in our dominion of Africa had begun to separate from one another with *mad fury*, and had *brought purposeless accusations against each other* about the keeping of the most holy catholic law" (emphasis mine).[118] He then summarized his attempt through the commission at Rome to resolve this quarrel around "Caecilian the Bishop of Carthage, *against whom*

---

113. In all of this Constantine was moving away from Miltiades and it is likely that by this time the emperor was also growing suspect of the bishop of Cordoba's insights into events in North Africa. First, the emperor's council could presumably override the bishop of Rome's council; second, neither Ossius nor Miltiades (or his successor) would be making an appearance at Arles. Cf. Stephenson, *Constantine,* 261, and Drake, *Constantine and the Bishops,* 218–19. Knowing as little as we do about the events at Arles, it might be that Ossius' absence led to the somewhat unstructured proceedings there (at least in contrast to Nicaea).

114. Eusebius, *HE* 10.5.23.

115. See Barnes, *Constantine and Eusebius,* 64–65, for details of Constantine's itinerary during this period.

116. One example is particularly telling: well before Arles, anti-Caecilianist efforts were under way in North Africa to secure the proof that was needed to confirm the allegations against Felix as a "betrayer." Within the year before August 314, an agent of the anti-Caecilianists, Ingentius, convinced the *duovir* who had been in charge at Abthungi in 303 to compose a letter to bishop Felix (as a favor), which summarized how the *duovir,* Alfius Caecilianus, had executed "his duties by burning the Scriptures" he found in the place of worship since he was "charged with local enforcement of the edict." However, Ingentius attached a postscript to this document adding "that Felix, afraid of having his house destroyed if the Scriptures were found there, promised to produce them in the place of worship." Barnes, *Constantine and Eusebius,* 58–59.

117. See, e.g., Barnes, *Constantine and Eusebius,* 58.

118. Optatus, *App.* 3.

especially they all often petitioned me." The commission's acts had been delivered to Constantine, along with verbal affirmation (presumably from the bishops from Gaul) of the equity of the proceedings. These not only declared Caecilian innocent of charges but that his accusers were guilty and had been forbidden to go back to Africa.[119] As a result, now further hearings were needed where Constantine "once hoped that . . . a fitting end [i.e., resolution at Rome] had been made" to the matter. Additionally Aelafius's description of anti-Caecilianist actions in Africa confirmed the emperor's concern that some of the thatparty were "persisting in a line of action which not merely leads to their shame and disgrace, *but also gives an opportunity of detraction to those who are known to turn their minds away from the keeping of the most holy catholic law"* (emphasis mine).[120]

Two significant developments are immediately clear. In stark contrast to the public elevation and worship of the Christian God in North Africa, which Constantine had tried to jumpstart from Rome at the end of 312, events in the African provinces were providing instead the basis for public ridicule of the peace of Christian beliefs and the worship of the Christian God. In the parallel letter of invitation to Chrestus, Bishop of Syracuse, Constantine complained that the African schism has provided "those whose souls are strangers to this most holy religion [a reason] to scoff."[121] Second, it is now down to Constantine "to provide that that which *ought to have ceased by voluntary agreement,* after the judgment already passed, may even now, if possible, be ended by the presence of many persons." Both Constantine's consternation that events in his realm had led to dishonor being ascribed to the Christian God and his opinion that the schism was over base things reasonable people could come to voluntary agreement upon required action.

Returning to the letter to Alfaelius, Constantine's identification of the core problem recalls his first assessment of the anti-Caecilianist party: a "party" responsible for "seditions and contentions," which he now feels they "suddenly called into being" and which they remain focused upon instead of "the reverence which is due to Almighty God." After detailed instructions regarding who should come from North Africa to Arles and how,

119. For instance, the synod had presumed upon Constantine's authority to remand the anti-Caecilianists either into custody or exile.

120. Optatus, *App.* 3. It is significant that Constantine described the problem with a skeptical eye on the anti-Caecilianists.

121. Eusebius, *HE* 10.5.21–24.

Constantine continues this theme describing the representatives of the group around Donatus who had again come to him asserting that "Caecilian is deemed not to be worthy of the worship of our most holy religion."[122] In response to Constantine's nod to the virtue of the actions and judgment at Rome, they "answer with *persistent obstinacy* that the whole case had not been heard, but that these Bishops had shut themselves up somewhere and given the judgment as was most convenient to themselves." Therefore, since resolution of the disturbance in Africa to the public worship of God was being delayed by failure to acknowledge Rome's judgments as just, the emperor now considered "that no end could be made of them without both Caecilian and three of those *who are making a schism against him* coming to the town of Arles, *for the judgment of those who are opposed to Caecilian,* and are bound to accept him as Bishop."[123] Yet, it is the end of this letter that most draws our attention:

> As to the rest, after the matter has been fully inquired into, let it be brought to an end. For when they shall all have come together, those things which are now known to be subjects of contention should with reason receive a timely conclusion . . . I confess to your Lordship, *since I am well aware that you also are a worshipper of the most High God, that I consider it by no means right that contentions and altercations of this kind should be hidden from me, by which, perchance, God may be moved not only against the human race, but also against me myself, to whose care,* by His heavenly Decree, *He has entrusted the direction of all human affairs,* and may in His wrath provide otherwise than heretofore" (emphasis mine).[124]

Not until Constantine is sure that "all [those assembled], bound together in brotherly concord, adore the most holy God with the worship of the catholic religion, that is His due" will he be "fully without anxiety." Here is genuine religious conviction that Christian "contentions and altercations of this kind" fall directly upon the emperor to address and not only in the good imperial tradition of the *pax deorum.* Failure to do so may result in God's wrath or even withholding favor from Constantine's special role "over all human affairs." All this makes sense of the efforts Constantine described in the letter to Bishop Crestus: "as we have commanded that very many bishops . . . should assemble at . . . Arles by the Kalends of August, we thought

122. Optatus, *App.* 3.
123. Ibid.
124. Ibid.

it good to write to you also . . . [so that] both by your Firmness and *by the unanimous wisdom of others assembled, this quarrel* also—disgracefully and miserably prolonged—when all has been heard . . . *by those who are now at variance among themselves*, whom we have also commanded to be present, *may*, however belatedly, *be replaced by genuine religion, faith and fraternal concord* (emphasis mine).[125] The implications are that Constantine hoped an unbiased venue that in some convincing sense represented the whole of the church would be enough to refine and vindicate the verdict of Rome in such a way for those in schism against Caecilian to be reconciled to his position at Carthage—since Constantine assumed Caecilian's innocence. Despite inevitable prejudgment from Rome, the anti-Caecilianist petition-ers should now have a fair hearing in Gaul, whence they originally wanted to receive judges, with full opportunity to air any and all of their allegations in an open environment where specific charges would be investigated. Al-though Constantine expected the previous decision at Rome to be upheld, once "all has been heard" he hoped that the gathered bishops may be able to persuade the factions may set aside their differences and move forward in a united front. That the council would be chaired by one of the Gallic bishops who was part of the Synod at Rome could cut both ways. If the bishops of Arles, Autun, and Cologne had not felt able in Rome to question the pope and Italian majority, they should now feel free to express their own opinion. Still, it is hard to see how any results at Arles that did not agree with Rome could avoid creating new divisions or political problems. Thus, such hopes betray either ignorance or underestimation of the motivations at play in the provinces and a failure to focus on regional differences (as at Nicaea) such as rebaptism,[126] which needed to be brought into discussion with respect if at all. No preparations toward such ends are evident.[127]

On 1 August 314, with bishop Marinus of Arles presiding, around forty-five bishops attended the Council at Arles representing the provinces under Constantine's control.[128] It is possible that the province with the

125. Eusebius, *HE* 10.5.23–24.

126. Donatus himself, never Majorinus, became the lighting rod on this issue and his aggressive application did not put things in a balanced light. In such ways, Donatus' persona quickly became representative for a broader anti-Caecilianist movement.

127. Unlike on the northern side of the Mediterranean, Constantine's own affiliation to the church had no ground presence and little positive association in Africa—other than buildings.

128. Gaul sent sixteen bishops; Italy and the islands ten; Spain six, Britain three or four, and Dalmatia one. Ricciltti, *Age of the Martyrs*, 238; cf. Frend *The Donatist* Church,

largest episcopal representation at Arles still may have been Africa. This helps put in perspective something that could only be felt by the Africans. They were used to larger councils such as the original council of seventy held under Secundus at Carthage in 307/308 or 311/312. While for those invited to Arles from other provinces this council would have been a "great spectacle,"[129] on numbers alone, the Donatist[130] contingent would not have been impressed by a council just over half the size of one they could assemble in haste, aware that if Africa were truly represented at Arles the picture would have looked quite different.

In terms of results, Arles appears to just reiterate Rome, with footnotes. What was decided at Arles in terms of canons is known but we have little sense for how things progressed. The short report of the council to the new bishop of Rome summarized the verdict against those opposed to Caecilian simply by affirming them to be "troublesome men, dangerous to our law and tradition . . . men of undisciplined mind who both the authority of our God, which is with us, and our tradition and the rule of truth reject . . . They have been either condemned or rejected" *because* they lacked "reasonableness in their argument . . . any moderation in their accusations," and "their manner of proof was not to the point."[131] The focus then shifted to miscellaneous items "from among the various matters which occurred to each of us [upon which] we should make decrees to provide for the present state of tranquility." Of the canons, only three are relevant to our discussion.

1. In Canon 3, those [in the army] "who throw down their arms in time of peace" are to be barred from communion. This was a boon to the leader of an army that would hold an increasingly large number of Christians.

2. In Canon 8, baptism by heretics is deemed valid so long as it is trinitarian in application (explicitly contra African tradition) and as such only the laying on of hands is needed.[132]

---

150. We can assume the number of African bishops present (including Caecilian, Donatus and both sides) were between twenty-one (the number at Rome) and ten (rough minimum estimates based on the instructions outline in Optatus, *App.* 3).

129. This is how the bishops there described it to Silvester, the absent Bishop of Rome, who had succeeded Miltiades. Cf. Optatus, *App.* 4.

130. From this point on, the appellation is appropriate if not always optimal. The anti-Caecilianist movement still lacked a true center.

131. Optatus, *App.* 4. No specifics about allegations are given in the report nor clarification of who or how many had been condemned or rejected.

132. "Moreover, with regard to the Africans, *inasmuch as they use their own law of*

3. In Canon 13, *traditores* are to be dismissed from clerical office *if* proved *ex actis publicis . . . non uerbis nudis* (by public record, not simply by verbal accusations). Moreover, the canon affirms that ordinations that had been performed by *traditores* were valid so long as the consecrated were worthy.[133]

Clearly, the council moved along lines that were very sensitive to verbal accusation and strongly in favor of uniformity under the new dispensation of political freedom and favor that they enjoyed through the emperor. The irregularities that carried such weight in Africa, just did not at Arles. The council was not looking for evidence of a suspicious consecration; they were looking for proof of criminal violations.[134] Moreover, the issue of rebaptism was again used against the Africans and it appears this area ("upon which they have their own law," Arles, Canon 8) was not seized upon either by Constantine or the bishops as a potential bridge building point to secure greater resolution. There is no evidence of backroom negotiations or any political unifying efforts save the genuine opportunity to vent grievances. This the Africans apparently did in poor form, which only confirmed presumptions that their motivations were worldly or even spiritually deceived.[135] Consequently, the final result of the council for Constantine was

---

rebaptizing, we have decreed that if any heretic comes to the Church, he should be questioned concerning the Creed, and if it be found that he has been baptized in the Father and the Son and the Holy Ghost, hands shall be laid upon him and no more. But if, on being questioned as to the Creed, he does not give the Trinity in answer, then let him rightly be baptized."

133. Thus, even if Felix were guilty, Caecilian's ordination would have been secure on that front (assuming Caecilian was worthy).

134. The focus for the allegations apparently remained on the lack of hard proof available either at Rome or at Arles. In such a context, the identification of suspicious irregularities by those against Caecilian: from his alleged ill treatment of confessors as a deacon, to the hurried manner in which he was elected in violation of protocol that should have included the Numidian primate, to the suspicions that he had been consecrated by a *traditor*—all of which, from an anti-Caecilianist view, would be taken seriously as they had the backing of a council of seventy bishops; were all met with dismissal (if even recognition) in the absence of a smoking gun. All the more strange then, that such "hard" evidence against Felix as would shortly appear in Cirta, did not reach Arles. The fact that such evidence may have been held until after Arles is important but hard to interpret. It may suggest that there was not much hope for things at Arles since if there was, then surely this data would at least allow the verdict of Rome to be ignored and allegations addressed in a new light. Such anticipated disappointment may again be in part explain of the arrogant behavior manifested by some anti-Caecilianists at Arles.

135. With the pseudo-universality of this council and the perception by its attendees

frustration and even disillusionment, as is seen when he addressed "an angry and impassioned letter to the bishops before they departed."[136] His main objective had not been judgment, which Constantine could affirm as correct; it remained resolution.[137]

There is also the question of how the assembled bishops felt spurred to act in the presence of the emperor at Arles (star struck?) and perhaps reactionary to behavior from the anti-Caecilianists in the proceedings or to words directed against Constantine (see below). We can imagine Constantine showing up as if such an event would have a good history of being organized.[138] Two significant sources of insight come from the experience, actions and reaction of the emperor himself to the proceedings. First, Eusebius later wrote about the event, describing how Constantine sat among the bishops and was content to fit in, dismissing his entourage and acting "as if he were one voice among the many."[139] He participated in the discussion at

---

that expressions of unity were the prime objective, there was no real incentive to do anything beyond affirming the condemnation of Rome, thereby placing most of North Africa at odds with the greater church over the issue of rebaptism. And since rebaptism, rightly administered in the African perspective, was one key to assure church purity, this could easily be taken by African Christians to mean that Arles affirmed in bold print that Constantine's church was in fact impure (or open to impurity). The results lay wide open to propaganda even without misrepresentation.

136. Barnes, *Constantine and Eusebius,* 58; cf. Optatus, *App.* 5.

137. In this regard, Stephenson's (*Constantine,* 261) treatment is representative of a somewhat truncated view when he concludes that at Arles, "In matter of greatest concern, the Donatists were once again ordered to relent, *which was certainly the emperor's preferred outcome*" (emphasis mine). In the instructions for both Rome and Arles, there are clear indications, missed by bishops at the time, that Constantine was expecting them to meet and join together, not just hold hearings, to bring an end to schism. That Constantine expected Caecilian to be affirmed is true. That he would have been willing to see Caecilian condemned or deposed and schism ended seems equally valid.

138. Though there had been church councils (with several numerically larger than Arles) and they had been variously organized, such organization was not yet formalized and other than Cyprian's models few had dealt successfully with open division.

139. Eusebius (*VC* 1.44–1.45.1) writes: "He did not disdain to be present and attend during their proceedings, and he participated in the subjects reviewed, by arbitration promoting the peace of God among all; and he took his seat among them as if he were one voice among many, dismissing his praetorians and soldiers and bodyguards of every kind, clad only in the fear of God and surrounded by the most loyal of his faithful companions. Then such as he saw able to be prevailed upon by argument and adopting a calm and conciliatory attitude, he commended most warmly, showing how he favored general unanimity, but the obstinate he rejected. There were even some who spoke harshly against him, and he tolerated them without resentment, with a gentle voice bidding them to behave reasonably and not be contentious. Some of them respected his rebukes and

points, commending those "he saw able to be prevailed upon by argument and adopting a calm and conciliatory attitude . . . *showing how he favored general unanimity*, but the obstinate he rejected."[140] He offered correction as much to demeanor as content, and remaining calmly comported when his suggestions were ignored and even when he was verbally assaulted. Eusebius continues: "There were even *some who spoke harshly against him, and he tolerated them without resentment*, with a gentle voice bidding them to behave reasonably and not be contentious. *Some of them respected his rebukes and desisted, while those who were past curing* and could not be brought to a sound mind *he left in the hands of God.*"[141] The picture is one of an emperor doing what he could to let a church council run its own course and encourage moves toward unity, with a focus more on manner than on content of the discussion.

Despite disappointments, the fact and manner of the council are of significant import and speak strongly for Constantine's religious understanding of church and state at the time. Shortly after or likely in closing the council we get a second glimpse into Constantine's mind at Arles as he addressed and dismissed the bishops. This significant communication contains two now well-established aspects in its opening section: a dependence upon Lactantius' *Divinae institutiones*,[142] and an articulation by Constantine of his own experience of God's salvation. Our interest in the address must start further into the piece. After greeting the bishops and outlining the "wonderful kindness" of the "Almighty God," which he has observed and experienced in both general and personal terms, Constantine described the assembled bishops' actions as "a most impartial inquiry" through which they had "recalled to a better hope and fortune those whom *the wickedness of the devil seemed by his wretched persuasion to have turned away* from the most noble light of the catholic law."[143] Yet, just as the rescue

---

desisted, while those who were past curing and could not be brought to a sound mind he left in the hands of God, being unwilling himself to devise anything whatever to any person's hurt." Unless otherwise noted, all translations from *VC* are from Hall and Cameron, *Life of Constantine*. The view taken here is that the description of 1.44 applies to Arles first, if not exclusively (per Barnes) and my sense that the flow of the passage into 1.45.1–2 is of a piece that fit the African references.

140. Eusebius, *VC* 1.44.3.

141. Ibid., 1.45.1

142. Which Digeser has demonstrated ("Dating the Divine Institutes," esp. 34–37) and is discussed in Brian Shelton's chapter.

143. Optatus, *App.* 5.

of Christ as Savior is triumphant, so for the schismatics, "if even now they will consent with pure faith to make their obedience to the most holy Law, they will be able to understand how great a provision has been made for them." Constantine hoped that such might result "even in those in whom the greatest hardness of heart has been engendered." This has not, he concluded, been the case, stating with frustration that *already* he has been appealed to by this group. The implications is that he will have to hear their appeal because the council's "right judgment has not been of any avail to them, nor has the merciful God made an entrance into their dispositions... since *so great a madness still holds them captive.*" So much that now "with unbelievable arrogance" they are: "departing from the right judgment that was given, *from which, as through the provision of Heaven I have learned they are appealing to my judgment . . .* oh, *mad daring of their rage!* They have made an appeal, as is done in the lawsuits of the pagans . . . *What of those* shirkers of the law *who refuse the judgment of Heaven, and have thought fit to ask for mine? Do they thus think of Christ the Savior? Behold, they are now 'Betrayers.'* Behold, without any need for . . . examination, they have betrayed themselves by their wicked deeds (emphasis mine).[144]

Constantine clearly grasped the focus of the Donatist' accusations, as he turns their phrase against them. He was disappointed that the Donatist party had emerged defiant, even affronted and arrogant, actions to him as bad as any they had alleged against others. His association of "madness" and the "devil's persuasion" with their behaviors is also significant. As the address concludes, he makes an important distinction. Namely, that the assembled bishops should exercise patience and give these "betrayers" a chance to choose the right things. Despite any obstinate actions they may observe, he exhorts the bishops to "go your way, and return to your own Sees, and remember me, that our Savior may always have mercy on me." Why, this prayer? Because Constantine has failed through the council to yet oversee resolution of the schism in North Africa and, as he immediately makes clear, he has directed his men to act as the arm of justice "to bring these wicked deceivers of religion to my court." Similarly, his officials in Africa have been ordered "as often as he finds any instances of *this madness,* he is to send the guilty, forthwith, to my court, lest any longer, beneath so great a shining of our God, such things be done by them, *as may provoke the greatest anger of the Heavenly Providence*" (emphasis mine).[145] So the prayer

144. Ibid.
145. Ibid.

requested is both for mercy against any divine displeasure over results thus far and to cover any lack of patience as Constantine takes actions to remove the contagion of contention from its source into his own presence where it can be addressed without the risk of ongoing Christian strife that still may provoke God's anger.

We have here a unique window into Constantine's personal spiritual and religious development. The spiritual picture Constantine has of the Donatists is highlighted by his use of "madness" to excuse behavior and justify both action and non-action and this phrase is used three times in conjunction with spiritual forces in his address.[146] So, as Constantine emerged from Arles, we can identify a significant shift with regard to the church and his understanding both of it and his relations to it.[147] Previously, he had been treating the church as a singly organized entity and consequently made some misassumptions about the level of that organization.

Arles also gives a snapshot of the church in the West. Its bishops, including an African contingent, are now linked and responsible to Constantine in explicit ways. His disciplinary arm has been appealed to and established as an enforcer of their collective decisions. His authority has emerged equal or greater than theirs on issues that relate to the church's right worship or, more specifically, whatever is not right worship. The bishops outside Italy have been given a framework that assumes a special place for the bishop of Rome, but also contains in a model of general council the capability to determine matters of practice that is at least equal to Rome's. The church, excluding the anti-Caecilianists in North Africa, had adopted uniform practices regarding a number of common situations such as celibacy and, like the case of rebaptism in point, has begun to determine orthodoxy by majority, in which uniformity is now a significant goal as opposed

146. The combination of passion, awareness of God's salvation and its ability to redeem, clear interaction with Lactantius's *DI* (so much so that he probably had a copy at hand), and determination to promote peace despite real spiritual adversaries but take responsibility on himself for corrective measures, all allow a valuable glimpse into Constantine's personal struggle to see how to lead the church away from division and contention, let alone open conflict. That he needs to lead thus he just assumes.

147. Stephenson's take (*Constantine*, 262) is that Constantine viewed no power higher than his own relative to any administration, religious or otherwise. While he was happy to delegate to Miltiades and a balanced hearing at Rome and then further to Arles when Miltiades did not achieve a resolution, Constantine understood that true authority could be refused if it lacked power that was recognized. But no one would deny Constantine's own authority on the matter (cf. his address to bishops at Arles and later letter to Celsus in Optatus, *App.* 7).

to a common but not necessary emergent property of the communion. The acceptance by Caecilian and his party of the Roman line on rebaptism is the most significant illustration at hand. A "Donatist" party now exists that is formally in schism not just with Caecilian's church but also with the general "great" church. Any in North Africa who stay true to the older African position on baptism are also now outside the majority orthodoxy of the church of the west. That no communication to the churches in Africa follows Constantine's dismissal address at Arles is a very significant silence, especially compared to Nicaea.

APPEAL FROM ARLES AND THE DELAY OF CONSTANTINE'S VERDICT

Constantine may have been assured of the rectitude of the judgments reached at Arles, but he realized and embraced that it was left to him to sort out the consequences for those condemned and to find a way to bring the council's decisions to bear on the situation to end division in North Africa. Then, shortly after the council, word arrived of a suit filed on 19 August 313 in Carthage against Felix of Abthungi that included formal evidence of *traditio* against the bishop.[148] The timing bears attention[149] and this news brought Constantine up short and redirected his actions.[150] He promptly ordered his vicar in Africa to make a full inquiry into the case against Felix in light of the new evidence. However, it took until 15 February 315 for the trial to conclude[151] finally under the Proconsul Aelianus and an additional delay of over two months for the results to reach

148. Barnes, *Constantine and Eusebius*, 58–59. As mentioned above, this was based on forged evidence that an anti-Caecilianist agent had started securing well before Arles.

149. Just over two weeks after Constantine's passionate dismissal to the bishops at Arles and disappointment at the failure of the church's council to achieve a meaningful reconciliation for the North African church.

150. He had by this point a clear idea that a strong opposition party existed in North Africa and that some sort of arbitration may therefore be needed without just one clear winner. But now there was reason for him to be suspect of the accuracy and approach of the two "hearings" that had occurred. Rome had not proceeded along his instructions, but events at Arles had done, although he had left the actual proceedings to the bishops. It is not surprising the he might enter a time where he kept his own counsel and was not so confident in his regular theological advisors.

151. The *vicarius* was replaced, his successor fell ill, leaving the prefect to finally step in and bring things to conclusion six plus months after Arles. Barnes, *Constantine and Eusebius*, 58–59.

Constantine.[152] Immediately after Arles, little was satisfactory to Constantine but everything was set for a gradual drain of the Donatist leadership from North Africa combined with some sort of mediation in the provinces and an extended rehabilitation period for the schismatic leaders remanded to Constantine's court. There would be plans to figure out but time for that once things began to move promptly forward. Now, however, everything shifted because of events on the ground in North Africa. The result was considerable delay of any such actions as there was the nagging possibility that Donatus and his colleagues at court might not be—at least solely—in the wrong. The ongoing contact with the Donatists in such a state does seem to have softened Constantine's stance towards them and made him more aware of the complexity of things in North Africa.[153] Optatus presents a record[154] of the events when at last Felix was exonerated and the forgery by Ingentius was discovered, confessed and also confirmed by the elderly Caecilianus. However, the six months before word of Felix's acquittal[155] arrived and even the months following the revelation of anti-Caecilianist forgery were periods of uncertainty for Constantine. The news from Africa was encouraging and he immediately called for the parties to come before him; but it was double-edged since it could imply at least some in the Donatist camp had anticipated the results at Arles and had been taking coordinated action well beforehand. It confirmed organized resistance on the ground, willing to take criminal actions, something Constantine would not want turned toward political unrest. Then compounding things further, for reasons unknown, Caecilian failed to appear at court in Rome, putting off things (and Constantine) until later at Milan.

This period of vacillation between the trial of Felix and Constantine's response to its results merits rethinking. It shows that Constantine was pondering the North African problem and in terms of resolution, not just verdict and enforcement. He increasingly understood that perhaps a majority of Christians in North Africa were anti-Caecilianists and that something would have to be resolved *there* in the provinces. Two aspects

---

152. Not until after April 28. See Barnes, *Constantine and Eusebius*, 59, and Optatus, *App.* 8, concerning the approval of some Donatists to leave Trier for Africa during this interval. It is hard not to imagine that this "buying time" was an intentional move by the anti-Caecilianists.

153. Cf. Optatus, *App.* 6.

154. *Optatus*, 1.22, and Optatus, *App.* 2.

155. Barnes (*Constantine: Dynasty*, 315) observed that, "Constantine's actions before he received Aelinus' verdict [in 315] seem vacillating and mysterious."

deserve more attention: The first is that Lactantius' ideas, even if he was no longer present, continued to attract but haunt Constantine, particularly the observation that "coercion is inimical to true religion." This was probably equaled by the concern that inter-Christian divisions could undermine Lacantius' model of universal gradual attraction to the true Christian God.[156] The second aspect is the indication that Constantine was actively thinking about who might effectively bring the message of unity to North Africa, for during this period he considered at least three and possibly four distinct approaches:

1. The idea of holding the final imperial hearings on the matter in Africa presided over by Constantine or his delegates. This is something that he initially dismisses, then appears to grant, only to change his mind back to his "first choice," which was to hear and render the decision at court.[157]

2. The idea of removing both Donatus and Caecilian from the picture and sending mediators to select a new unified bishop of Carthage (e.g., the mission of bishops Eunomius and Olympius).[158]

3. The idea of recruiting particularly admirable Christians, such as Eunomius and Olympius, to be his advocates on the ground in North Africa towards gradual reconciliation or his mediators of more direct reconciliation negotiations. Here we also note the comments in his later letter to Alexander and Arius in 324.[159] Was Constantine thinking this broadly even earlier?

4. Coming himself to put down opposition that was not open to reconciliation.[160]

The chronology and overlap of these various possibilities is convoluted and when viewed from the outside would communicate hesitancy—not confidence or threat. Nevertheless, they all show Constantine's intention to determine an effective course of action during the period between Arles

---

156. Something that would result, in the Lactantian ideal, if Christians were given opportunity to worship God in an empire free of religious coercion.

157. Optatus, *App.* 6.

158. *Optatus* 1.26. According to Barnes (*New Empire*, 244), this would have been in the summer of 315.

159. Eusebius, *VC* 2.66–2.68.1.

160. Optatus, *App.* 8. Consider "Constantine's letter to Celsus, vicar of Africa" discussed below.

and his final judgment of the case. He still lacked understanding of the situation on the ground and especially the theological nature of the North African church, though signs of movement in his understanding are evident. Responsibility for such deficits partly lies with his theological advisors, however, it also highlights that as Constantine came to Christianity, he remained firmly fixed in the basic Roman conception of religion as individual observance of cult and ritual—actions not necessarily reflective of the internal or spiritual. He did not yet have the doctrinal antennae of what it meant to be part of an ecclesial body, wherein interdependence and effects on collective witness were crucial on individual, local, regional and now empire-wide scales. This interdependent aspect was foreign to Constantine. That he was never experientially on the inside of this relative to the church or the interdependent witness of the *ecclesia* in the face of persecution may have been the most costly aspect of his decision to delay baptism until just before death.

Constantine's vacillations also reveal important deficits in the North African context with which he dealt. In particular, the two sides did not appear to be equal opponents *in situ*. Caecillian appears quite passive and, in our records, he is always silent, sometimes absent, and most likely to be found in or on his way to his church.[161] Moreover, figures like Felix who might have been a vocal advocate for and with Caecilian were kept on the sidelines with suspicion by all parties.[162] With only one real set of activists in the situation, Constantine was bottlenecked by Carthage. Donatus was not so hindered. The emperor rightly sensed that things could go against him on the ground in North Africa. In the spring of 315 he wrote: "if the case were tried in Africa [by judges sent there] it would be determined, not as is fitting, and as the demands of truth require, but that through your exceedingly great obstinacy something might easily result which would both be displeasing to God in Heaven, and also would be exceedingly detrimental to my good reputation."[163] Such deficits, context, and internal questions explain at least part of vacillations in 314–315 up to Constantine's final adjudication at Milan in October 315. However, they do not account for the delay of over a year between that verdict and any corresponding

---

161. He seems primarily concerned with maintaining what was his, especially at Carthage, and appears willing to adopt whatever Constantine's delegates sent his way, with little evidence of efforts to create a growing college of bishops around his cause.

162. *Optatus* 1.27, *ad fin.*

163. Optatus, *App.* 6.

implementation—November 316 at the earliest. In this, Constantine seems to have made several faulty assumptions about his subjects and options. As Stephenson comments, Constantine thought that the power of the synods, councils, and mediators should be followed but felt that "power must be recognized, and where theirs [i.e., bishops] is not, none would deny his own."[164] Since the final hearing before him at Milan was *the* final appeal, he assumed things would now have to adjust to his judgment and spark changes to accommodate it. What took him a long time to see was that it was unlikely anything would change in North Africa unless something there made things change.

Constantine's Verdict and Delayed Judgment

In this situation, we encounter a fascinating and angry letter where Constantine refers to a potential visit to Africa and which shows, among other things, that he is beginning to understand a connection between Caecilian's opponents and martyrdom.[165] On first glance, Constantine appears almost out of control, ready to come to Africa in a vengeance to show where and with whom "right religion" and the "due form of worship" were to be found.[166] Those who opposed it would "suffer the due penalties of their madness and reckless obstinacy." Our dating of this crucial piece follows Barnes' narrative putting it perhaps early winter 315/316.[167] Other accounts place it as early as spring 315, a matter that needs focused reevaluation beyond the scope of this chapter. Regardless of when this outburst occurred between 315 and early 316, it is a significant marker for understanding Constantine's mind with regard to the church and politics.[168] He keenly felt the respon-

164. Stephenson, *Constantine*, 261.

165. *Optatus*, 1.26, and Optatus, *App.* 7; Frend, *Donatist Church*, 158.

166. This was possibly the only thing that might have achieved the sought after concord.

167. For instance, in the autumn of 315 after Constantine's final decision in October, and after he had been consulted twice regarding its lack of observance. See Barnes, *Constantine and Eusebius*, 58–60. Stephenson *(Constantine, 263)* assigns the date much earlier to the spring of 315, which is possible in light of the potential error of both parties, but I consider Constantine's frustration more consistent with the situation after his own judgment had been ignored.

168. In Roman society there was always overlap between the officials of state and religion. As we have seen, Constantine was far from an exception to this. He was in fact prudent but aggressive in his integration of religion and the empire.

sibility to ensure concord and right worship for the Christian community lest God be displeased and alter his favor. Moreover he had been on a path, inspired by Lactantius, to create an empire in which religious freedom was the general rule on a playing field tipped toward orthodox Christianity. The key stumbling block to this pursuit had been an existing and stubborn division between Christians themselves, as reflected in the North African schism, and it was for the resolution of this issue that he remained engaged, all the more since his verdict had been snubbed.[169]

Almost before Constantine's verdict upholding Caecilian as the rightful bishop of Carthage was given, it seems that the principal actors (Donatus then Caecilian) had returned to Africa, where the schism continued with renewed vigor.[170] Constantine received grim reports back from the *vicarius Africae*, Celsus, to whom he responded in this remarkable letter.[171] It opens acknowledging Celsus' handling of a "seditious tumult" that one Menalius "and the others who have departed from the truth of God" had been planning. Constantine reflects that those in the Donatist group at court who had endeavored to flee when he prepared to "inquire most fully between them and Caecilian, concerning the charges brought against him" in fact "were hastening to return to the things which they both had done previously and are now persisting in doing" in North Africa. Despite all this, Constantine instructs Celsus, to "leave alone" those who have returned understanding that "we *must temporize* with them (emphasis mine)." The surprising indication that those dismissed from his court condemned may still have a potential role to play in Constantine's plans should not be overlooked. When combined with the real fireworks to come in this letter, it suggests that Constantine was not on the verge of launching persecution on the Donatists. What he was contemplating is more complex and apparently hinged on leaders from both sides being shown the truth and having the truth about themselves revealed so that they may join in the fight against the "war" that is violating God's worship. He continued: "you should make

---

169. Stephenson (*Constantine,* 262–63) reads this as indicating "how close (Constantine) had come to instituting persecution." Far from reverting "to his tried methods: summary judgment, autocracy and force" post Arles, as is argued below, I see a figure genuinely worried that he may not be able to bring resolution to the divided church in North Africa, processing options to do so on several levels that go beyond "summary judgment, autocracy and force." Thus, Constantine probably eventually adopted Christian repression reluctantly.

170. Barnes, *Constantine and Eusebius,* 60; cf. *Optatus* 1.26, and Optatus, *App.* 7.

171. Preserved in Optatus, *App.* 7.

it plain both to Caecilian and to [these leaders of the anti-Caecilianits], that when by the Divine Goodness I come to Africa, *I shall render it most clear to all*, both to Caecilian, and to those who are acting against him, *by reading a perfectly plain judgment, as to what and what kind of worship is to be given to the Supreme God*, and with what manner of service He is pleased" (emphasis mine).[172] Constantine aims to come as judge to both groups relative to the single goal of the Supreme God receiving proper worship. Twin references to Caecilian here raise the possibility that he may not remain unscathed if Constantine comes. The emperor promises "to drag into the light by diligent examination" those things "some fancy they can keep dark," namely, of "those same persons who now *stir up the people in such a war* as to bring it about *that the supreme God is not worshipped with the veneration that is His due*. Such instigators, he says, "I shall destroy and dash in pieces." The focus remains on eliminating whoever is causing the worship of God to lack correct veneration. Significantly, Constantine uses the picture of war among the many but caused by leaders on both sides.[173]

Constantine next addressed martyrdom and, as Frend recognized, indicating that "In one way or another, Caecilian's opponents had become associated in his mind with the martyrs."[174] Constantine wrote, "It is sufficiently clear that no one may hope to obtain the honors of a martyr with that kind [of martyrdom] which is seen to be foreign to the truth of religion." Therefore he will waste no time before causing "those men whom *I shall ascertain* to have acted against that which is right and against religion itself, and *whom I shall discover to have been guilty of violence in their worship*, to undergo the destruction which they have deserved by their *madness* and reckless obstinacy" (emphasis mine).[175] So if any disputant has doubts about their claim on salvation in the face of death they should demonstrate it in appropriate actions now since Constantine warns he will "most diligently search into the things that concern not merely the people, but *also those clerics who are in the first places*." The recurring theme is that Constantine is coming to do three things: first, to show and demonstrate "what

172. Ibid.

173. Ibid. The war itself that stirred up people is the causal agent sapping the proper veneration from the worship being offered to God. Constantine is not principally concerned with specific practice or beliefs here, but with the overriding reality of open conflict between Christians caused by those who are stirring up the factions.

174. See Frend, *Donatist Church*, 158 and n109; although "whether they had any claim to the blessing of the martyrs was the point they must prove."

175. Optatus, *App. 7*.

kind of worship is to be given to the Supreme God"; second, to eliminate those on any side that are stirring up people into a "war" amongst those who should be engaged in right worship; and third, to make clear to all the true nature and actions of those in leadership and pursuing division. Constantine claims that all such actions are part of the responsibility of the "office of a Prince . . . after having driven away errors and destroyed all rash opinions, to bring it about that all men should show forth true religion and simplicity in concord, and to render to Almighty God the worship which is His due."[176]

Modern commentators rightly observe that war with Licinius got in the way of any such mission and Constantine never went to Africa, leaving us to wonder what would have happened if this "when I come" ultimatum had taken place. The texts suggest that precise cultic uniformity was not what Constantine would have insisted on at this point, but rather a clear demonstration by leaders that they were committed to the goal of peaceful reconciliation, wherein worship offered was being done in a community at peace; not public war. Had Constantine's agenda been brought into being, it need not have been merely an inverse kind of persecution on those Christians that were deemed "rigorist, having no truck with Christians who would compromise, or, as Constantine saw it, tolerate others."[177] As the canons of Arles (and Iliberris!) reflect rigorist leanings, the key for Constantine was not uniformity per se, but a mutual desire for God's worship to be as universally in concord as possible.[178] A searching, well-publicized display of what was practically keeping the church divided may have gone a long way toward quieting a people stirred up by biased exaggeration and toward identifying a core group of leaders who could champion the cause of unity *and* holiness after the tradition of Cyprian. Such results are speculation, but Constantine's savvy with propaganda and his willingness to take swift, dramatic action, might have left a quite different result.

What requires no speculation was that the situation left as it was leaned more towards the side of Donatus in terms of theological tradition and long conditioned suspicions of church cooperation with the state. Without Constantine's presence, official action against the anti-Caecilianist

---

176. Ibid.

177. Stephenson, *Constantine*, 262.

178. In the event, he suspected, quite rightly, that the underlying motives of many of the leaders, on both sides, when revealed would not show the motives of true martyrs, but rather the pursuit of worldly things at the expense of God's "due reverence."

party, especially in Carthage, was bound to elicit violence. Indeed, it may have been because Constantine did not come to Africa that persecution did come.

CONSTANTINE'S PERSECUTION OF ANTI-CAECILIANIST PARTY (317–321)

After yet another year (through 316) of ongoing disputes between the rival North African churches showed that no mind was being paid to his "final" verdict, Constantine made the decision to enforce sanctions against the anti-Caecilianists.[179] That it took this long for such action to occur, especially in light of the threat to come in person just considered, indicates ongoing deliberation by the emperor, and then a conscious choice to focus his personal efforts elsewhere. The "when I come!" threat faded and the hammer of sanctions dropped from a distance.

Meanwhile, once Constantine's final verdict concurred with the ecclesiastical decisions of Rome and Arles, the catholic church considered all outside communion with Caecilian to be in schism and the long tradition of African rebaptism of schismatics and heretics to be unorthodox.[180] Thus, when division was formalized by enforcement of these positions, a critical freezing point was reached that fixed in place so many things about the split North African communion and the positions of the various players involved. As we consider the period during which Constantine legislated persecution against the Donatists, we can look for changes in his motivations and for the genesis of a certain resignation to a "Donatist" Africa.[181]

In his entry on Donatism in the *Encyclopedia of Early Christianity,* Frend wrote that with the repression of the Donatists beginning in 316: "This should have been the end of the matter, especially when in December 320 a spectacular trial was held before the *consularis* (governor) of Numidia, Zenophilus, at which it became clear that the chief opponents of Caecilian in that province had been themselves *traditores* . . . the Donatists,

---

179. We do not have his specific instructions, but as Barnes (*Constantine and Eusebius*, 60) explains, the letter sent on November 10, 316, to the *vicarius Africae* in which Constantine reviewed the conflict probably communicated provisions by which to repress the schismatics.

180. As well as the more recent and irregular rebaptism of the lapsed.

181. Preliminary evidence suggests the emperor was increasingly having second thoughts about how to proceed toward his goal of a truly unified empire and church.

however, went from strength to strength."[182] What allowed such a result? Constantine's orders against the Donatists were executed and Optatus indicates that there was initial violence when they were enforced and churches were confiscated. During the same period, some Donatist bishops were exiled.[183] In a sense, the Donatist church was placed back into the familiar position from the Great Persecution where, naturally, the state was against them. This gave a tangible connection to their long verbalized claim that the connection of Caecilian's church to the state confirmed it was the church of the "betrayers." The effect should not be underestimated. Repression was "largely at Carthage"[184] and it was there on 12 March 317, the African "schismatic sect gained its first martyrs when Roman soldiers and a catholic mob attacked Donatist churches, allegedly at the instigation of Caecilianus, and killed several Donatists, including two bishops of small African towns."[185] We do not have much data on the extent of the repressive measures or what violence they inspired,[186] but from this period, the Donatist party would mark a tangible link in the chain between themselves and the church of the martyrs.[187] As Decret notes, the persecution of Donatists, cooperation of catholic churches with the state, and moves to bribe schismatic congregations back into communion with Caecillian, were not just doomed to fail. They also affirmed the very position the African church had always celebrated, a martyr church standing fast against the world.[188]

Did Constantine begin to worry that he was, even if rarely and accidently, creating true martyrs or souring his connection with the long tradition of the church's martyrs in Africa? Certainly the possibility bears future study beyond the limits of this chapter, as does a revived influence of Lactantius as Constantine digested the publications of *De Mortibus* and *De Ira Dei* during the period of anti-Caecilianist persecution.[189] Nevertheless, it is

---

182. Frend, "Donatism," 274–75.

183. *Optatus*, 1.26, and Optatus, *App.* 7; Tilley, *Donatist Martyr Stories*, xv–xvi; cf. *Optatus* 3.1; Augustine *Cresc.* 3.70.81.

184. Decret, *Early Christianity in North Africa*, 105.

185. Barnes, *Constantine and Eusebius*, 60.

186. Ibid., 317nn157–60.

187. See the passion accounts in Tilley, *Donatist Martyr Stories*, 51–52 (cf. 52–60).

188. Decret, *Early Christianity in North Africa*, 104–5.

189. Additionally war with Licinius dragged through 316 and negotiations well into 317 (Lenski "Constantine," 264). As a result, Constantine would have occasions to be reminded of certain legal provisions that dealt with the legacy of martyrs as he incorporated the territories (in the Balkans) that came to him in 317.

possible that realization and concern regarding the connection in Africa of schismatics to traditional and even recent martyrs[190] tied into Constantine's eventual toleration of the Donatists. Regardless, the increasing association of the church of Constantine with the church of the betrayers (or worse the persecuting church) would have caused him concern both spiritually and politically, and not just in North Africa since bad news is wont to spread.[191]

Certainly a real change of perspective did take place at some point between what we find in Optatus' *Appendix* 5 (August, 314) or *Appendix* 8 (315-early 317)[192] and Constantine's letter of toleration for the Donatists in *Appendix* 9 (321).[193] Did a conception of how to set up the catholics in North Africa for martyrdom claims and to undercut such Donatist claims cause the "patience" perspective to become the policy that figures so prominently in Optatus' accounts of 321 and even as late as 330?[194]

Here we return to the rest of the passage Eusebius gave when describing Constantine's actions and demeanor at councils such as Arles: "it came about that *those in Africa reached such a pitch of dissension that crimes were committed, some evil demon* apparently resenting the unstinted present prosperity and *driving those men on to criminal actions, in order to provoke the Emperor's fury against them.* His envy however did not prosper: *the emperor treated what was being done as ridiculous* and said he understood the provocation of the Evil One (emphasis mine).[195] We cannot pinpoint the exact period in Africa that this describes.[196] However, the spiritual claims being ascribed to Constantine are striking on several important levels. Constantine's mode of response in the face of verbal abuse and rejection was the same as in the face of crimes designed to bait him. Those perpetrators

190. Eusebius (*VC* 3.1.6) writes, "while he never ceased honoring the memorials of the holy martyrs of God." For more on reverence for martyrs, restoration of places of martyrs, and inheritances of martyrs, see Eusebius, *VC* 2.21, 35, 40.

191. He was very attuned to propaganda and the potential for it. We have already seen him assert a counter charge of who were the real "betrayers" in his address at Arles (314) and his affirmation of where "true" martyrs lay in his letter to Celsus (315–early 316).

192. Constantine's dismissal address from Arles and threat to come to Africa in the letter to Celsus respectively.

193. Constantine's letter of toleration for the Donatists, which prefigures *Appendix* 10—Constantine's resignation to Donatist control in much of Africa.

194. Optatus, *App.* 10.

195. Eusebius, *VC* 1.45.1–3.

196. Probably it was before the letter to the *vicarius*, Celsus, but possibly into 316, or even the period of persecution—in which corporeal harm was not desired.

considered not of sound mind and possibly demonically possessed at the instigation of the "Evil One" against Constantine[197] the emperor "left in the hands of God" and considered they "ought to be pitied rather than punished." The spiritual tenor here combined with a dual understanding of "madness" as either "insane" or possessed of "spiritual madness" is critical. If this passage is compared with the letter to Celsus threatening to come to Africa, where "madness" is only used in connection with "destruction which they have deserved by their *madness* and reckless obstinacy" of ones "whom I shall discover to have been *guilty of violence in their worship*,"[198] a more nuanced picture begins to emerge of Constantine's understanding of schismatics. Taking the passages together, in the face of such "madness" one needs:

- To leave those who claim Christ but who refuse to be corrected in the hands of God having made clear where the right path lies (since He is judge and they may choose to choose well);[199] or

- If crimes are committed, to save these insane from themselves by removing them from temptation or danger and this from pity, not seeking by action to harm or coerce them, but to bring them to the a safe place to again be left in the hands of God; or

- If someone remains either in obstinate spiritual frenzy or obstinate conscious criminal action that brings violence to the worship of God, Constantine reserves the state's right to incapacitate these factions.

The implications of this picture for Constantine's experience of the period of Donatist persecution are significant. Effectively, between 317 and 320 Constantine was removing the leaders of this stubborn schism against God's church to where they cannot continue harm and may come back to their senses.[200] Also, he was removing the temptations—opportunity, example and location—of those followers who may have been "stirred up to madness" of this kind. Finally, in those rare cases where the insane or consciously determined schismatic cannot be safely removed from doing violence to God's worship and communion, removal by incarceration or

197. Cf. the address at Arles (Optatus, *App.* 5) and the discussion above.

198. Optatus, *App.* 7.

199. Cf. Optatus, *App.* 5.

200. As he had attempted to do earlier by remanding them to his own court and intended to do further after Arles before the evidence against Felix interrupted things (Optatus, *App.* 8).

death may be required. This last option is only associated in texts describing "war" and "violence" by the offenders.[201] It is interesting to compare the letter Constantine sent to Alexander and Arius at the beginning of his interaction with their controversy around 324.[202] There, the whole of Africa is described as "seized with madness," and Constantine is in search of peaceful strategies to address it.[203] But what if the religious activists were to be stirred up earlier by renewed, more solidly based repression, leveraged by the new revelations against them? Could Constantine afford the possibility of open sedition if the schismatic cause started to experience perhaps dramatic loses? Would the factional dispute become open political opposition?

Events at Cirta may have forced Constantine's hand. The inquiry at Cirta in December 320 by the governor of Numidia[204] into the allegations of a disaffected Donatist deacon Nundinarius against his bishop Silvanus led to the bombshell news that several key Donatist leaders themselves were guilty of *traditio* and other crimes. Barnes indicates that the inquiry at Cirta by *consularius* Zenophilus was perhaps a prelude to firmer measures in Numidia.[205] If correct, this sets up a major missed opportunity from the trial's results. It may have represented a tough road, but the beachhead was certainly open for Constantine's (or a delegate's) coming to press the advantage. In light of the earlier communication to Celsus, the option to bring pressure for reunification leveraged by the guilt of so many of Caecilian's opponents instead of issuing toleration was certainly on the table. Yet, the

---

201. Optatus, *App.* 7. It should be noted that once the understanding the schism was connected to a spiritual "war," it would certainly effect how a seasoned military leader would approach things.

202. Eusebius, *VC* 2.64–72.

203. Eusebius writes (*VC* 2.66–68.1): "Indeed, when *an intolerable madness had seized the whole of Africa because of those who* had dared with ill-considered frivolity to *split the worship of the population into various factions,* and when I personally desired to put right this disease, the *only cure sufficient for the affair that I could think of was that,* after I had destroyed the common enemy of the whole world, who had set his own unlawful will against your holy synods, *I might send some of you to help towards the reconciliation* of those at variance with each other . . . But (O best, divine Providence!) what a deadly wound my ears suffered, or rather my very heart, for the information that the division originating among you was much graver than those I had left behind there, so that your regions, from which I had hoped medicine would be supplied to others, were now in greater need of healing"; emphasis mine.

204. Optatus *App.* 1.

205. Barnes, *Constantine and Eusebius*, 60; cf. Optatus, *App.* 1,

dramatic events of Cirta passed without collateral effect and a little over a year later, Constantine would reverse course and issue toleration for the schismatics. What remains intriguing is that this change of mind came just when things looked to be starting to turn against the Donatists. Among the questions this raises are whether the situation with Licinius in 320 alone was sufficient to stimulate such a change and whether this change of mind was more politically or theologically motivated? Future research and discussion beyond the limits of this chapter are needed to address such questions.

CONCLUSION

This chapter has provided an outline of the interaction with the North African schism that would be formative for Constantine's later perspectives and actions related to church matters. In terms of conciliar direction, presumption of authority, the importance of initial communication, and the consequences of both delayed action and "correction" by force, the "Donatist" controversy set various trajectories upon which Constantine would selectively continue as he related to the whole of the church. Response to the schism also set significant precedents in several areas: identifying right belief with a representative council under the emperor; creating parallel authority structures that intertwined church and emperor;[206] reducing regional distinctives of religious practice for the sake of more uniform worship; and in setting some practical limits on the ideals of toleration and religious freedom. The interaction also provided Constantine a key framework within which his own developing Christianity would be shaped and understood. While we do not have much data beyond his official communiqués and policies, dealing with the schism in North Africa sparked two of the most personal and theologically revealing communications prior to his *Oration to the Saints*: the dismissal address to the Council of Arles in 314 and his letter to Celsus, *vicarius* of Africa (c. 315–316). The course of the controversy to 316 revealed that Constantine, and his religious advisors, underestimated the depth of feeling and division on the ground in North Africa and allowed too much delay before engaging the problem directly. Such results would spur a more interactive and expedient engagement in the later Arian crisis. Theologically, Constantine clearly wrestled with the ideal of religious freedom and a state wherein worship of the one "Supreme

206. Especially with regard to enforcement of decisions.

God," his patron God, would be optimally observed and practiced. Movement in this area started from the baseline of traditional imperial responsibility for the *pax deorum* and on the public side this amounted to dramatic efforts to bring Christian cult practice to the level of Rome's traditional religions. This was especially visible in the identification of Christian clergy with the special public and financial privileges accorded to traditional priests as well as in the grants for improvements and new construction of Christian places of worship.[207] On the private side, such established imperial responsibility combined with Constantine's own sense of destiny as being especially chosen by God (a sense that was affirmed by many in the Christian community) to create serious pressure to achieve that communal worship, concord, and decorum, which Constantine thought the "most holy God is due in the worship of the catholic religion."[208] This concern seems to have been driven by three fears: that the God who had granted Constantine victory and peace for those under his jurisdiction would revoke His benefits for the state; that the Highest Deity would bring down consequences on Constantine himself; and that the level of Christian division and discord was insurmountable. These fears would gradually subside or undergo theological reframing from 312 to at least 321 in essentially the same order.[209]

Constantine's interaction with the Caecilianist controversy also unavoidably set some interesting and challenging precedents relative to existing ecclesiastical structures and practices. With regard to Rome, Constantine's actions both elevated the church in a uniquely dramatic way, in part required by the impressive existing religious spaces there, and gave what Christians could see as confirmation of their one true God in the new monuments to the emperor. Also, Constantine's initial delegation to Miltiades to arbitrate the North African dispute, whether consciously or not, created a pattern of precedence for the emperor to refer such cases to the bishop of Rome. However, when the bishop of Rome took advantage of this to confirm his own position by creating an Italian dominated church council to judge the issues and then centered the results on the longstanding difference between Italy and North Africa over rebaptism with relatively little regard for the troubling nature of the accusations made by the

---

207. Such boons were most striking where persecution had been most intense.

208. Optatus, *App.* 3.

209. This development is beyond the bounds of this chapter but will be discussed in a future article.

Majorinists against Caecilian, Constantine did not respond favorably. By treating Miltiades' Synod at Rome as subject to a general council called by himself, Constantine implicitly undermined some claims for Rome's authority. The Council of Arles, being called as a representative council of all the churches in Constantine's domain itself, formally linked and labeled the council's determinations as the belief of the broader catholic church and tied them to the emperor and his enforcement. The emperor's own actions of humility during the council at Arles indicate a desire and perceived appropriateness of his participation as if he was one of the bishops. Yet, the fact that Constantine closed the council with the statements implying that he would consider an appeal of the council's verdict to himself, however audacious such an appeal might be, suggested that he held ultimate or at least equal authority to the council on an ecclesiastical matter. Certainly, Constantine expected that his own decision would carry more weight than the council's. It seems likely that his experience of these two councils, and their failure to effect reconciliation, radically altered his perception of the unity of the Christian community. Instead, he saw it as ineffective and not sufficiently motivated toward the ideals of harmony and reconciliation. Thus, it would need political guidance and be treated as a political entity, especially through its bishops.

Constantine's interaction with the North African schism allows significant glimpses into his personal growth as a Christian.[210] The first indications around the battle of the Milvian Bridge are of a straightforward contractual relationship to a monotheistic patron God who is uniquely connected with the risen Lord of the Christians. Developments on this front are more fully explored elsewhere in this volume and also most recently, in Bryan Litfin's recent article discussing Eusebius on Constantine.[211] However, the urgency underlying Constantine's initial communications with the church in North Africa is reflective of a very new dramatic commitment to the Christian God and the public elevation of His worship as true. In response to the schism around Caecilian, Constantine's assumptions evidence what he understood to be Christian ideals—most significantly connected to Lactantius. His assumption that the bishops he trusted from Gaul and Miltiades of Rome would seriously desire to arbitrate the North

---

210. Despite his lack of baptism and full participation in church life, Constantine's actions as well as his comments at Arles (Optatus, *App.* 5) and in his letter to Alfaeus (Optatus, *App.* 3) clearly demonstrate this self-perception of the emperor.

211. Litfin, "Eusebius on Constantine."

African situation toward reconciliation belies his conviction that Christian concord was a most basic ideal of devotion. Once response to the dispute was codified by the result of the Roman synod, Constantine assumed that the dispute was solely based on basic disagreements of a few key individuals, not on doctrinal emphases that translated deeply in the African church. He did not seem to understand the deep connections of purity to a recently persecuted church that already held a unique place for the martyrs and the traditions of martyr figures like Cyprian. Responsibility for this oversight lies squarely on the shoulders of Constantine's Christian advisors and Constantine's lack of firsthand knowledge of the African provinces. The fact that Constantine did not understand certain issues at hand, like rebaptism, also highlights both his position as a believer still outside the core sacraments and most intimate communion of his fellow Christian believers as well as his own relative interest in the cult practices of his chosen religion. Issues like rebaptism represented an opportunity—just as the Pascha date would at Nicaea—to affirm regionally recognized traditions while still seeking to reach a place where the church could hopefully move forward in unified practice and beyond particular clerical disputes.[212] Constantine's increasing appreciation for prayer and for the tradition of the martyrs in the context of a spiritual war both show development over the course of the North African controversy up to toleration and beyond. It is probable that the relevance of these two things were related in his mind, wherein the martyrs represented those whose prayers were most particularly effective.[213] Finally the outbursts of the emperor during this period reveal that he had personally experienced God's grace as well as demonstrate Constantine's dramatic confidence that he was capable of ascertaining spiritual truths and rendering spiritual judgments in protection of the right worship of God.[214] It is out of these communications that we most clearly see how by the time he approached the Arian controversy, Constantine was prepared to approach division in the church as a kind of "war."[215]

212. Neither the Synod at Rome nor the general council at Arles appear to have ever widened the point of discussion much beyond questions about a few individuals to find bases for such potential agreement moving forward.

213. This would lead to the odd inversion, to be discussed in a future article, in Constantine's letters of 320 and 330 to North Africa that set up the catholic church there *to* experience martyrdom.

214. Optatus, *App.* 5, 7.

215. Eusebius, *VC* 3.5.3.

As a Christian emperor responsible for the spiritual well-being of the state, establishing new precedents relative to church and state while growing in his own understanding of the Christian God, community and practice, the North African controversy forced Constantine to make decisions and develop perspective right from the beginning of his new Christian devotion and at a rushed pace. It may be that as the emperor reflected on course of things up to 321, he recognized this deficit and decided to make such amends as he could. That this was connected in some way to his plans and propaganda for eventual war with Licinius is undoubtedly true, but that this war was sufficient motivation for the reversal of policy in North Africa in 321, just as fresh indications were coming of some weakness in the Donatists' front, is open to question. At least one other factor, and in my view theological factors, must have motivated such a change at this particular point. This chapter has identified some of the areas of contemplation that would have been a part of this, but more research into the Christian stimulus around Constantine between 317 and 320 is needed to identify specific contributors that may have effected a change. This may have included a Lactantian renaissance for Constantine as he interacted anew with the rhetor's work.

In closing, we can take a snapshot assessment of the legacy of the North African controversy for Constantine and the church by exploring some key parallels and differences between his approach to the North African and Arian disputes. That Donatist action specifically anticipated, shaped, or altered imperial response to the Arian disputes is clear; the issues are in terms of developments and degrees. Throughout both the North African and Arian controversies, the "real issues" at play were not immediately or intrinsically significant to Constantine. In Africa, the issues seemed to him to center on stubborn unseemly, unruly, uncharitable, and contentious problems. In the Arian situation, the issues initially just seemed trivial hair splitting of questionable relevance to salvation[216] and even once grasped, especially with respect to Christ's honor with which Constantine resonated, were still to him about parameters that ultimately did come down to fine differences of terminology. The current study shows that Constantine was moving toward an increasingly refined understanding of schism and heresy as states of spiritual war. The degrees to which that "war" in North Africa only reached a stalemate primed and informed Constantine's determination to address new spiritual wars in the East in strategic ways. As the

216. Cf. Eusebius, *VC* 2.68.1–2.71.6.

basis for further research, our inquiry raises the question of whether an illuminating cohesion may be found between Constantine's responses to both controversies in his conception of "madness." As such explorations are stimulated, hopefully this rethinking of Constantine and the North African schism will help spark and frame other needed reconsiderations of the first Christian emperor and Donatism's rise in North Africa.

4

Reevaluating Constantine's Legacy in Trinitarian Orthodoxy

New Evidence from Eusebius of Caesarea's Commentary on Isaiah

Jonathan J. Armstrong

SCHOLARS HAVE LONG BEEN conflicted concerning the real influence that Constantine exerted over the proceedings and theological conclusions of the Council of Nicaea.[1] In addition to the problems one could expect to encounter in the attempt to determine the theological interests of a major political figure from classical history, at least three factors conspire to make the determination of Constantine's true faith commitments and priorities at Nicaea uniquely problematic. First, no official record of the council proceedings survives.[2] Second, there is no consensus among the ancient historians concerning who—other than Constantine—presided

---

1. For a survey of the relevant literature, see Grant, "Religion and Politics at the Council of Nicaea," 1–12; Barnes, *Constantine and Eusebius*, 208–23; Hanson, *The Search for the Christian Doctrine of God*, 152–78; Simonetti, *La Crisi Ariana nel IV Secolo*, 25–41.

2. Tanner, *Decrees of the Ecumenical Councils*, 1:2; for further discussion, see Hefele, *Histoire des conciles d'après les documents originaux*, 1:1:391. These scholars conclude that it is most probable that no official record of the council was ever produced.

over the council.[3] Third, ever since Eduard Schwartz's discovery in 1905 of a Syriac text purporting to relate the events of a certain Council of Antioch, at which Eusebius of Caesarea was provisionally excommunicated for his pro-Arian views, scholars have generally been suspicious of the accuracy of Eusebius' portrayal of the Council of Nicaea.[4] Schwartz's Syriac text has been found in three manuscripts in all, but it has never been found in a language other than Syriac, and the Council of Antioch, which it claims to report, is not known from any other ancient source.[5] If one accepts the authenticity of the Syriac document, then Eusebius of Caesarea must have professed support for Arius only months before the Council of Nicaea, at which time he quickly retracted his support of Arius in order to follow the prevailing theological winds at the council. It is this scenario that has led many scholars to conclude that Eusebius was theologically disingenuous in his reports of the Arian Crisis and the Council of Nicaea. According to the traditional portrait of the council, Constantine played a significant role in establishing orthodoxy.[6] Prior scholarship accepted that Eusebius had been a major orthodox voice at the council. It was even concluded that Eusebius had advanced the creed of his church in Caesarea as the new theological standard, and that it was this creed that was effectively accepted as the Nicene Creed, with the addition of the term *homoousios* as suggested specifically by Constantine. Eusebius' clearest statement of the role

3. See Eusebius, *VC* 3.4–14; Socrates, *HE* 1.8–13; Sozomenus, *HE* 1.17–24; Theodoret, *HE* 1.6; Rufinus, *HE* 10.1–6. The absence of consensus among the ancient historians can be quite conspicuous, as in the case of Socrates (*HE* 1.1, translation from *NFNF* 2:1) who writes concerning Eusebius of Caesarea's portrait of the council: "Also in writing the life of Constantine, this same author has but slightly treated of matters regarding Arius, being more intent on the rhetorical finish of his composition and the praises of the emperor, than on an accurate statement of facts."

4. Schwartz, *Zur Geschichte des Athanasius* 3:117–68; Hanson, *The Search for the Christian Doctrine of God*, 146–51. Stead gives us a summary of the reasons why Eusebius of Caesarea has usually been thought to be "semi-Arian," based in large part upon evidence drawn from the *Demonstratio Evangelica* ("Eusebius and the Council of Nicaea," 85–100, esp. 90–92). Glen L. Thompson pointed out to me that the fragments of Eusebius' letter to Euphration of Balanea and the fragments of his letter to Alexander of Alexandria confirm Eusebius' pre-Nicene Arian sympathies.

5. Not all scholars are convinced that Schwartz's reconstruction is accurate. See Strutwolf, *Die Trinitätstheologie und Christologie des Euseb von Caesarea*, 31–44. See also Lienhard's analysis of Eusebius as an essentially orthodox theologian in *Contra Marcellum*, 104–35.

6. See, for example, Faulkner, "The First Great Christian Creed," 47–61.

of Constantine in formulation of the teachings of Nicaea is given in a letter
that he wrote to his congregation in Caesarea shortly after the council:

> When we presented this faith, there was no opportunity for resis-
> tance by anyone. But our emperor, most beloved of God, himself
> first of all witnessed that this was most orthodox. He agreed that
> even he himself thought thus, and he ordered all to assent to sub-
> scribe to the teachings and to be in harmony with them, although
> only one word, *homoousios*, was added, which he himself inter-
> preted, saying that the Son might not be said to be *homoousios*
> according to the affection of bodies, and is from the Father neither
> according to division nor according to a cutting off, for the imma-
> terial, intellectual, and incorporeal nature is unable to subsist in
> some corporeal affection, but it is befitting to think of such things
> in a divine and ineffable manner. And our emperor, most wise and
> pious, thought philosophically in this manner.[7]

However, if Eusebius' testimony is withdrawn as compromised or somehow
untrustworthy, then we are left only to imagine what Constantine's motives
at the Council of Nicaea may have been, and modern commentators tend
to imagine that Constantine could not have had a legitimate theological
interest in the outcome but was rather, more or less, entirely politically
motivated.

The argument of this essay is that there is an inadequate amount of
evidence to justify an abandonment of the traditional reconstruction of the
Council of Nicaea—a reconstruction in which Constantine played a significant role and even recommended the inclusion of the term *homoousios*. Specifically, although there is considerable evidence that Eusebius' pre-Nicene
views were less than completely orthodox, in light of the new evidence
surfacing from my translation of Eusebius of Caesarea's *Commentary on
Isaiah*, it appears that Eusebius' post-Nicene views were unreservedly orthodox. Therefore, I conclude that Eusebius' depiction of the Council of Nicaea cannot be dismissed as unhistorical, and that the traditional portrait
of Constantine's legacy in Nicene theology merits sustained reevaluation.
Eusebius' *Commentary on Isaiah* had never before been translated into any
modern language, and therefore this storehouse of theological information
had previously been available only to a few intrepid Greek readers. As I argue in the introduction to my translation, the commentary can be dated to
the end of Eusebius' life, based on several clear allusions to the baptism of

---

7. Cited in Rusch, *The Trinitarian Controversy*, 58. See also Eusebius, *VC* 3.13.

Constantine.[8] We can therefore fix the date of the commentary to sometime after Emperor Constantine's baptism on May 22, 337, and sometime before Eusebius' death on May 30, 339. Thus, Eusebius wrote the *Commentarius in Isaiam* at the same approximate time that he also wrote *De ecclesiastica theologia* and *Contra Marcellum*, two other tractates in which Eusebius is concerned to advance trinitarian orthodoxy. As we shall see, Eusebius presents a clearly orthodox trinitarian theology in his *Commentary on Isaiah*.

THE COMMENTARY ON ISAIAH AND EUSEBIUS' TRINITARIAN THEOLOGY

Eusebius is unequivocal in his affirmation of the deity of Christ. If Eusebius had voiced a clearly Arian Christology at the Synod of Antioch in 325, then one could say that his theology had certainly acquired orthodox terminology in the years afterward. Eusebius affirms in no uncertain terms that Isaiah foretold that Christ is God: "And in accordance with the promise, the Christ of God was designated as Lord and God among the nations by the Father who freely gave this glory to him alone."[9] In his comments on Isaiah 7:1, Eusebius attests that the prophet "presented the divinity of the only-begotten Son of God [τὴν θεότητα τοῦ μονογενοῦς υἱοῦ τοῦ θεοῦ],"[10] and passages in which Eusebius affirms the divinity of the Word of God could be multiplied.[11] In his exposition of Isaiah 48:12, Eusebius takes the opportunity to arrange together a mosaic of passages all celebrating a high Christology:

> And he reminds them of the theology [θεολογία] about him when he says that he is the first and the last. For this reason, according to the other Greek translations, the text reads: I am the first and the last. And it has been written elsewhere "concerning the only-begotten of God [περὶ τοῦ μονογενοῦς τοῦ θεοῦ]" (cf. Jn. 3:18) that he is "the first and the last" [Rev. 1:17, 2:8, 22:13], and "the Alpha and the Omega" [Rev. 1:8, 21:6, 22:13]. And he shows plainly how he is the first and the last when he next says: "The living one,

8. See "The Date of the Commentary" in the introduction of Eusebius, *Commentary on Isaiah*. Unless otherwise, noted all translations of *Comm. in Is.* are my own.

9. *Comm. in Is.* 42:8.

10. Ibid., 7:1.

11. See especially ibid., 11:5, 26:11, 32:10–12, 40:9, 45:20–21, 51:9–10, 51:15–16, 60:1–2, 66:18–20.

although I died" [Rev. 1:18]. On the one hand, he is the beginning of life, because "he was the life" [cf. Jn. 1:4], and on the other hand, again, he is the last, since "he emptied himself, taking the form of a servant, and he humbled himself and became obedient to the Father unto death, even death on a cross" [Phil. 2:7–8].[12]

Eusebius' emphasis that the Word of God is the first and the last makes it at least difficult to imagine that he could affirm that there was a time when the Son was not. In his comments on Isaiah 26:11, Eusebius speaks of "the divinity of the Savior [τὴν θεότητα τοῦ σωτῆρος]" and says that those who "had fallen far away from the knowledge of his divinity [τῆς γνώσεως τῆς θεότητος]" would experience eternal damnation.[13] Eusebius' word choice deserves comment. He is not simply speaking of the pagans who never knew the divinity of Christ. He is speaking, rather, of those who once confessed Christ's divinity but who later "fell far away" from this confession. One plausible interpretation of Eusebius' words is that they were written specifically against the Arians. Eusebius then writes that "the impious groped about in the darkness of their own ignorance." It is easy to imagine, too, that this line was written against the muddled theological outcomes for the Arians of the past decade.

In his study, *Holy City, Holy Places? Christian Attitudes to Jerusalem and the Holy Land in the Fourth Century*, Peter W. L. Walker writes: "Eusebius was not strictly a theologian of the Incarnation at all; he was a theologian of theophany."[14] I find this to be an extraordinarily clear insight into Eusebius' trinitarian theology. It is true that Eusebius seems to avoid the term "incarnation," often choosing rather expressions such as Christ's "passage into humanity [τῆς εἰς ἀνθρώπους παρόδου]."[15] Eusebius does indeed state his Christology in terms of theophany rather than incarnation, and this can lead the reader to conclude too quickly that Eusebius' incarnational theology is defective. In his depiction of Isaiah's vision of the majestic throne room of God, we see Eusebius' theological imagination guiding him to describe the vision in terms of theophany, not incarnational theology. Eusebius' focus is intently set on the theological dilemma of how

---

12. Ibid., 48:12.

13. Ibid., 26:11.

14. Walker, *Holy City, Holy Places?*, 88.

15. *Comm. in Is.* 19:1. See also ibid., 52:14–15, 53:1–4. In ibid., 30:1–5, Eusebius speaks, too, of Christ's "appearance among humanity" (εἰς ἀνθρώπους ἐπιφάνειαν).

the invisible God could be said to have been seen by human eyes. Eusebius writes of the Prophet Isaiah:

> He thus introduces God as he was seen. However, concerning the unbegotten divinity [περὶ τῆς ἀγεννήτου θεότητος], it has been said: "No one has ever seen God; the only Son, who is in the bosom of the Father, he has made him known" [Jn. 1:18]. And the Savior himself taught: "Not that anyone has seen the Father except him who is from God; he has seen the Father" [Jn. 6:46]. Surely then the Lord of hosts who appeared to the prophet was another than the unbegotten and invisible and incomprehensible divinity [τῆς ἀγεννήτου καὶ ἀοράτου καὶ ἀκαταλήπτου θεότητος]. And who could this be but "the only-begotten God, who is in the bosom of the Father" [Jn. 1:18], who stepped down from his own exalted position, and, lowering himself from that position, made himself visible and comprehensible to humanity?[16]

Eusebius enumerates the various times in the Old Testament that it is said that the Lord appeared to one of the saints: Abraham's encounter with God at the oak in Mamre, Isaac and Jacob and Moses' and Ezekiel's visions of the Lord. Eusebius concludes: "For it has been said by Moses: 'You shall not be able to see my face; for a person shall never see my face and live' [Ex. 33:20]. For the face of God the Word and the divinity of the only-begotten Son of God could never be apprehensible to mortal nature [τὸ γὰρ πρόσωπον θεοῦ λόγου καὶ ἡ θεότης τοῦ μονογενοῦς υἱοῦ τοῦ θεοῦ θνητῇ φύσει οὐκ ἂν γένοιτο καταληπτή] . . . Thus, as we discussed above, he saw the glory of our Savior Jesus Christ."[17]

If Eusebius' theology is anywhere equivocal, it would seem to be in his articulation of the incarnation. Eusebius' theology of the incarnation could be interpreted as inadequate in as far as God the Word only indwelt, or somehow rested upon, the human flesh of Jesus of Nazareth. In his comments on the septuagintal phrase "they will do obeisance to you and pray in you, because God is in you," Eusebius writes: "And they will pray in him, inasmuch as God was in him and because God dwelled in him, and he was God [καὶ τὸ προσεύξασθαι ἐν αὐτῷ, ἐπειδήπερ ὁ θεὸς ἐν αὐτῷ ἦν καὶ διὰ τὸν ἐνοικοῦντα ἐν αὐτῷ θεὸν καὶ αὐτὸς θεὸς ἦν]."[18] Eusebius' imprecision is again unsettling in his comments on Isaiah 49:24–26, when he writes: "The

16. Ibid., 6:1.

17. Ibid.

18. Ibid., 44:14–17.

divine is incorporeal, immaterial, intangible and indivisible. And there is no one who has done anything like what he has done in taking on a corporeal appearance [ἀσώματον τὸ θεῖον, ἄϋλον, ἀναφὲς καὶ ἁπλοῦν καὶ οὐκ ἄν τις ἐπ' αὐτῷ τὰ εἰκότα δρῶν φαντασίαν τινὰ λάβοι συματικήν].ʺ[19] Unsettling as these statements may be, it is nonetheless perfectly clear that Eusebius is not advocating an Arian theology. In his interpretation of Isaiah 11:2–3, Eusebius writes: "Therefore the little rod or the branch or the shoot, perceived according to the flesh, was our Savior the man. But it is clear from the statements adduced next that God the Word indwelled him." Eusebius demonstrates an affinity for the language of indwelling rather than incarnation in this passage, and yet, Eusebius can also affirm that the Spirit of God mentioned here in Isaiah 11:2–3 represents "'the whole fullness of deity' of the only-begotten God." After commenting on a catena of significant Christological passages, Eusebius affirms that the various titles for the Spirit of God in Isaiah 11:2–3 all refer to the "one and the same Word who proceeds [πρόειμι] from God and who rested on him who descended from the root of Jesus and 'from David according to the flesh.'"[20] Eusebius' imprecision in differentiating between the Word of God and Spirit of God may raise concerns of another sort, but it is clear that, for Eusebius, the Word of God is deity. This is not the only instance in which Eusebius struggles to articulate a consistent theology of the incarnation, as when he interprets the man in Isaiah 32:2 as Christ, "who is not a man by nature but by nature superior to a man [οὐκ ὢν τῇ φύσει ἀνήρ, ἀλλὰ κρείττων ἢ κατὰ ἀνθρώπου φύσιν]."[21] Eusebius, too, can speak of Christ "donning a human body," as a shepherd clothing himself in sheep hide.[22] If we did not have clear examples of a complete theology of the incarnation in the passages discussed in the paragraphs following, one could certainly read these statements as betraying a defective Christology.

Even if some of Eusebius' statements of the incarnation are decidedly unconventional, Eusebius can also posit entirely clear affirmations of the doctrine of the incarnation. In contrast to the faithfulness of Abraham and Sarah, Eusebius speaks of the failure of the Jews "who had seen the one only-begotten Word of God in an appearance like ours—that is, as one who

19. Ibid., 49:24–26.
20. Ibid., 11:2–3a.
21. Ibid., 32:1–4.
22. Ibid., 40:10–11.

had become a man [τοῦτ᾽ ἔστιν γενόμενον ἄνθρωπον]."[23] In his comments on Isaiah 52:13, Eusebius says that the Servant of the Lord "contained God the Word in himself [τὸν θεὸν λόγον εἰς ἑαυτὸν χωρήσας]."[24] Eusebius continues on to affirm: "And all these things were fulfilled in the man who is our Savior because of his union with God the Word [διὰ τὴν πρὸς τὸν θεὸν λόγον ἕνωσιν]."[25] Commenting on Isaiah 61:1–3, Eusebius' affirmation of the doctrine of the incarnation becomes perfectly unequivocal:

> *The Spirit of the Lord is on me, because he has anointed me.* This verse is clearly directed at those who suppose that the Christ of God was neither a real man nor a fleshless and bodiless Word or who believe that he never partook of mortal nature. But they say that he was both God and man. He is God according to the verse which states that he is "the only-begotten God, who is in the bosom of the Father" [Jn. 1:18], and he is considered to be man according to the verse, "who was descended from David, according to the flesh" [Rom. 1:3].

One could scarcely hope for a clearer articulation of the incarnation. It is to this doctrine that Eusebius points when, in his comments on Isaiah 7:15–17, he states that prophet proclaims that the birth of "God, the Savior of the human race"[26] will be a real human birth, "for it will not be as an apparition that he will appear among people, nor will it be that he merely seems to be present. . . . This indeed is perhaps indicative of his humanity and divinity [τοῦτο μὲν οὖν ἀνθρώπινον, τὸ δὲ τῆς θεότητος αὐτοῦ παραστατικὸν ἐκεῖνο ἂν εἴη]."[27]

Eusebius' most significant affirmations of Nicene orthodoxy, however, come in his treatment of the "Servant Song" of Isaiah 42. In his comments on Isaiah 42:1, Eusebius argues that "neither the other Greek translations nor the Hebrew text mentions Jacob and Israel," and therefore that the text is theoretically open to a christological interpretation of the servant.

---

23. Ibid., 51:1–2; see also ibid., 1.2–3.

24. Ibid., 52:13.

25. Ibid.

26. Ibid., 7:14.

27. Ibid., 7:15–17. One of Eusebius' favorite biblical texts for expressing the theology of the incarnation is the vision of the stone chiseled out by no human hand that became a great mountain from Daniel 2:34–35. Eusebius affirms: "Indeed, the stone is to be understood as the human body of the Savior and the mountain as his divinity" (Ibid., 28:16). In his earlier comments on Isaiah 2:1–4, Eusebius states: "'Stone' actually speaks of the humanity of the Savior and 'mountain' speaks of God the Word." See also Ibid., 51:5–7.

Eusebius briefly entertains the possibility that the servant could be identi-fied as the "apostolic band," but concludes almost immediately thereafter that, in the text, "a superior person is introduced," a person whom Eusebius identifies as "the Christ of God." Having excluded Jacob and Israel and even the apostles from being the servant, Eusebius writes:

> Therefore, there is here another one who is spoken of as the ser-vant of God and of his chosen one. For this reason, the following statement is then added: *My soul has accepted him.* For this one alone was the chosen of God, the one accepted by him who is re-ferred to as the soul of God. Usually, the one to whom the name soul is applied in the divine Scriptures is God. . . . But the chosen one cannot be referring to the apostles, since it has been said to the chosen one alone: "Whom my soul has chosen" [cf. Mt. 12:18], and: "The Spirit of God descended upon him alone" [cf. Isaiah 11:2]. "For in him the whole fullness of deity dwelt bodily" [Col. 2:9]. And the Spirit that was given to the one who came "from the root of Jesse" [Isaiah 11:1] was the only-begotten Word of God [ὁ μονογενὴς τοῦ θεοῦ λόγος], as also the Apostle Paul made clear when he said: "Now the Lord is the Spirit" [2 Cor. 3:17]. Therefore, he alone understands the Spirit of the Father . . .[28]

Eusebius here identifies the "soul" that accepted the Servant as God, and the Servant as God the Word, and the Spirit that descended on the Servant as God the Spirit. Eusebius uses the opportunity here to affirm trinitarian imagery.

Should there be any confusion as to his interpretation of the "Servant Song" of Isaiah 42, Eusebius reaffirms this conclusion: "Therefore, God himself is even this servant, my chosen one, as the Savior made clear in the Gospels when he said: 'Whoever acknowledges me before men, I also will acknowledge him before my Father who is in heaven' [Mt. 10:32]. I will serve as a witness for my witnesses, so that you may know and believe and understand that I am. Before me there was no other god, nor shall there by any after me."[29] Eusebius then delivers his most decisive statement thus far: "For this reason, he bursts forth: *Be my witnesses; I too am a witness, says the Lord God, and the servant whom I have chosen.* And he continues on to say: *So that you may know and believe and understand that I am. Before me there was no other god, nor shall there by any after me.* For, being from one beginning, the divine nature must be one, as the theology concerning

28. Ibid., 42:1.
29. Ibid., 43:8–11.

his only-begotten Son counsels [μιᾶς γὰρ οὔσης ἀρχῆς μία εἴη ἂν θεότης, ἢ συμπαραλαμβάνεται καὶ ἡ τοῦ μονογενοῦς αὐτοῦ θεολογία]" (emphasis mine).[30] Eusebius, here again, clearly disallows an Arian interpretation of the Scriptures. Eusebius defends the Nicene definition of the eternal generation of the Son, affirming that the Son and the Father are coeternal ("being from one beginning"), and therefore that the Son is consubstantial with the Father ("the divine nature must be one"). It would seem that this is as close as one can come to affirming the Nicene doctrine of ὁμοούσιος without actually using this theological term.[31]

Eusebius also seems to affirm his orthodox convictions in his comments on Isaiah 52:14–15 ("many nations marveled at him, and kings closed their mouths"), where Eusebius writes: "The word concerning him still even now produces astonishment and perplexity and befuddlement in many." Eusebius then goes on to explain that the phrase, "many nations marveled at him,"

> speaks about those who believe in him and worship his divinity, and on the other hand, it speaks about those who, although marveling at his power, "persist in unbelief" [cf. Rom. 11:23], even though his power is higher and stronger than those who attempt to fight against it. After uttering many blasphemous and godless and profane words against him and persecuting his church, kings closed their mouths and submitted to his teaching, since they were not able to bring about an end to their meaningless sufferings. For at various times and seasons, their spirits were broken, and they were driven on by the scourges of destiny. And we who record these things have had the same experience.[32]

Eusebius then finishes his comments on this passage: "These people from all the nations—although they never learned about him or knew the Scriptures concerning him—nevertheless they have seen him and understood, and they accepted the knowledge of his divinity."[33] This would seem to be a series of clear allusions to the period after Nicaea and the battle for

30. Ibid., 43:8–11.

31. See also Eusebius' comments on Isaiah 44:6, where he again differentiates between the Father and the Son while yet affirming their unity, claiming that the teaching in Isaiah favors the unity of the Godhead because the Jews were not yet ready for further revelation.

32. Ibid., 52:14–15.

33. Ibid.

orthodoxy that ensued, and as read in this light, Eusebius stands clearly as an advocate of orthodoxy.

D. S. Wallace-Hadrill complained that Eusebius indulges in "wordiness, confused syntax, long passages of unalleviated dullness."[34] Scholars of late have not been kind in their assessment of the theological contribution of Eusebius' sprawling *Commentarius in Isaiam*. Michael J. Hollerich states: "The theological yield of the *Commentary on Isaiah* is rather slight, especially if one seeks fresh insight into Eusebius' mind in the aftermath of Nicaea."[35] Timothy D. Barnes can write candidly: "The commentaries on Isaiah and the Psalms are not the product of a keen philosophical intelligence."[36] Berkhof goes so far as to say: "Eusebius is not a theologian in the proper sense of the word."[37] While I would concede that Eusebius' primary purpose for the *Commentary on Isaiah* is clearly not an exposition of trinitarian theology, yet the commentary contains rich, apparently overlooked clues concerning Eusebius' trinitarian views. Eusebius' true convictions concerning the Arian crisis and the Council of Nicaea—and therefore the accuracy of his portrait of Constantine's legacy in trinitarian orthodoxy—may continue to be a matter of considerable scholarly controversy, but neither because there is no textual evidence nor because the textual evidence available is demonstrably untrustworthy.

HOW DOES THIS NEW EVIDENCE REFLECT ON CONSTANTINE?

How does a reevaluation of Eusebius' theology influence our assessment of the theological convictions of Constantine and the role that he played in the formulation of trinitarian orthodoxy at the Council of Nicaea? Once Eusebius is exonerated as no longer "semi-Arian"[38] and an unreliable

34. Wallace-Hadrill, *Eusebius of* Caesarea, 99.

35. Hollerich, *Eusebius of Caesarea's Commentary on Isaiah*, 61.

36. Barnes, *Constantine and Eusebius*, 100.

37. Cited in Lienhard, *Contra Marcellum*, 127.

38. I am aware of the storm of research in recent years that has challenged the traditional reconstruction of the "Arian Controversy," and even the serviceability of such terms as "Arian," "semi-Arian," and "orthodox." See especially Williams, *Arius*, 48–61; Ayres, *Nicaea and Its Legacy*, 15–20; Gwynn, *The Eusebians*, 245–49; see also perhaps the more fruitful work by Anatolios, *Retrieving Nicaea*, 33–98. While some of the sources mentioned here in fact support the exoneration of Eusebius, definitive reevaluation must await Hanns C. Brennecke's forthcoming critical edition of the works of Athanasius, an

source of information concerning the council, the account that he provides of Constantine's role becomes invaluable. If Eusebius is no longer dismissed as, in Jacob Burckhardt's inimitable phrase, "the first thoroughly dishonest historian of antiquity," then suddenly Constantine's role in the formation of Christian orthodoxy becomes once again of irreplaceable significance. The traditional sources tell the story that Constantine was a man of conviction who was personally invested in the outcome of the Council of Nicaea and who was personally involved in lobbying for the use of *homoousios* as part of the definition of Trinitarian orthodoxy. In Faulkner's classic portrait of the unfolding of the Arian crisis and the Council of Nicaea, Constantine is one of the principle reasons why Athanasian trinitiarianism won the day at the Council of Nicaea, although Athanasius' view was not the majority view at the beginning of the council.[39]

In his letter to Alexander and Arius, it is true that Constantine writes: "I do not say these things as though I were forcing you to come to agreement on every aspect of this very silly question, whatever it actually is,"[40] seemingly betraying marked indifference to the real theology of the debate. At the same time, the Constantine whom Eusebius portrays clearly understood himself as responsible for the success of the Christian church. Eusebius reports that Constantine even thought of himself as a bishop: "Hence it is not surprising that on one occasion, when entertaining bishops to dinner, he let slip the remark that he was perhaps himself a bishop too, using some such words as these in our hearing: 'You are bishops of those within the church, but I am perhaps a bishop appointed by God over those outside.'"[41] Constantine certainly wished to communicate a deep personal piety to the church leaders assembled at Nicaea, and Eusebius can write in apparent great admiration of Constantine's involvement[42] at the Council:

---

edition that is projected to replace Opitz's edition, on which all scholarship on the Arian crisis is currently based.

39. Faulkner, "The First Great Christian Creed," 59–60.

40. Eusebius, *VC* 2.71 (unless otherwise noted, all translations are from Cameron and Hall). However, in his letter to the churches, Constantine clearly intends to communicate his fervent concern for the question of Arianism (see especially *VC* 3.17). Barnes (*Constantine and Eusebius*, 212) writes: "If Constantine hoped to mediate the quarrel, it was because he set a lower value on theological definitions, which he considered pedantic, than on making the Roman Empire Christian."

41. Eusebius, *VC* 4.24.

42. It should be noted that, contra Cameron and Hall, Barnes (*Constantine and Eusebius*, 58) interprets this paragraph as in reference to the Council of Arles).

"He did not disdain to be present and attend during their proceedings, and he participated in the subjects reviewed, by arbitration promoting the peace of God among all; and he took his seat among them as if he were one voice among many, dismissing his praetorians and soldiers and bodyguards of every kind, clad only in the fear of God and surrounded by the most loyal of his faithful companions."[43] Constantine's translators and commentators, Cameron and Hall, write concerning the evaluation of Constantine's convictions: "Once the letters [i.e., Constantine's letters as recorded by Eusebius in *VC*] are accepted as authentic, Constantine's conviction of divine calling and service must be accepted. But was he at heart a Christian, and if so, of what kind? Opinions differ as to the degree of his theological awareness, and as to his ultimate motives."[44]

Estimations of Constantine's legacy in the theological definitions forged at the Council of Nicaea have differed markedly. On one hand, some historians view Constantine as a Machiavellian politician, orchestrating his every maneuver solely to achieve greater power for the imperial office. Other historians have portrayed Constantine as a man of genuine faith, legitimately invested in the theological issues debated at the council. In the face of the confusion of the historical record and the seeming impossibility of arriving upon a more solid basis for a historical understanding of the council, Jacob Burckhardt abandons himself to prejudice and can write spiritedly but libelously of Constantine as "the murderous egoist who possessed the great merit of having conceived of Christianity as a world power and of having acted accordingly."[45] On the other hand, R. P. C. Hanson contends that Schwartz's reconstruction of affairs reflects "the *Realpolitik* of Bismarck rather than the mind of Constantine."[46] Recent accounts aimed at a more popular-level audience generally fail even to give real consideration to the viewpoint that Constantine may have been motivated by theology in

43. Eusebius, *VC* 1.44. See also Eusebius' account of Constantine's study of the Scripture concerning the question of the nature of God (*VC* 1.32).

44. Eusebius, *Life of Constantine*, trans. Cameron, 44. At the same time, as Leithart (*Defending Constantine*, 175) points out, Constantine certainly did not have the church under his absolute sway, as the many twists and turns in the narrative amply demonstrate.

45. Burckhardt, *The Age of Constantine the Great*, 293. MacMullen (*Constantine*, 171) finds himself in largely the same predicament: "For so historic an event, the Nicene Council remains surprisingly obscure. But of course it represented a determined effort by a most determined man to bury differences, and in the process he inevitably buried much else besides."

46. Hanson, *The Search for the Christian Doctrine of God*, 153.

any of his political decisions. In this essay, I have attempted to demonstrate that the evidence from Eusebius of Caesarea's *Commentarius in Isaiam* points toward the conclusion that Eusebius had fully accepted Nicene orthodoxy at the end of his life, and this in turn supports the conclusion that Eusebius' depiction of the role that Constantine played in the council in *Vita Constantini* was not dramatically rewritten to mask Eusebius' own unorthodoxy. In removing reason to suspect Eusebius of compromised orthodoxy, this same evidence removes reason to suspect that Eusebius' portrait of Constantine's advancement of orthodoxy at the Council of Nicaea was fabricated for reasons of political expediency.

5

Constantine, Sabbath-Keeping, and Sunday Observance

Paul A. Hartog

THE FOLLOWING CONVERSATION TAKES place in the literary classic *The Swiss Family Robinson*:

> Next morning all were early awake, and the children sprang about the tree like young monkeys.
>
> "What shall we begin to do, father?" they cried. "What do you want us to do, today?"
>
> "Rest, my boys," I replied, "rest."
>
> "Rest?" repeated they. "Why should we rest?"
>
> "'Six days shalt thou labor and do all that thou hast to do, but on the seventh, thou shalt do no manner of work.' This is the seventh day," I replied, "on it, therefore, let us rest."
>
> "What, is it really Sunday?" said Jack, "How jolly! Oh, I won't do any work; but I'll take a bow and arrow and shoot, and we'll climb about the tree and have fun all day."
>
> "That is not resting," said I, "that is not the way you are accustomed to spend the Lord's Day."[1]

---

1. Wyss, *Swiss Family Robinson*, 95. The impulse to use this opening illustration came from Wilson, "Principles for Observing Sabbath."

D. A. Carson claims that the Sabbath/Sunday question is "one of the most difficult areas in the study of the relationship between the Testaments, and in the history of the development of doctrine."[2] The issue of a Christian "sabbatarian" observance of either Saturday or "the Lord's Day" (Sunday), keeping a day of rest from labor and "worldly" recreation, has a storied heritage. A major chapter of this narrative centers upon the role of the Emperor Constantine, whose character and conversion have been keenly contested,[3] especially in Protestant circles.[4] Scholars have long debated the *Konstantinische Wende* ("Constantinian turn").[5] Such quarrels have frequently discussed Constantine's influence on Sabbath/Sunday observance.[6] This essay will re-examine the role of Constantine, focused through an exploration of inter-denominational disputes concerning Sabbath and Sunday observance. On the one hand, Constantine has often been blamed for producing shifts he did not bring about. And, on the other hand, Constantine has often not received recognition for the shifts he did effect.

LUTHERANS AND CATHOLICS

Luther taught that the Decalogue's Sabbath commandment is not binding on Christians as a legal requirement.[7] Luther's Small Catechism maintained that the Sabbath commandment merely means "We should fear and love

---

2. Carson, *From Sabbath to Lord's Day*, 17.

3. For classic studies, see Staehelin, "Constantin der Grosse"; Dörries, *Das Selbstzeugnis Kaiser Konstantins*; Dorries, *Constantine the Great*; MacMullen, *Constantine*; Bleicken, *Constantin der Große une die Christen*; Leeb, *Konstantin und Christus*; Bleckmann, *Konstantin der Grosse*; Ritter, "Constantin und die Christen"; Barnes, "Constantine and Christianity." Cf. Lieu and Montserrat, *Constantine*. For recent overviews, see Stephenson, *Constantine*; Potter, *Constantine the Emperor*.

4. Leithart (*Defending Constantine*) has recently tried to resuscitate Constantine's reputation among Protestants. Leithart's work has surprisingly little to say about Sunday worship (see ibid., 81).

5. See Bringmann, "Die Konstantinische Wende"; Girardet, "Die Konstantinische Wende"; Winkelmann, "Die 'Konstantinische Wende'"; Dassmann, *Konstantinische Wende*; Girardet, *Die Konstantische Wende*; Ruhbach, *Die Kirche angesichts der Konstantinischen Wende*; Hausammann, *Alte Kirche*.

6. See Hough, *Who Changed the Sabbath?*; Fisher and Davis, *Sunday Question*; Wardner, *Constantine and the Sunday*.

7. Augustine tended to spiritualize the conception of the Sabbath, and he taught that the Christian "celebrates" (*celerare*) and "observes" (*observare*) the Lord's Day (see Beckwith and Stott, *This Is the Day*, 137).

God that we may not despise preaching and His Word, but hold it sacred, and gladly hear and learn it."[8] The Lutheran Reformation did not insist that Sunday should be the day of worship, because "there is freedom in matters that lack a specific command of God."[9] John Theodore Mueller, a renowned confessional Lutheran theologian (1885–1967), declared: "But they err in teaching that Sunday has taken the place of the Old Testament Sabbath and therefore must be kept as the seventh day had to be kept by the children of Israel . . . These churches err in their teaching, for the Scripture has in no way ordained the first day of the week in place of the Sabbath. There is simply no law in the New Testament to that effect."[10]

This non-sabbatarian view of Sunday continues within confessional Lutheranism.[11] One Wisconsin Evangelical Lutheran Synod pastor explains:

> The same is true for us today. Sunday is not a New Testament Sabbath for us. There is no ceremonial law for us living in the New Testament times. So we don't want to make all kinds of rules and regulations for Sunday observance. In Christian freedom, Sunday was chosen by the early Christians as their regular day of worship, because that was the day on which our Savior Jesus rose victorious.
> . . . We have a true and lasting Sabbath rest—one which will last for

8. English translation available at http://www.bookofconcord.org/smallcatechism. php. Earlier, Luther's Large Catechism had stated, "Secondly, and most especially, that on such day of rest (since we can get no other opportunity) freedom and time be taken to attend divine service, so that we come together to hear and treat of God's Word, and then to praise God, to sing and pray" ("The Third Commandment"; English translation from http://www.bookofconcord.org/lc-3-tencommandments.php). The emphasis upon physical rest was dropped by the time the Smaller Catechism was composed. In his annotations on the Sabbath commandment of the Decalogue, Luther had stated, "Although the Sabbath is now abolished, and the conscience is free from it, it is still good, and even necessary, that men should keep a particular day in the week for the sake of the word of God, on which they are to meditate, hear, and learn, for all cannot command every day; and nature also requires that one day in the week should be kept quiet, without labor either for man or beast" (as quoted in Fairbairn, *Typology of Scripture*, 2:452).

9. Arand, "Response to Craig L. Blomberg," 392. The Augsburg Confession of Faith declared that the Sabbath has been abrogated, along with all Mosaic ceremonial injunctions (Article XXVIII). For Melanchthon's view, see Arand, "Response to Craig L. Blomberg," 393.

10. Mueller, "Sabbath or Sunday," 15–16; as cited in Hullquist, *Sabbath Diagnosis*, 176. Ferguson also refers to "the absence of any NT teaching that Sunday is the Christian Sabbath" (Ferguson, "Sabbath," 173).

11. Gurgel, "In the Cross Hairs."

all eternity and all because our Savior carried the burden for us so that we might rest eternally.[12]

Early Lutheranism specifically argued that Sunday sabbatarianism was an ecclesiastical development rather than a biblical mandate: "For those who judge that by the authority of the church the observance of the Lord's Day instead of the Sabbath-day was ordained as a thing necessary, do greatly err. Scripture has abrogated the Sabbath-day; for it teaches that, since the gospel has been revealed, all the ceremonies of Moses can be omitted. And yet, because it was necessary to appoint a certain day, that the people might know when they ought to come together, it appears that the church designated the Lord's Day for this purpose; and this day seems to have been chosen all the more for this additional reason, that men might have an example of Christian liberty, and might know that the keeping neither of the Sabbath nor of any other day is necessary."[13] "They [Roman Catholics] refer to the Sabbath-day as having been changed into the Lord's Day, contrary to the Decalogue, as it seems. Neither is there any example whereof they make more than concerning the changing of the Sabbath-day. Great, they say, is the power of the church, since it has dispensed with one of the Ten Commandments!"[14]

Historically, various Roman Catholic authors have indeed emphasized the church's role in Sunday traditions. Thomas Aquinas stated, "In the New Law the observance of the Lord's Day took the place of the observance of the Sabbath, not by virtue of the precept [in the Decalogue] but by the institution of the Church."[15] In the Reformation-era debates, Roman Catholic theologians "often appealed to the ecclesiastical origin of Sunday in order to prove the power of their church to introduce new laws and ceremonies."[16]

12. Neumann, "Enjoy Your Sabbath Rest."

13. *Augsburg Confession of Faith*, Art. XXVIII.57–60. Unless otherwise noted, all translations are from *Triglot Concordia*. This essay cannot cover all denominational views of Sabbath/Sunday observance, of course. But we may cite the view of Alexander Campbell, an early leader of the Restorationist movement: "I do not believe that the Lord's day came in the room of the Jewish Sabbath, or that the Sabbath was changed from the seventh to the first day, for this plain reason, that where there is no *testimony*, there can be no *faith*. Now there is no testimony in all the oracles of heaven that the Sabbath was changed, or that the Lord's day came in the room of it" (as quoted in Ballenger, "Protestantism True and False," 16–17).

14. *Augsburg Confession of Faith*, Art. XXVIII.33.

15. As quoted in Bacchiocchi, *Divine Rest for Human Restlessness*, 229.

16. Ibid.

Stephan Keenan's *A Doctrinal Catechism* (1865) included the following assertions concerning the Catholic Church: She "substituted the observance of Sunday the first day of the week, for the observance of Saturday the seventh day, a change for which there is no Scriptural authority."[17] In the *Catholic Mirror* of September 23, 1893, Cardinal Gibbons stated, "The Catholic Church by virtue of her divine mission changed the day from Saturday to Sunday." The 1913 *Convert's Catechism of Catholic Doctrine* maintained, "We observe Sunday instead of Saturday because the Catholic Church, in the Council of Laodicea (AD 336 [*sic*]), transferred the solemnity from Saturday to Sunday . . . The church substituted Sunday for Saturday by the plenitude of that divine power which Jesus Christ bestowed upon her."[18]

In turn, such Roman Catholic assertions have become fodder in denominational and sectarian debates, sometimes mixed with a fervent anti-Constantinianism.[19] According to the Christian Biblical Church of God, "Most Christians assume that Sunday is the biblically approved day of worship. The Roman Catholic Church protests that, indeed, it is not. The Roman Catholic Church itself without any Scriptural authority from God transferred Christian worship from the Biblical Sabbath (Saturday) to Sunday, by the command of the pagan Roman Emperor Constantine in 325 AD [*sic*]; and that to try to argue that the change was made in the Bible is both dishonest and a denial of Catholic authority. If Protestantism wants to base its teachings only on the Bible, *it should worship on Saturday*."[20] Fred Coulter, a leader of the Christian Biblical Church of God, explains, "But *when* did Sunday, which was venerated by pagan sun worshippers, become the holiest day of the week for Christians? It was the Roman emperor Constantine who first issued an edict concerning Sunday in AD 321."[21]

Saturday sabbatarians have frequently connected the change of day to the influence of paganism and sometimes specifically the role of Mithraism.[22] One Saturday sabbatarian source claims: "When Constantine

17. See Lewis, *Protestant Dilemma*, 78.

18. Geiermann, *Convert's Catechism of Catholic Doctrine*, 50. For a sabbatarian Messianic-Jewish read of the evidence, see Sanford, "Constantine's Council of Nicea."

19. "Historians and Church Authorities."

20. Christian Biblical Church of God, "Rome's Challenge"; italics original. For a critique of the theory of dependence upon Mithraism, see Strand, "From Sabbath to Sunday," 90.

21. Coulter, "Occult Holidays," 96.

22. See Lewis, *Protestant Dilemma*, 55, 62; Green, *Power of the Original Church*, 77–81; Lewis, *Paganism Surviving in Christianity*.

pressed his pagan hordes into the church they were observing the day of the sun for their adoration of the sun god. It was their special holy day. In order to make it more convenient for them to make the change to the new religion, Constantine accepted their day of worship, Sunday, instead of the Christian Sabbath which had been observed by Jesus and His disciples."[23] Joseph Green argues:

> So not only did Constantine adapt Christian meanings to pagan holidays, but he also forbade Christians or anyone else in the empire from observing the Sabbath or any of the Jewish observances! If Constantine had been scripturally literate, he would have known that these appointed times were not the feasts of the Jews, but rather the feasts of YHVH (Jehovah), which he was demeaning and neglecting! . . . God never changed this calendar. He never changes. As long as we follow His method of making the days, weeks, months, years, Sabbath years, jubilee years, and millennia, we won't be ignorant of His times and His seasons.[24]

Seventh-Day Adventists

In particular, Seventh-Day Adventists have used Roman Catholic claims against Protestants to their own advantage.[25] For example, Skip Mac-Carty insists, "Reason and common sense demand the acceptance of one or the other of these alternatives: either Protestantism and the keeping holy of Saturday, or Catholicity and the keeping of Sunday. Compromise is impossible."[26]

Moreover, through the years, various Adventists have claimed that Constantine changed the day of Christian worship from Saturday to Sunday.[27] In a 2003 article within the *Adventist Review*, Trudy Morgan-Cole states:

23. Crews, "How the Sabbath Was Changed." The context targets the role of Mithraism. Similar materials are plentiful on the web. For examples, see "Constantine Changes the Sabbath"; "Sunday—The Perfect Deception"; "Historians and Church Authorities"; Sanford, "Constantine's Council of Nicea."

24. Green, *Power of the Original Church*, 80–81.

25. Contrast Ferguson, "Sabbath," 181. Lewis argued that the Catholic hierarchy "may well use this basis of unity [Sunday observance] as a powerful invitation to Protestants to return to the fold" (Lewis, *Protestant Dilemma*, 5).

26. MacCarty, "Seventh-Day Sabbath," 46n91. Cf. O'Brien, *Faith of Millions*, 399–401.

27. MacCarty himself does not make this claim.

> I can't remember when I first heard the name of the Roman em-
> peror Constantine, but I'm sure it was in church and I'm sure I was
> very young. Along with most lifelong Seventh-Day Adventists, I
> learned early on that Constantine was the "bad guy" in the big
> switch from Sabbath to Sunday, proclaiming the "Venerable Day of
> the Sun" as the day on which all should worship. Of course, Con-
> stantine didn't invent Sunday worship—he legitimized a practice
> the church had drifted into the past two centuries as it struggled to
> assimilate pagan converts and dissociate itself from Judaism. Still,
> for most Adventists Constantine's name is indissolubly linked with
> that fatal error.[28]

This Adventist reconstruction is sometimes embedded within a larger understanding of the "Constantinian turn."[29] One recent Adventist author declares that "the conversion of Constantine was a major setback for God's kingdom and a victory for the domination system. When the church accepted violence, state control of religion, and secular power structures, it turned aside from Jesus' example as surely as when it mandated the 'Venerable Day of the Sun' in place of God's Sabbath. As a people who have always rejected Constantine's innovative decision to legislate Sunday worship for God's followers, I believe Seventh-Day Adventists should also take a stand against the rest of Constantine's innovations."[30]

Ellen G. White wrote, "The keeping of the counterfeit Sabbath [Sunday observance] is the reception of the mark [of the beast]."[31] She continued,

> In the first centuries the true Sabbath had been kept by all Chris-
> tians . . . Constantine, while still a heathen, issued a decree enjoining
> the general observance of Sunday as a public festival throughout
> the Roman Empire. After his conversion, he remained a staunch
> advocate of Sunday, and his pagan edict was then enforced by him
> in the interests of his new faith. But the honor shown this day was
> not as yet sufficient to prevent Christians from regarding the true
> Sabbath as the holy of the Lord. Another step must be taken; the
> false Sabbath must be exalted to an equality with the true. A few
> years after the issue of Constantine's decree, the bishop of Rome
> conferred on the Sunday the title of the Lord's Day.[32]

---

28. Morgan-Cole, "Christ or Constantine."

29. Naylor, *Did Constantine Change the Sabbath?*

30. Morgan-Cole, "Christ or Constantine."

31. White, *Spirit of Prophecy*, 4:281.

32. Ibid. 4:55.

According to White, Constantine attempted "to unite the conflicting interests of heathenism and Christianity," so that "the day of the sun was reverenced by his pagan subjects and was honored by Christians."[33] The bishops of his era "perceived that if the same day was observed by both Christians and heathen, it would promote the nominal acceptance of Christianity by pagans, and thus advance the power and glory of the church."[34]

White maintained, "Vast councils were held from time to time, in which the dignitaries of the church were convened from all the world. In nearly every council the Sabbath which God had instituted was pressed down a little lower, while the Sunday was correspondingly exalted. Thus the pagan festival came finally to be honored as a divine institution, while the Bible Sabbath was pronounced a relic of Judaism, and its observers were declared to be accursed."[35]

In order to emphasize a Constantinian shift toward Sunday observance, White claimed that faithful early Christians as a whole practiced Saturday Sabbath observance. "In the first centuries the true Sabbath had been kept by all Christians. They were jealous for the honor of God, and believing that His law is immutable, they zealously guarded the sacredness of its precepts. But with great subtlety Satan worked through his agents to bring about his object. That the attention of the people might be called to the Sunday, it was made a festival in honor of the resurrection of Christ. Religious services were held upon it; yet it was regarded as a day of recreation, the Sabbath being still sacredly observed."[36]

E. K. Slade, writing for the Australian Seventh-Day Adventist periodical *Signs of the Times*, asserted, "No account is given in the New Testament of the observance of Sunday, or the first day of the week by early Christians. We have no such fact recorded in history until the third or fourth century, when Sunday gradually came into . . . prominence through the strange blending of pagan rites with apostate Christianity."[37] Some recent Seventh-Day Adventist articles have continued such argumentation.[38]

33. White, *Great Controversy*, 53. "Royal edicts, general councils, and church ordinances sustained by secular power were the steps by which the pagan festival attained its position of honor in the Christian world. The first public measure enforcing Sunday observance was the law enacted by Constantine" (White, *Great Controversy*, 574).

34. Ibid.

35. Ibid.

36. Ibid., 52.

37. As quoted in Deck, *Lord's Day or the Sabbath*, 141.

38. Odom, "Pagan Sunday Observance." Cf. Veith, "Constantine and the Sabbath Change."

Nevertheless, contemporary Seventh-Day Adventist scholars acknowledge that a charge of Constantine initiating Sunday (the "Lord's Day") observance in the fourth century cannot be confirmed by the historical evidence.[39] Samuele Bacchiocchi, an accomplished Adventist academic trained at the Gregorian Pontifical University, re-formatted Adventist discussion by pressing Sunday worship back to AD 135.[40] Bacchiocchi traced the alteration to anti-Jewish sentiments in the second century,[41] "at the time when Hadrian's (about 135) anti-Judaic repressive measures made it expedient for Christians to differentiate from the Jews by abandoning their characteristic festivals such as the Passover and the Sabbath."[42] Bacchiocchi emphasized the role of the church of Rome,[43] and he further theorized that "the diffusion of the Sun cults" explains the choice of the first day of the week as the new Christian day of worship.[44] Hadrian identified himself with the Sun or *Sol Invictus*.[45] "An interplay of political, social, pagan-religious and Christian factors—similar somewhat to those which gave rise to the December 25 observance of Christ's birth—made it expedient to adopt Sunday as a new day of worship."[46]

Bacchiocchi recognized that he had diverged from Ellen G. White's explanation. He acknowledged, "I differ from Ellen White, for example, on the origin of Sunday. She teaches that in the first centuries all Christians observed the Sabbath and it was largely through the efforts of Constantine that Sunday-keeping was adopted by many Christians in the fourth century. My research shows otherwise."[47] Thus, while White and early Adven-

39. See Ferguson, "Sabbath," 176. Besides Samuele Bacchiocchi's *œuvre*, see also the many writings of Kenneth Strand, as represented in the bibliography.

40. Bacchiocchi, *From Sabbath to Sunday*. "The earliest explicit references to the Christian observance of Sunday are by Barnabas (about 135) and Justin Martyr (about 150)" (Bacchiocchi, *Divine Rest for Human Restlessness*, 233).

41. See also Bacchiocchi, *Anti-Judaism and the Origin of Sunday*; Strand, "Sunday in the Early Church."

42. Bacchiocchi, *Divine Rest for Human Restlessness*, 247. For a critique of Bacchiocchi on this point, see Ferguson, "Sabbath," 179. For a study of Jewish Sabbath observance, see McKay, *Sabbath and Synagogue*; Weiss, "Sabbath." Cf. Cox, *Sabbaths*.

43. See also Bacchiocchi, "Rome and the Origin of Sunday Observance." For a representative critique of this aspect of Bacchiocchi's reconstruction, see Morrison, "Sabbath and Sunday."

44. Bacchiocchi, *Divine Rest for Human Restlessness*, 248.

45. Ibid.

46. Ibid., 250.

47. Bacchiocchi, email message posted to the "Free Catholic Mailing List," catholic@

tists had charged Constantine and/or the popes of late antiquity with the Saturday to Sunday alteration, Bacchiocchi, though a firm Adventist, had moved the transition back to the first half of the second century—by the reign of the Emperor Hadrian, in 135.[48]

EARLY CHRISTIAN OVERVIEW

Much of contemporary Adventist scholarship, including Skip MacCarty's 2011 essay within *Perspectives on the Sabbath: Four Views*, follows the tenor of Bacchiocchi's proposal.[49] In order to do so, these scholars downplay pre-Hadrianic evidence for Christian worship on Sunday. I do not have the space to re-examine the early Christian evidence here.[50] Everett Ferguson may overstate the case by asserting that the early Christian day of worship as Sunday is supported by "numerous, unanimous, and unambiguous" references and "clear and unmistakable" evidence.[51] But a sound case can be made for a consistent Christian pattern of Sunday worship, although not universally practiced, reaching back *prior* to Hadrian.[52]

---

american.edu, Feb. 8, 1997. Though see White, *Great Controversy*. 52.

48. Cf. Bacchiocchi, "Rise of Sunday Observance," 139-42.

49. See Schreven, *Now That's Clear*, 97. Cf. MacCarty, "Seventh-Day Sabbath," 42; Brimsmead, *Sabbatarianism Re-examined*; Wynne, "Lying for God."

50. Relevant texts and authors in these discussions and debates concerning earliest Christianity include (but are not limited to) Matt 12:1–8; Mark 2:23–28; John 20:26; Acts 2:46, 20:7; Rom 14:5; 1 Cor 16:2–3; Gal 4:9–10; Col 2:13–17; Heb 4; Rev 1:10; *Didache*; Pliny's letter to Trajan; Ignatius of Antioch; *Epistle of Barnabas*; *Gospel of Peter*; *Epistle of the Apostles*; Justin Martyr; *Epistle to Diognetus*; *Gospel of Thomas*; *Acts of John*; *Acts of Peter*; Dionysius of Corinth; Melito of Sardis; Theophilus of Antioch; Irenaeus; Bardesanes; Tertullian; and Clement of Alexandria. See Bacchiocchi, "Rise of Sunday Observance"; Bauckham, "Lord's Day"; Bauckham, ""Sabbath and Sunday"; Beckwith, "Daily and Weekly Worship"; Cairus, "Clement of Alexandria"; California Institute for Ancient Studies, "Brief History of the Sabbath"; Carson, *From Sabbath to Lord's Day*; Coleman, "Historical Sketch"; Cotton, *From Sabbath to Sunday*; Dugmore, "Lord's Day and Easter"; Guy, "Lord's Day"; Kraft, "Some Notes on Sabbath Observance"; Lewis, "Ignatius"; Llewelyn, "Use of Sunday"; Maxwell, "Early Sabbath-Sunday History"; Maxwell, "Sabbath and Sunday"; Morrison, "Sabbath and Sunday"; Odom, *Sabbath and Sunday*; "Saturday (Sabbath) or Sunday?"; Shigley, "Historical Review"; Strand, "From Sabbath to Sunday"; Strand, "Sabbath and Sunday"; Strand, "Some Notes"; Strand, "Tertullian and the Sabbath"; Young, "Use of Sunday." Cf. Andrews, *Complete Testimony of the Fathers*; Andrews and Conradi, *History of the Sabbath*.

51. Ferguson, *Early Christians Speak*, 1:69.

52. In another essay, I intend to examine the relevant materials in the Apostolic

On the other hand, Joseph Pipa claims in sweeping terms: "All Christians transferred their day of worship from Saturday to Sunday; their gathering at the synagogues was for evangelistic purposes and not to fulfill the responsibilities of corporate worship."[53] Nevertheless, an examination of the diverse spectrum of Jewish-Christian sects will reveal that matters were more complex than Pipa's generalized phrase "All Christians"—as one might indeed expect.[54]

There is no inherent incompatibility between Saturday Sabbath-keeping and assembling for corporate worship on Sundays, such that both could not be observed by the same person or church.[55] Various texts confirm that "there were Jewish Christians who celebrated the Sabbath."[56] Some Jewish-Christian groups continued to worship on Saturday throughout the early centuries,[57] and some factions held distinct observances on both Saturday

---

Fathers and associated literature. A consortium of Evangelical scholars published a collected volume tracing a continuous line of Sunday worship from the first century through Constantine's era (Carson, *From Sabbath to Lord's Day*, 2000). Bacchiocchi called this collection "the most objective and realistic attempt made by Sunday keeping scholars to establish the historical genesis of Sunday observance" (Bacchiocchi, *Divine Rest for Human Restlessness*, 14–15).

53. Pipa, "Response to Craig L. Blomberg," 375. For a full discussion of Pipa's Sunday sabbatarian views, see Pipa, *Lord's Day*.

54. Ferguson recognizes some complexity in "Sabbath," 178–79. See the backpedaling from a general summary to more detailed nuances in Ferguson, *Early Christians Speak*, 1:69. On the complexities of Patristic evidence, see Hartog, "Complexity and Variety."

55. Ferguson, "Sabbath," 178–79. See Rouwhorst, "Liturgical Time and Space," 267; Rouwhorst, "Continuity and Discontinuity." On the complexities of "Jewish Christianity," see Jackson-McCabe, *Jewish Christianity Reconsidered*.

56. Rouwhorst, "Jewish Liturgical Traditions," 86; Rouwhorst, "Reception of the Jewish Sabbath." See especially Hippolytus, *Refutatatio omnium haeresim* 9.16.3; Epiphanius, *Panarion* 19.5.1; 29.7.5; 30.2.2; 30.17.5; Jerome, *Ep.* 112.13; Jerome, *Commentariorum in Evangelium Matthaei* 12.2; Timothy of Alexandria, *Responsa* (PG 33:1305).

57. Kraft, "Some Notes on Sabbath Observance." Chadwick (*Early Church*, 22) summarizes, "The Jewish Christians, excluded by their fellow-country-men, continued to observe Sabbaths, circumcision, and other Jewish feasts. As this distressed many Gentile Christians, they became lonely, unsupported groups. In the fourth century and later, there were small Jewish churches in Syria . . . But the orthodox Jews could not forgive them for being Christians, and the Gentile majority in the Church could not comprehend their continued observance of the traditional customs and rites of Judaism. Slowly the communities lost importance." See Justin Martyr, *Dialogue with Trypho* 47.

and Sunday.[58] For example, some Syriac Jewish-Christian groups apparently observed Saturday as the Sabbath and assembled for worship on Sundays.[59]

The *Apostolic Constitutions* (*Constitutiones Apostolorum*) reflect a Christian movement that assembled "every day, morning and evening," but "principally on the Sabbath-day," while meeting "more diligently" on the "the Lord's Day" ("the day of our Lord's resurrection").[60] The work asserts:

> On this account He permitted men every Sabbath to rest, that so no one might be willing to send one word out of his mouth in anger on the day of the Sabbath. For the Sabbath is the ceasing of the creation, the completion of the world, the inquiry after laws, and the grateful praise to God for the blessings He has bestowed upon men. All which the Lord's Day excels, and shows the Mediator Himself, the Provider, the Lawgiver, the Cause of the resurrection, the First-born of the whole creation, God the Word, and man, who was born of Mary alone, without a man, who lived holily, who was crucified under Pontius Pilate, and died, and rose again from the dead. So that the Lord's Day commands us to offer unto Thee, O Lord, thanksgiving for all.[61]

"On the one hand," notes Gerard Rouwhorst, "the Sabbath is paid a high tribute in a way that may be called surprising in a Christian writing. On the other hand, it is conspicuous that the text of the prayer emphasizes the superiority of the Sunday vis-à-vis the Saturday/Sabbath."[62]

---

58. See Rouwhorst, "Reception of the Jewish Sabbath"; Rouwhorst, "Jewish Liturgical Traditions," 80–87; Stewart-Sykes, "Seating of Polycarp," 327–29; Bradshaw and Johnson, *Origins of Feasts*; Morrison, "Sabbath and Sunday in Early Christianity."

59. For a critical response, see Wynne, "Lying for God." Rouwhorst ("Jewish Liturgical Traditions," 80) argues that the observance of the Sabbath was the minority view even within early Syriac Christianity: "In fact, most of the known Syriac sources do not bear any evidence of the continuing influence of the Sabbath or even of elements related to it. If they make mention of the weekly Jewish day of rest at all, it is only in a polemical sense and particularly with the intention to restrain Christians from observing that day. This fact in itself, of course, demonstrates that some Christians felt attracted by the Sabbath or rituals connected with it and celebrated it together with the Jews or, what seems more probable, had developed their own Christian Sabbath practices. This does, however, not alter the fact that the relevant sources in question themselves are opposed to any celebration of the Sabbath."

60. *Constitutiones Apostolorum* 2.7.59 (all translations are from *ANF* 7). See Deck, *Lord's Day or the Sabbath*, 142. Cf. Gane, "Significance of the Apostolic Constitutions." Contrast the *Didascalia* (see Beckwith and Stott, *This Is the Day*, 51).

61. *Constitutiones Apostolorum* 7.2.36.

62. Rouwhorst, "Jewish Liturgical Traditions," 85–86.

Stewart-Sykes has theorized, "Whilst we may agree that the redactor of *Constitutiones Apostolorum*, by giving a subordinate recognition to the Sabbath, is meeting Jewish Christianity half-way, we might ask whether the Sabbath keeping of these Syrian Jewish Christians is actually a relic of a more ancient custom which the redactor of the Syrian *Didascalia* opposes because of its apparent Judaizing tendencies, and with which the redactor of *Constitutiones Apostolorum* seeks to reach a compromise."[63] Stewart-Sykes points to parallels with the *Vita Polycarpi* (which he dates to the third century) as confirmation: "Because the manner in which the Sabbath is observed in the community of *Vita Polycarpi* is in keeping with the manner in which Jews observed the day before the parting of the ways, we may suggest that the keeping of the seventh day by Christians as a day devoted to study and learning was an ancient custom."[64]

Eusebius spoke of "Ebionites" who "used to observe the Sabbath and the rest of the Jewish ceremonial, but on Sundays celebrated rites like ours in commemoration of the Savior's resurrection."[65] Socrates Scholasticus (fifth century) claimed: "For although almost all churches throughout the

63. Stewart-Sykes, "Seating of Polycarp," 328. Rouwhorst ("Jewish Liturgical Traditions," 84) has a different take, arguing that "the celebration of the Saturday/Sabbath appears only in one source, that is moreover relatively late, whereas several other sources which are, in addition, older, explicitly condemn it. This means that the antiquity of this tradition, as far as the majority of the Syriac Churches is concerned, is very unlikely." Rouwhorst adds that "it is striking that those parts of the Apostolic Constitutions (books 1–6), which notoriously constitute an adapted version of the Syriac Didascalia, have left out the passages of the latter source that contain polemics against the observance of the Sabbath! Moreover, Christians are even explicitly called on to observe not only the Sunday, but also the Saturday which is considered as the day on which the creation of the world is commemorated (VII,23,2; VII,36,1.5 and VIII,33,2). On both days they are supposed to assemble together for a liturgical service (II,59,3) and, what must seem more surprising, to rest, viz. to abstain from work (VII,36,1.5 and VIII,33,2), whereas it is forbidden to fast on these days (VIII,47,64) . . . These facts should be seen in the right perspective. The Apostolic Constitutions are not the only source dating from the end of the fourth century to allot a particular place to the celebration of the Saturday. Liturgical services on that day are testified to by several sources describing liturgical practices in the East during the same period. As far as I know, however, there are no indications that during that period elsewhere Christians abstained from work on Saturday and certainly there are no other examples known of Christianized Sabbath blessings" ("Jewish Liturgical Traditions," 81–82).

64. Stewart Sykes, *Life of Polycarp*, 57. Stewart-Sykes elsewhere ("Seating of Polycarp," 326) maintains "there is evidence for other Jewish practices among the Christians of Smyrna in the third century provided by *Vita Polycarpi*, most notably gatherings for instruction on the Sabbath."

65. Eusebius, *HE* 3.2.7 (all translations are from from *LCL*).

world celebrate the sacred mysteries [the Lord's Supper] on the sabbath [Saturday] of every week, yet the Christians of Alexandria and at Rome, on account of some ancient tradition, have ceased to do this [do not do this]."[66] Sozomen (fifth century) similarly acknowledged, "Assemblies are not held in all churches on the same time or manner. The people of Constantinople, and almost everywhere, assemble together on the Sabbath, as well as on the first day of the week, which custom is never observed at Rome or at Alexandria."[67] Such data reflect more complexity in the diverse strands of early Christianity than is often acknowledged.

CONSTANTINE AND SUNDAY

Opinions concerning Constantine's conversion and policies vary greatly. "The nature of Constantine's 'conversion,' the interpretation of the events at the Milvian Bridge, and Constantine's subsequent attitude to Christianity, are the subjects of endless debates among scholars. Ranging from the persistently cynical to the naively credulous, scholarly opinions judge Constantine to be anything from a brilliant statesman and political opportunist to a sincere and unselfish Christian believer."[68] Evidence does suggest that Constantine retained a continuing devotion (in some form) to the sun even after 324, although considering himself a Christian.[69]

66. Socrates, *HE* 5.22 (all translations are from *NPNF2* 2). The *NPNF2* translation of "have ceased to do this" is actually a mistranslation. Instead, the original asserts that the churches "do not observe this" (the Lord's Supper on the Sabbath). See Maxwell, "Early Sabbath-Sunday History," 142. Cf. Lewis, *Protestant Dilemma*, 48.

67. Sozomen, *HE* 7.19 (all translations are from *NPNF2* 2). See Lewis, *Protestant Dilemma*, 66. Cf. Augustine, *Ep.* 36.27.

68. Cardman, "Emperor's New Clothes," 195. On Constantine's vision, see Weiss, "Die Vision Constantins." On his conversion, see Alföldi, *Conversion of Constantine*; Eadie, *Conversion of Constantine*. On the subsequent religious shifts in the Roman Empire and Europe, see Jones, *Constantine and the Conversion of Europe*; Baynes, *Constantine the Great and the Christian Church*; Odahl, *Constantine and the Christian Empire*. See also Rebenich, "Vom dreizehnten Gott zum dreizehnten Apostel?"

69. Wallraff, "Constantine's Devotion to the Sun after 324." Wallraff concludes (ibid., 267–68), "We can probably assume correctly that he considered himself a Christian, but what he understood by Christianity was quite different from what we understand, and from what even the contemporary theologians understood by Christianity. Therefore, the theologians found themselves in an embarrassing situation. On the other hand, they had to acknowledge that the situation for the Church had improved very much thanks to Constantine's initiative, and they were sincerely grateful for that. On the other hand, they did not know what to make of the highly individual form of Christianity Constantine

On March 7, 321, Constantine issued the following edict: "All judges, townspeople and all occupations should rest on the most honorable day of the sun. Farmers indeed should be free and unhindered in their cultivation of the fields, since it frequently occurs that there is no more suitable day for entrusting seeds of corn [grain] to the furrows and slips of vine to the holes (prepared for them), lest haply the favorable moment sent by divine providence be lost."[70]

One notes the nomenclature of "the most honorable day of the sun (*dies solis*),"[71] the exemption for farmhands to work still on special occasions,[72] and the reference to "divine providence."[73] It is interesting that Constantine specifically exempted farm workers from the edict, because in Jewish tradition it was *especially* farm work that was prohibited on the Sabbath.[74] This shows that Constantine was not attempting simply to copy Jewish law and paste it on to Sunday observance.[75]

While many have interpreted the edict as "an act motivated by respect for Christian teaching and practice," Paul Jewett finds it difficult to

---

claimed for himself." Cf. Gross-Albenhausen, "Zur christlichen Selbstdarstellung Konstantins."

70. *Codex Justianus* 3.12.3, cited in Rordorf, *Sunday*, 162. For the relevant parallel in *Codex Theodosianus* (*CTh*) 2.8.1 (concerning the differentiation of legal actions on Sunday, including litigation and manumission), also from 321, see Rordorf, *Sunday*, 164–65. Rordorf notes (*Sunday*, 165), "In this passage it is plain that the emperor was concerned with a religious differentiation of Sunday, but it did not have an expressly Christian character." See also Gaudemet, "La législation religieuse de Constantin."

71. Jewett (*The Lord's Day*, 126) asserts, "The fact that it is called 'the day of the sun' does not prove that he had in mind the heathen veneration of the day, for it was common usage by this time to designate the days of the week by their planetary names." On the other hand, Constantine may have subtly nodded at non-Christian interests, such as the Mithraist veneration of the sun. See also Wallraff ("Constantine's Devotion to the Sun after 324," 258–60) who argues that Constantine's edict "is certainly not as Christian as Eusebius wants us to believe."

72. This, of course, differs from the observance of the Sabbath in the Mosaic Law.

73. Jewett, *Lord's Day*, 126.

74. Rordorf (*Sunday*, 163–64) argued that Constantine may have wanted to unite the empire around a loose monotheism. In Rordorf's view, the legislation was not so much religious as "the product of political and social considerations" (*Sunday*, 166).

75. Contrast the "*quanto magis* formula" later used by Christians, as in the Carolingian period (Rordorf, *Sunday*, 172). Rordorf argued that the "Sabbath commandment" became important for the justification of Sunday rest only in the sixth century (*Sunday*, 171).

assume that Constantine's motives were "purely Christian."[76] He contends that Constantine's edict "must be viewed, not only as a milestone in the development of Sunday observance, but also as a monument to his political sagacity."[77]

On the other hand, Martin Girardet von Klaus has recently argued that Constantine's legislation hints that the *dies solis* was established in connection with laws about the clergy and church buildings in 312/313.[78] Von Klaus adds, "Early Egyptian papyri show that the Christian name of the day (*dies dominicus, dominica*) is used even in documents written by pagan administrators from 325 onwards."[79] He concludes, "So, the character of the *dies solis* cannot be considered as a pagan or syncretistic one, but as an early step towards a Christianisation of the Roman Empire."[80]

After Constantine's era, Christians enjoyed more time and greater freedom to engage in corporate worship on Sunday.[81] More specifically, Constantine allowed his Christian soldiers to attend church on Sunday without hindrance.[82] One should not overstate Constantine's influence, however. Willy Rordorf (following Hans Huber) demonstrated how immediately subsequent writers did not cite Constantine's Sunday legislation. Moreover, according to Rordorf, "In the Latin fathers of this period we meet absolutely no law about rest from work on Sunday, not even the merest allusion to prohibition of work on Sunday."[83] Jerome reported concerning women returning to their convents on the Lord's Day: "When they had returned, they devoted themselves eagerly to work and made clothes either for themselves or for other people."[84] Benedict's Rule declared, "On

---

76. Jewett, *Lord's Day*, 126.

77. Ibid. When the edict was proclaimed, most Christians lived in the East under Licinius's rule, so that Constantine may have targeted their support and his own political advantage.

78. Von Klaus, "Vom Sonnen-Tag zum Sonntag," 310.

79. Ibid.

80. Ibid.

81. Jewett, *Lord's Day*, 127.

82. Eusebius, *VC* 4.18–20; cf. *Laud. Const.* 9.9–10; Rordorf, *Der Sonntag*, 165; Jewett, *Lord's Day*, 126.

83. Rordorf, *Sunday*, 167.

84. Jerome, *Ep.* 108.20 cited in Rordorf, *Sunday*, 167. By later standards, working by making clothes for others might be categorized as a "work of mercy." Jerome distinguished between *opera servilia* ("servile work") and work in general. "They [the Jews] did no servile work on the sabbath: we do none on the Lord's Day" (cited in Rordorf, *Sunday*, 172).

Sundays likewise all shall apply themselves to reading, except those who are assigned to various duties. But if there be anyone so careless and slothful that he will not or cannot study or read, let him be given some work to perform, so that he may not be idle."[85] Nevertheless, the requirement to rest on Sundays "was more and more couched in legal terms," and within fifty years of Constantine, the requirement for rest had been extended at times to agricultural work as well.[86]

BAPTISTS AND SUNDAY

Among Protestant movements stemming from the Reformation, various Sunday views developed.[87] Along with others, Baptists have disagreed concerning Sabbath/Sunday observance. One historic strand of Baptists, the Seventh-Day Baptists, have traditionally observed Saturday as a day of worship and rest.[88] Many Baptists have insisted upon the observance of Sunday as the Christian Sabbath, as a day of rest from "secular" work.[89] For example, the Lord's Day article from the Westminster Confession (and its insistence upon Sunday rest)[90] was transferred almost word-for-word into the Second London Baptist Confession of 1689.[91]

One sees the continuing influence of the Westminster material upon the Philadelphia Baptist Confession of Faith of 1742. The later New Hampshire Baptist Confession of Faith (1833) tightened the wording, but preserved Sunday as a day of Sabbath rest: "Of the Christian Sabbath We believe that the first day of the week is the Lord's Day, or Christian Sabbath; and is to be kept sacred to religious purposes, by abstaining from all secular labor and sinful recreations; by the devout observance of all the

85. Cited in Rordorf, *Sunday*, 167.

86. Rordorf, *Sunday*, 168, 169n3.

87. For Calvin's views, see Gaffin, *Calvin and the Sabbath*.

88. For an overview, see Kersten, "Seventh Day Baptists," 29. In 1650, John Ockford wrote a work combining Saturday Sabbatarianism with Baptist principles. By 1657, Saturday-observing Baptist churches were meeting in the greater London area. The first Seventh Day Baptist church in North America was planted in 1671 in Newport, Rhode Island. The Seventh Day Baptist General Conference was formed in 1802.

89. For a modern explanation, see Saunders, *Sabbath*.

90. On Sunday as the "Christian Sabbath," see Wardner, *Lord's Day*; Lee, *Covenantal Sabbath*, ch. 6.

91. Among the small changes, the chief was the addition of the phrase "the observation of the last day of the week being abolished."

means of grace, both private and public; and by preparation for that rest that remaineth for the people of God."

Sunday sabbatarians came not only from Calvinistic Baptists, but from Arminian Baptists as well. The Liberty Association Articles of Faith (1824) and the General Association Articles of Faith of both 1870 and 1949 all state: "We believe in the sanctity of the first day of the week (or Lord's Day) and that it ought to be observed and spent in the public or private worship of God and that on it we should abstain from our worldly concerns except in a case of necessity or mercy."[92] The Treatise of the Faith and Practice of the Free Will Baptists (1935) similarly declared, "This is one day in seven, which from the creation of the world God has set apart for sacred rest and holy service. Under the former dispensation, the seventh day of the week, as commemorative of the work of creation, was set apart for the Lord's Day. Under the gospel, the first day of the week, in commemoration of the resurrection of Christ, and by authority of Christ and the apostles, is observed as the Christian Sabbath. On this day all men are required to refrain from secular labor and devote themselves to the worship and service of God."

This Sunday sabbatarian view is also reflected in such key Baptist statements as Jessey's Catechism of 1652,[93] Keach's Catechism of 1677,[94] the Baptist Catechism for Girls and Boys of 1798, the Baptist Catechism of the Charleston Association of 1813,[95] Spurgeon's Catechism of 1855,[96]

---

92. Only the punctuation differs between these three documents in their Lord's Day articles.

93. "Q. What must we and you do on the Lord's Sabbath day? A. We must not work, nor prate, nor play, on the Sabbath day."

94. "The Sabbath is to be sanctified by a holy resting all that day, even from such worldly employments and recreations as are lawful on other days, and spending the time in the public and private exercises of God's worship, except so much as is to be taken up in the works of necessity and mercy" (Answer 66).

95. "The Sabbath is to be sanctified by a holy resting all that day (Ex. 20:8, 10), even from such worldly employments and recreations as are lawful on other days (Ex. 16:25–28; Neh. 13:15–22); and spending the whole time in the public and private exercises of God's worship (Lk. 4:16; Acts 20:7; Ps. 92:title; Is. 66:23), except so much as is to be taken up in the works of necessity and mercy (Mt. 12:1–13)."

96. Spurgeon's explanation is similar to the Charleston Association's (above): "The Sabbath is to be sanctified by a holy resting all that day, even from such worldly employments and recreations as are lawful on other days (Lev. 23:3), and spending the whole time in the public and private exercises of God's worship (Ps. 92:1–2; Isa. 58:13–14), except so much as is taken up in the works of necessity and mercy (Matt. 12:11–12)" (Answer 20).

the Abstract of Principles of 1858,[97] Everts' Catechism of 1866,[98] Boyce's Catechism of 1867,[99] and Broadus' Catechism of 1892.[100] These documents (and the list is by no means exhaustive) exhort the faithful to abstain from all secular labor and amusements, and to reserve Sunday as a day of worship, spiritual endeavor, and rest.

Other Baptist confessions have supported a less rigid Sunday rest observance, such as the Confession of Faith of the Minnesota Baptist Association[101] and John Piper's recent Baptist Catechism.[102] An interesting shift toward greater laxity occurred in the 2000 revision of the Baptist Faith and Message of the Southern Baptist Convention. The 1925 and 1963 versions had stated, "The first day of the week is the Lord's Day. It is a Christian institution for regular observance. It commemorates the resurrection of Christ from the dead and should be employed in exercises of worship and spiritual devotion, both public and private, and by refraining from worldly

97. "The Lord's Day is a Christian institution for regular observance, and should be employed in exercises of worship and spiritual devotion, both public and private, resting from worldly employments and amusements, works of necessity and mercy only excepted."

98. "The observance of a seventh part of time (the first day of the week, according to apostolic order) as a holy day, to be devoted to religious worship and duties; forbidding all profanation of that day by secular business, the pursuit of pleasure, vacant idleness, or indifference to religion" (Answer 20).

99. Christians are to keep "The first day of the week or Sunday" as "the Sabbath." The Sabbath "is one day of the week, which God requires to be kept as a day of rest, and holy to Him."

100. "Ought we to keep the Lord's day as the Sabbath? Yes, we ought to keep the Lord's day as a day of rest and holy employments" (Question and Answer 9).

101. "We believe that the first day of the week is the Lord's Day, and is a Christian institution; it is to be kept sacred to spiritual purposes, by abstaining from all unnecessary secular labor and sinful recreations, for it commemorates the resurrection of the Lord Jesus Christ from the dead; by the devout observance of all the means of grace, both private and public; and by preparation for the rest that remaineth for the people of God." Cf. the Confession of Faith of Central Baptist Theological Seminary of Plymouth, Minnesota; Bauder, "Shall We Keep Sabbath?"

102. "Question 66: How is the Sabbath to be sanctified? Answer: One day in seven should be especially devoted to corporate worship and other spiritual exercises that restore the soul's rest in God and zeal for His name. It should provide physical refreshment and fit one for a week of devoted service to Christ. Question 67: What is forbidden in the fourth commandment? Answer: The fourth commandment forbids dishonoring the Lord's Day by actions or thoughts that divert the soul from spiritual refreshment, or deprive the body of renewed energy or distract the mind from its special Sabbath focus on the Lord."

amusements, and resting from secular employments, works of necessity and mercy only being excepted."[103] The 2000 version of the Baptist Faith and Message deleted these specific prohibitions: "The first day of the week is the Lord's Day. It is a Christian institution for regular observance. It commemorates the resurrection of Christ from the dead and should include exercises of worship and spiritual devotion, both public and private. Activities on the Lord's Day should be commensurate with the Christian's conscience under the Lordship of Jesus Christ."[104]

IRONY

An irony is found within the phenomenon of Baptist Sunday sabbatarianism. Traditionally, Baptist authors have negatively assessed Constantine and "Constantinianism." For example, Roger Williams claimed that Constantine "did more hurt to Christ Iesus, his Crowne, and Kingdome, then [sic] the raging fury of the most bloody Neroes."[105] Like many of their brethren among the free church movements, Baptists have regularly criticized Constantine's role within church history. The so-called "Constantinian fall" has often been viewed as a precipitous moment of decline in the purity and vigor of the church. In a twentieth-century thesis for Northern Baptist Theological Seminary, August Morrow Vanderark declared that "The acts of Constantine, climaxed with the publication of Milan, set in motion the process of departure and digression from the practices of true Christianity. Let Baptists and Evangelical Christians heed the warning of history."[106]

Yet the sabbatarian observance of Sunday, as mandated by early modern Baptist confessions, owed its ease of compliance to the results

103. The 1925 version has "works of necessity and mercy" while the 1963 version has "work of necessity and mercy."

104. For a comparison of the 1925, 1963, and 2000 versions of the Baptist Faith and Message, see http://www.sbc.net/bfm/bfmcomparison.asp.

105. Cf. Vanderark, "Constantine's Edict of Milan," 112. Concerning sabbatarian views, "Williams was notoriously skeptical about Sunday as the chosen day for no work. He had considerable sympathy with the theological arguments of the Seventh-Day Baptists. More generally, he saw the burden that comes with imposing a majority practice on all. Rhode Island had no Sunday law during his lifetime" (Nussbaum, *Liberty of Conscience*, 50). Williams maintained this posture even though Sunday sabbatarianism was prevalent in his Puritan context (Maxwell, "From Sabbath to Sunday"). For a comparison of the concepts of "religious liberty" in Patristic sources and the American founders, see Hartog, "Religious Liberty."

106. Vanderark, "Constantine's Edict of Milan," 112.

of "Constantinianism." As Jewett affirms, "It is not until the reign of Constantine that the idea of Sunday rest from work as such begins to be prominent."[107] Numerous authors, including Phillip Schaff and Everett Ferguson, have noted that many of the early Christians (especially slaves) in the first few centuries could not have fully excused themselves from labor on Sundays.[108] For example, Jewett insisted, "Since most Christians belonged to the working class, it was unthinkable at first that they should not work on Sunday."[109] Rordorf explained, "In the early centuries of the Church's history down to the time of the Emperor Constantine it would, in any case, not have been practicable for Christians to observe Sunday as a day of rest, on which they were obliged, for the sake of principle, to abstain from work."[110] Rordorf maintained that Christians would have rested *partially* on Sunday, in order to attend worship services.[111]

The early Christians often met before dawn (or after dusk), perhaps enabling slaves and day-laborers to attend services and to work as well.[112] We have no pagan materials criticizing a Christian practice of a day's rest

107. Jewett, *Lord's Day*, 124.

108. Ferguson, *Early Christian Speak*, 1:69. Philip Schaff (*History of the Christian Church*, 2:202) declared, "Considering that the church was struggling into existence, and that a large number of Christians were slaves of heathen masters, we cannot expect an unbroken regularity of worship and a universal cessation of labor on Sunday until the civil government in the time of Constantine came to the help of the church and legalized (and in part even enforced) the observance of the Lord's Day." Moule (*Birth of the New Testament,* 49) adds: "Whereas circumcision would have been practicable for Gentile converts, Sabbath observance simply was not. Unless they came inside the Jewish ghetto, where there was an ordered life adjusted to the cessation of work on the Sabbath, they could not earn their living or subsist while observing the Sabbath. If they were slaves, Gentile masters would not release them from work; and if they were independent and earning their own living, they would still have had to pursue their trade on a Sabbath. It was no doubt because circumcision was a practical possibility for Gentile Christians, as the Sabbath was not, that it was the centre of controversy." See also Porvaznik, "Emperor Constantine: Pagan, Christian, or First Pope?"

109. Jewett, *Lord's Day*, 125.

110. Rordorf, *Sunday*, 154.

111. Ibid., 156–58.

112. As McQuilkin (McQuilkin, *Introduction to Biblical Ethics*, 174–75) acknowledges, "The strong presumption is that a large portion of the early Christians, as slaves, really had no rest at all as we understand the term . . . For the first three centuries, then, the Fathers were bound by a society in which neither they nor their disciples could rest." But McQuilkin insists, "So they 'made Scripture serve Caesar'—they taught that the Bible enjoined work on Sunday. But as soon as freedom to rest was granted, the theologians returned to a theological base."

(in comparison with extant criticisms of the Jewish tradition of Saturday rest). Kerry Wynne reasons, "If the early church had maintained a Sabbath stance, the Romans would have made record of it. Supporting this idea is the fact that the Jews had such a bad reputation with the Romans for their Sabbath keeping that they were generally exempt from military service and were not valued for slaves, but this was not true for Christians."[113] Although there are hints of Sunday rest in the ante-Nicene church writings, they are usually couched as recommendations rather than mandates.[114] "It is never distinctly maintained by the early fathers that it is a sin to work on the first day."[115]

Mark Searle concludes, "There is absolutely no evidence to suggest that the early church saw Sunday as a Christian Sabbath. . . . Moreover, it should be noted that the first day of the week was a day for assembling to worship; never, among Christians, a day for abstaining from work."[116] Some evidence is difficult to fit within Searle's reconstruction, however.[117] Tertullian wrote:

> In the matter of kneeling also prayer is subject to diversity of observance, through the act of some few who abstain from kneeling on the Sabbath; and since this dissension is particularly on its trial before the churches, the Lord will give His grace that the dissentients may either yield, or else indulge their opinion without offence to others. We, however (just as we have received), only on the day of the Lord's Resurrection ought to guard not only against kneeling, but every posture and office of solicitude; deferring even our businesses (*differentes etiam negotia*) lest we give any place to the devil (*ne quem diabolo locum demus*). Similarly, too, in the

---

113. Wynne, "Lying for God." See also Barclay, *Ten Commandments for Today*, 31–32; Forster, *Palestinian Judaism in New Testament Times*, 72; Lohse, "Sabbath"; Brinsmead, "Digest of the Sabbath Question"; Brinsmead, *Sabbatarianism Re-Examined*.

114. Cf. Tertullian, *Ad nationes* 1.13.

115. Lewis, *Protestant Dilemma*, 62.

116. Searle, "Sunday," 63. "Until well into the second century we do not find the slightest indication in our sources that Christians marked Sunday by any kind of abstention from work" (Rordorf, *Sunday*, 157; cf. 154).

117. Materials attributed to Peter of Alexandria have been summoned as evidence of the Lord's Day as a day of rest (Beckwith and Stott, *This Is the Day*, 100). But the relevant discourse probably was not written by him (see Rordorf, *Sunday* 171n4). In his *Canonical Epistle*, canon 15, Peter did affirm, "We celebrate the Lord's day as the day of joy, because on it He rose again" (see Lee, *Covenantal Sabbath*, ch. 6).

period of Pentecost; which period we distinguish by the same solemnity of exultation.[118]

Nevertheless, although some have argued that Tertullian's exhortation entailed a total rest from all work, Rordorf maintained that the parallel of the fifty-day period from Easter to Pentecost would preclude such a *total* rest; and the fear of giving place to the devil was reason to attend worship services not reason to abstain from work (as early Christians frequently viewed respite as a source of temptation).[119] In this understanding of the passage, Tertullian was calling for time of rest in order to attend corporate worship, not for a full day of rest. "Sunday *worship* was the reason for 'deferring business affairs.'"[120] Rordorf compared this to the Syriac *Didascalia*, which exhorted, "But on the Lord's Day leave everything and run eagerly to your church; for she is your glory."[121] Yet the *Didascalia* also urged, "Do you the faithful therefore, all of you, daily and hourly, whenever you are not in the church, devote yourselves to your work; so that in all the conduct of life you may either be occupied in the things of the Lord or engaged upon your work, and may never be idle."[122]

A universal prohibition of Sunday labor would have proved extremely difficult if not impossible for pre-Constantinian Christians to enforce.[123] As Rordorf asserted, "The Christians, who for a long time belonged principally to the lower strata of society and in particular to the slave class, could not observe a day of rest which recurred after every six days, in addition to

---

118. Tertullian, *De Oratione* 23 (translation from *ANF* 3).

119. Rordorf even shows how Constantine's Sunday laws brought "new, serious, practical problems which resulted from the total rest from work on Sunday" (Rordorf, *Sunday*, 162).

120. Ibid., 160.

121. Translation adapted from Connolly, *Didascalia Apostolorum*, 58–59. Cf. also *Constitutiones Apostolorum* 7.33.1–2: "Slaves should work for five days; on the Sabbath and on the Lord's Day they should be free from work on account of the religious instruction in the church . . . During Holy Week and during that week which immediately follows, the slaves should rest"; and *Testamentum Domini* 2.12: "Let those who bear the burdens of labor refresh themselves a little in the days of Pentecost, and on every first day of the week" (translation from Cooper and Maclean, *Testament of our Lord*, 130). Geraty proposed that Sunday observance arose from Easter observance (Geraty, "Pascha"). In response, see Morrison, "Sabbath and Sunday."

122. Translation adapted from Connolly, *Didascalia Apostolorum*, 61.

123. Especially in times of persecution, Sunday rest would have immediately set the Christians off from society (Rordorf, *Sunday*, 155).

observing the official days of rest; their economic and social circumstances would never have permitted this."[124]

Therefore, although Constantine did not change the day of worship for Christianity as a whole, he did play an important role by insisting upon Sunday as a day of rest from labor within imperial legislation. And the *Konstantinische Wende* did affect Christian liturgy.[125] After Constantine, the term "Sabbath" came to be used regularly for Sunday—the "Lord's Day."[126] The Council of Laodicea (ca. 364/365) declared that Christians should do no work on Sunday, "if possible."[127] Eventually, increasing legislation guaranteed Sunday as an entire day of rest.

A Theodosian edict of 386 prohibited Sunday performances in the circus and the theatre.[128] The Council of Carthage of 401 stipulated that no plays were to be performed on Sundays, and it petitioned the emperor "that public shows might be transferred from the Christian Sunday . . . to some other days of the week."[129] Emperor Leo I issued another Sunday law in 469, which abolished non-religious celebrations and events,[130] and Emperor Justinian incorporated the previous Sunday legislations of Constantine and

124. Ibid. See also Lee, *Covenantal Sabbath*.

125. See Shepherd, "Liturgical Expressions of the Constantinian Triumph." A debate still rages concerning Constantine's role in the development of Christmas celebration. See Roll, "Origins of Christmas." Constantine's role is downplayed in Talley ("Constantine and Christmas," 272) who argues against the view that Constantine "was personally interested in the establishment at Rome of the festival of Christ's nativity on the *natalis invicti.*"

126. See Pipa, "Christian Sabbath," 150; Pipa, "Response to Craig L. Blomberg," 376. Cf. John Chrysostom, *Commentary on Matthew*, homily 5:1.

127. Canon 29 of the Council of Laodicea stipulated, "Christians shall not Judaize and be idle on Saturday but shall work on that day; but the Lord's Day they shall especially honor, and, as being Christians, shall, if possible, do no work on that day. If, however, they are found Judaizing, they shall be shut out from Christ" (translation in Strand, "The Sabbath and Sunday," 329; cf. Lewis, *Protestant Dilemma*, 73). For an early counter-Adventist examination of the Council of Laodicea, see Riggle, *Sabbath and the Lord's Day*, 155–57.

128. See Rordorf, *Sunday*, 166, who adds in n3, "One may wonder why this prohibition was enacted; did the sporting events disturb the church services, or did they keep Christians from their worship?"

129. Lee, *Covenantal Sabbath*, ch. 6; see Pipa, "Christian Sabbath," 153.

130. Leo decreed that there would be no Sunday games or hunting, no stage plays, no playing of musical instruments, no business activities, and no legal proceedings (cf. Lewis, *Protestant Dilemma*, 74).

Leo within his revised Roman law code of 534.[131] "The Council of Orleans in 538 prohibited labor, even for farmers, so they could attend worship services on Sunday."[132]

CONCLUSION

In sum, the trajectory symbolized by Constantine's legal influence greatly assisted a Sunday respite from work, particularly for disenfranchised Christians. Sunday eventually became a requisite day of rest and worship throughout Christendom, and remained so throughout much of the Reformation and its ecclesial descendants.[133] Rordorf fittingly concluded, "through the centuries the church has been living on the heritage of the post-Constantinian period."[134]

In this manner, confessional Baptists and other free-church Christians have enjoyed, to some degree at least, the fruits of a "Constantinianism" that they might otherwise generally disdain.[135] Over three decades ago, Everett Ferguson insisted that both Adventists and the Reformed can learn from Patristic scholarship in this matter of Sabbath/Sunday observance. Based upon this present study, one might add that Baptist movements influenced by the Reformed confessions should return to the Patristic sources as well. May we all humbly study the entirety of ecclesiastical history rather than simply those historical segments most conducive or most associated with our own systems. Such a return can only enhance our understanding of the nature and scope of the vast narrative of church history, and can concurrently and even unexpectedly enhance our understanding of our own slice of the larger story as well.[136]

131. See MacCarty, "Seventh-Day Sabbath," 43.

132. Ibid.

133. See Chantry, *Call the Sabbath a Delight*.

134. Rordorf, *Sunday*, 173. He added, "We should not forget that this heritage does not derive from pre-Constantinian Christianity."

135. This is not to deny various ill effects resulting from the so-called "Constantinian turn." Moreover, on the practical benefits of a weekly rest, see Baab, *Sabbath Keeping*; Buchanan, *Rest of God*; Kent, *Rest*; Muller, *Sabbath*; Ray, *Celebrating the Sabbath*. A Jewish classic is Heschel, *Sabbath*.

136. This essay was also presented at the Patristic, Medieval, and Renaissance Conference held at Villanova University in October of 2012. I wish to thank George Kalantzis and the Wheaton Center for Early Christian Studies for allowing me to be a Visiting Scholar in the summer of 2012, and thereby assisting my research.

6

Did the Rise of Constantine Mean the End of Christian Mission?

Edward L. Smither

Christianity is a missionary faith. This is certainly evident from the "Great Commissional" type passages of Scripture, verses preached from and visibly posted in modern evangelical missions conferences, but even more so from the overall thrust of Scripture. That is, the mission of God (*missio Dei*) is the grand narrative of the Old and New Testaments and thus, in the opinion of some scholars, Scripture should be read with a hermeneutic of mission.[1] Whether this approach to Scripture is fully accepted or not, mission remains in the DNA of the Christian faith and the Christian movement prior to the fourth century demonstrated this value.

But did mission—proclaiming the death, burial, and resurrection of Christ and ministering to all nations in word and deed—cease with Constantine's conversion and his giving Christianity a preferred status within the Roman Empire? Did Christendom, which expanded through political, military, and economic power replace Christian mission?

In this chapter, I will argue that Christian mission did continue past Constantine, though the narrative certainly becomes more confusing

1. See Bauckham, "Mission as Hermeneutic for Scriptural Interpretation"; and Wright, *Mission of God*, 29–70.

following his rise to power. Beginning with a working definition of mission, I will discuss some representative elements of this diverse history showing examples of Christendom that appear to abandon mission altogether. However, this inquiry will largely reveal accounts of missionaries working within a state-church paradigm or at least approaching mission in full view of political authorities. In terms of scope and limitations, I will focus on missions within or from the Roman Empire from the fourth to eighth centuries. Finally, in my concluding section I will offer some points of reflection for modern Christians, particularly evangelicals, contemplating the history of missions.

WHAT IS MISSION?

What do we mean by Christian mission? Following the consensus of missiological thought shared across traditions, I am persuaded that Christian mission flows from God's mission *(missio Dei)* to glorify himself and expand his kingdom.[2] With doxology as the driving motif, we affirm that "God is the one who initiates and sustains mission."[3] Hence, I define *mission* as all that the church does to promote God's glory among the nations, while *missions* is the specific activity of the church and its missionaries to make disciples of all nations through evangelism, discipleship, church planting, and related ministries.[4]

I should add that I define *missionaries* as those who are engaged in the task of missions. Although in the early church period, there is evidence for some who were involved in a sort of full-time vocational missionary labor, that seems to be the exception as most missionaries ministered while engaged in other types of vocation. Hence, we observe missionaries who were primarily bishops, monks, teachers, businesspeople, and even soldiers.

One may reasonably ask—at what point did mission become mission in the history of the church? Is it not anachronistic to refer to mission in the early church? David Bosch is correct in asserting that in the Patristic period "the Latin word *missio* was an expression employed in the doctrine of the Trinity, to denote the sending of the Son by the Father, and of the

2. See Guder's helpful summary of Barth's *missio Dei* thought in Guder, "Defining and Describing 'Mission,'" 56–60.

3. Moreau et al., *Introducing World Missions*, 17; also Kreider, *Worship and Mission*, 43–55.

4. Moreau et al., *Introducing World Missions*, 17.

Holy Spirit by the Father and the Son."[5] Yet, modern theologians such as Leslie Newbigin, Darrell Guder, and Timothy Tennent have worked from this trinitarian framework and articulated their missional theology within it.[6] Dana Robert focuses the discussion by reminding us how mission is conveyed in the New Testament. She writes: "the idea of 'mission' is carried through the New Testament by 206 references to the term 'sending.' The main Greek verb 'to send' is *apostollein*. Thus apostles were literally those sent to spread the 'Good News' of Jesus' life and message."[7] In short, mission has been central to the identity of the Christian movement since its inception even when the term mission is not always present. Summarizing this point, Bosch writes: "For fifteen centuries the church used other terms to refer to what we subsequently call 'mission': phrases such as 'propagation of the faith,' 'preaching of the gospel,' apostolic proclamation,' 'promulgation of the gospel,' 'augmenting the faith,' 'expanding the church,' 'planting the church,' propagation of the reign of Christ,' and 'illuminating the nations.'"[8]

WAS CONSTANTINE THE FIRST CHRISTIAN EMPEROR?

Before proceeding, I would like to set the stage with some clarifying remarks on Constantine. In his recent work *Defending Constantine*, Peter Leithart asserts that Constantine was the first Christian emperor.[9] With the emperor's declaration of faith, Leithart emphasizes many of the benefits of the gospel that Constantine brought to bear within the empire. Though Leithart is clearly focused on a Christian leader within the context of Rome, it is worth nothing that the so-called Constantinian revolution and the Christendom paradigm probably got started outside of Rome with the conversion of King Trdat of Armenia around 301.

If we believe the accounts of the Armenian historian Agathangelos, we learn that Gregory the Illuminator (ca. 240–332) came from Asia Minor to

5. Bosch, *Transforming Mission*, 228.

6. See Newbigin, *The Open Secret*; Guder, "Defining and Describing 'Mission,'" 56; and Tennent, *Invitation to World Missions*.

7. Robert, *Christian Mission*, 11.

8. Bosch, *Transforming Mission*, 228.

9. This premise resounds throughout Leithart's *Defending Constantine* and was evident in his lectures at the 2012 eastern regional Evangelical Theological Society meeting (March 2, 2012) to which I gave the response.

serve the Armenian king. Because of his refusal to make sacrifices to an Armenian goddess and the fact that his father was an enemy of Trdat, Gregory was tortured and then thrown in a pit for some thirteen years but did not die. The chronicler reports that Trdat, along with his household and servants, became afflicted by demons and fell ill, and Gregory was summoned to minister to them. As he prayed, they were healed and freed from the demonic influence after which Gregory was given freedom to proclaim the Christian faith. Together with the royal household and Armenian nobility, Trdat embraced Christianity, was catechized, and then baptized. The king took it one step farther and declared Christianity to be the new national religion and some four million Armenians were reportedly baptized. While critics might easily dismiss Agathangelos' account as a trope that greatly resembles Daniel's interactions with the kings of Babylon and Persia, this narrative remains a focal point in the Christian memory of the contemporary Armenian Orthodox church.[10]

As Trdat's conversion occurred a good decade before Constantine's experience in 312, this casts doubt on the assertion that Constantine was the first Christian monarch. Rather, Constantine's story should be properly located in the history of Roman Christianity within a broader narrative of global Christianity. But it should be further noted that Constantine never went as far as Trdat in declaring Christianity as the official religion of his dominion. Instead, around 312, following the victory at Milvian Bridge, he extended the policies of Galerius' Edict of Nicomedia from the previous year and tolerated Christianity within the empire. In addition, the church began to receive other benefits as clergy were given a tax free status, churches were constructed, and other property was donated to the church. It is not actually until the decree of Theodosius around 390 that Christianity is declared the official religion of the empire.[11]

In short, the Armenian account shows us that the notion of a Christian monarch and even the seeds of Christendom probably do not originate with Constantine. However, the reason that we do not talk about a Tiridatian revolution is that Rome's global and historical stage was clearly much grander than that of Armenia. Nor do we speak of Theodosianism because Christendom was already in development prior to the adoption of

10. See Agathangelos, "History of the Armenians," 122–30; also Moffett, *History of Christianity in Asia*, 118; Irvin and Sunquist, *History of the World Christian Movement*, 113; Sterk, "Captive Women and Heretical Monks," 21; Sterk, "Missions from Below," 8–9; and Sterk, "'Representing' Mission from Below," 278–79.

11. Kreider, *Worship and Mission*, 38.

the late-fourth-century Theodosian Code. Without a doubt, Constantine's person and timing were remarkable.

The Nature and Scope of Christendom (and Its Missionaries)

What is Christendom? Kreider helpfully defines it as "a Christian civilization with common understandings of belief, belonging, and behavior, and with widely shared forms of religious experience."[12] Though Constantine set these things into motion during his reign, Christendom did not come into full bloom until the end of the first millennium.[13] Expanding on his definition, Kreider describes some of its key characteristics,[14] which include:

- A common belief (Christian orthodoxy).

- Religious instruction (catechesis) becoming very basic.

- Infant baptism becoming normalized and universal.

- A common belonging ("everyone is a Christian").

- Heresy not being tolerated by the government.

- The symbiosis of the church and state.

- Society's symbols, art, and rituals becoming Christian.

In relation to the last point, in some contexts, the "baptizing" of public spaces can be observed. Leithart has argued that Constantine's construction of Constantinople reflected this value.[15] After Constantine, Bishops Theophilus of Alexandria and Synesius of Cyrene waged a similar campaign to cleanse the public spaces of their cities from pagan idolatry.[16] Describing the process and outcome in Alexandria, the church historian Socrates remembers, "the images of their gods [were] molten into pots and other convenient utensils for the use of the Alexandrian church."[17] Baptizing

---

12. Kreider, *Change of Conversion*, 42.

13. Peter Brown traces this trajectory in his *Rise of Western Christendom*.

14. Kreider, *Change of Conversion*, 91–98.

15. Leithart, *Defending Constantine*, 303, 326–33.

16. Oden, *Early Libyan Christianity*, 180.

17. Cited in ibid.

public spaces implied the suppression of paganism and its places of worship, which came to a climax in 529 with Justinian's legislation.[18]

To be sure, from Constantine's reign through the eighth century, there is evidence of the spread of Christianity through power and coercion. For instance, in 496, the Frankish King Clovis experienced his own Constantinian-like conversion. While losing on the battlefield at Alamanni, Clovis cried out to the God of the Christians for help in exchange for his conversion. Clovis emerged victorious and was baptized on Christmas of 496 without undergoing catechesis. Not unlike the account of Trdat, Clovis was joined in baptism by three thousand of his soldiers who were surely motivated more by loyalty and job security than by faith. While the motivation for conversion and the lack of proclamation and teaching are troubling, it should be noted that Clovis was probably evangelized in part by his Christian wife who is remembered for her witness and prayers.[19]

Perhaps the clearest example of Christendom expansion from this period is Charlemagne's (742–814) eighth-century conquest of the Saxons. Following the example of his father Pippin, who had received blessing from the bishop of Rome to invade the Lombard Kingdom in Northern Italy, Charlemagne led a series of violent campaigns against the Saxons between 772 and 798. In one particular battle, over 4000 Saxons were put to death. More than merely settling a longstanding feud between two warring peoples, Charlemagne went further and ordered the conquered Saxons to be baptized or face death, while also instituting anti-pagan legislation.[20] Despite the accounts of violence and coercion, it should be noted that missionaries—whose strategies included preaching, catechizing, and baptizing—followed in the wake of Charlemagne and some of them even suffered martyrdom.[21] Hence, even in this extreme account of Christianization, a glimmer of authentic mission can be observed.

---

18. Kreider, *Change of Conversion*, 39.

19. Ibid., 87–88; Sterk, "Missions from Below," 11–12; Dunaetz, *Early Religious History of France*, 59–62.

20. Irvin and Sundquist, *History of the World Christian Movement*, 334–35; Neill, *History of Christian Missions*, 67–69; and Dunaetz, *Early Religious History of France*, 100–101.

21. Neill, *History of Christian Missions*, 69. See also the accounts of the efforts to translate the Gospels into Saxon in the ninth century in Coakley and Sterk, *Readings in World Christianity*, 271–80.

AMBIGUOUS CASES OF MISSION WITHIN CHRISTENDOM

Kreider argues that following Constantine and the advance of Christendom that the nature of conversion changed. This is particularly evident in the decrease of kerygmatic proclamation and thorough catechesis along with the universal practice of infant baptism being adopted. He argues, "after the sixth century, when all the inhabitants of a society were baptized, mission largely disappeared from western Christendom."[22] While Kreider has made a strong case, I have two lingering questions: did mission truly disappear to this extent, and did monarchs such as Justinian and Charlemagne replace the church as the agents of mission?

In his comprehensive work, *Christianity and Paganism in the Fourth to Eighth Centuries*, Ramsey MacMullen makes a compelling argument for the persistent presence of paganism within the Roman Empire. For instance, he describes the thoroughly pagan city of Calama in North Africa—where Augustine's disciple and biographer Possidius pastored—that did not assimilate into the Christian empire. He also highlights the ongoing pagan practices of Constantine himself—practices that are seemingly ignored by Leithart in his defense of the emperor.[23] While discussing at length the enduring presence of paganism as well as the post-fifth-century attempts to Christianize Rome through legislation, MacMullen shows that the establishment and scope of Christendom was not quite as comprehensive as Kreider has claimed. Ironically, MacMullen concedes that much of the conversion of pagans to Christianity in this period occurred largely as it had prior to Constantine—through pagans observing miracles and hearing Christian preaching.[24]

In light of MacMullen's assertions, it would be profitable to consider some of the ambiguous narrative of Christian expansion within the Christendom paradigm. That is, clear accounts exist of bishops and missionaries who had access to the power and privilege of Christendom but who approached their ministry in a more missional manner. Let us consider a few representative examples.

22. Kreider, *Worship and Mission*, 39.

23. MacMullen, *Christianity and Paganism*, 34–36, 41.

24. Ibid., 30.

Basil of Caesarea

When Kreider writes, "except for a brief period in the 360s [Emperor Julian], the emperors were Christian of one flavor or another,"[25] we are led to believe that after Constantine, the church largely had the emperor as an ally and defender. Implicit in Kreider's "one flavor or another" comment is that the emperors differed in their theological persuasions and many of the fourth-century emperors had Arian leanings. This was the environment in which Basil of Caesarea (329–379) labored in the late fourth century.[26]

Aside from his role as bishop of Caesarea and metropolitan bishop for the surrounding provinces of Asia Minor, Basil was engaged in ministry in the intercultural crossroads of Caesarea that was frequented by diverse cultural groups from Armenia, Syria, Persia, the northern Gothic regions, and Asia Minor.[27] Apart from his preaching in the context of the church, much of Basil's tangible mission work could be observed in the *basileas* ("new city")—"a complex of buildings constructed at the edge of Caesarea during the early years of [his] episcopate."[28] The impetus for the *basileas'* construction was probably the great famine that struck Caesarea in 368.[29] The ministries of the *basileas* included a home for the poor, probably an orphanage, a hospital for the sick, a food distribution center, and a hospice for travelers.[30]

While Basil directed these ministries with much resolve, which probably led to his early death at age forty-nine, he also did so while fighting the imperial influence. If we believe Basil and Gregory of Nazianzus' reports, the conflict that Basil experienced with the Emperor Valens was over the emperor's distaste for Basil's Nicene convictions.[31] Gregory referred to the emperor as "a cloud full of hail, with destructive roar, overwhelming every church upon which it burst and seized . . . Valens, most fond of gold and most hostile to Christ." He adds, "Those who clung to the orthodox faith,

---

25. Kreider, *Change of Conversion*, 38.

26. For more discussion of Basil and his ministry, see Smither, "Basil of Caesarea: An Early Christian Model of Urban Mission."

27. Rousseau, *Basil of Caesarea*, 133–34; also Holman, *Hungry are Dying*, 69–70.

28. Sterk, *Renouncing the World*, 69.

29. Basil, *Epp.* 94, 150, 176; Holman, *Hungry are Dying*, 76.

30. Holman, *Hungry are Dying*, 80; Sterk, *Renouncing the World*, 69; and Rousseau, *Basil of Caesarea*, 133, 142.

31. Basil, *Epp.* 80, 82, 90.1, 91, 92.2–3, 203.1, 242.1, 243.4, 244.8, 256; Sterk, *Renouncing the World*, 45.

as we did, were expelled from their churches; others were imposed upon, who agreed with the imperial soul-destroying doctrines, and begged for testimonies of impiety."[32] Gregory continues by recording an encounter that Basil had with the Prefect Modestus who openly challenged Basil for not respecting the Emperor Valens. Basil related that he only followed the teachings of a true Sovereign—the Lord. When Modestus asked if Basil feared him, the following exchange occurred:

> "Fear of what?" said Basil, "How could it affect me? . . . confisca-
> tion, banishment, torture, death. Have you no other threat?" said
> he, "for none of these can reach me . . . Because . . . a man who has
> nothing, is beyond the reach of confiscation; unless you demand
> my tattered rags, and the few books, which are my only posses-
> sions. Banishment is impossible for me, who am confined by no
> limit of place, counting my own neither the land where I now
> dwell, nor all of that into which I may be hurled . . . As for tor-
> tures, what hold can they have upon one whose body has ceased
> to be? . . . Death is my benefactor, for it will send me the sooner
> to God." Amazed at this language, the prefect said, "No one has
> ever yet spoken thus, and with such boldness, to Modestus." "Why,
> perhaps," said Basil, "you have not met . . . a bishop . . . where the
> interests of God are at stake, we care for nothing else, and make
> these our sole object."[33]

In short, while Basil may appear as a bishop working at the early stages of Christendom, his work seems quite missional and his relationship with the Arian emperor, which should have been amicable, was quite adversarial.

Augustine of Hippo

Augustine (354–430) has not typically been remembered as a mission-ary bishop. On the contrary, much ink has been spilled through the years regarding his coercion of the Donatists toward unity with the catholic church. Though I have argued elsewhere that Augustine's engagement to-ward the Donatists could be understood as missional, let us explore just a few thoughts.[34] First, though the Donatists and Augustine were prob-ably from a similar ethno-linguistic group, there were clearly frontiers of

32. Gregory of Nazianzus, *Oratio* 43.30, 36 (all translations are from *NPNF* 2:7).
33. Gregory of Nazianzus, *Oratio* 43.48–50.
34. Smither, "Augustine, Missionary to Heretics?"

culture and belief between them. For Augustine, the biggest barrier was the Donatist schism, which he believed had morphed into heresy.[35] Second, his interactions with the Donatists through teaching, preaching, debating, and writing seemed to be part of his greater ministry of evangelizing the church—a mission that was probably also focused on those with a lingering pagan worldview.[36] Third, though Augustine welcomed the state's intervention against the Donatists in 405 and 411, his general approach toward the Donatists from 392 to 419 was more characterized by persuasion than coercion. Perhaps the clearest example of this missional approach was in 418 when Augustine traveled 1500km to visit Emeritus of Mauretania Caesarea, a Donatist bishop who had refused to unify with the church. That is, seven years after the official decree was given at Carthage, Augustine, without any law enforcement, merely debated Emeritus and preached to his congregation only to return home having failed to convince the elderly bishop to reunite with the church. In short, Augustine's interaction with the Donatists seems to be a case of cross-cultural ministry by a bishop who could have invoked political power but chose to preach, teach, write, and persuade instead.

Boniface

A final ambiguous account of mission within Christendom is that of the English missionary monk Boniface (ca. 680–754). Originally called Wynfrith, he was given the name Boniface by Pope Gregory II who commissioned him in 716 to be a missionary to what is now Germany. In 722, he was ordained by the pope as a missionary bishop and was responsible for teaching in Mainz and Hesse. While Boniface had the pope's moral support, he also enjoyed the financial and military backing of the Frankish King Charles Martel.[37] Such protection was available in 724 when he confronted the Pagans at Hesse and cut down the Sacred Oak of Thor. Though Martel's protection was important, this "power encounter" apparently communicated the superiority of the Christian God to Boniface's Pagan audience.[38]

---

35. Augustine, *De Haeresibus* 69.1.

36. See Kreider, *Change of Conversion*, 55–56.

37. Charles Martel was Pippin's father and Charlemagne's grandfather.

38. Irvin and Sundquist, *History of the World Christian Movement*, 345–46; also Neill, *History of Christian Missions*, 64–65.

Though Boniface enjoyed the position of being an established bishop, Irvin and Sundquist write that "the spirit of *peregrini* and the call of missions in the end proved to be too strong for Boniface."[39] In 753, at the age of seventy-three, he set out to evangelize the Frisian people—a Germanic people who lived beyond the borders of Frankish control. Neill writes, "On 5 June 754, Boniface and his companions were waiting in . . . Dokkum for the arrival of a number of newly converted Christians who were to be confirmed. They were suddenly attacked . . . the old man and his fifty companions were all killed."[40] Despite having the support of the pope and Frankish king, Boniface diverged from a pure Christendom approach to Christianization by focusing on evangelism and teaching. The irony of his account is that despite having ecclesiastical, military, and financial support, his missionary zeal pushed him beyond the scope of that security, which resulted in his martyrdom.

Mission within the Framework of Political Power

Are there examples of mission in this period in which missionaries repudiate all political power and deliberately serve and minister from the margins of society? While the clearest example of dissent in the fourth century toward the Constantinian revolution is monasticism, this phenomenon did not have a primary missional focus. However, later, as missionary activity became a central value to monastic life in the medieval period, missionary monks were eager to engage political leaders in the process of mission. In short, it is difficult to find examples of "mission from the margins" in this period and, as we have seen, many missionaries acknowledged the Christendom framework and labored within it, while others served in full view of the political authorities. Let us consider some representative examples of missionary monks and other missionaries that support this claim.

Augustine of Canterbury

Augustine of Canterbury (d. 604) and a group of forty Benedictine monks were sent by Pope Gregory I to evangelize the English in 596. Bede vividly describes their approach to ministry—an integration of monastic and

---

39. Irvin and Sundquist, *History of the World Christian Movement*, 346.
40. Neill, *History of Christian Missions*, 66.

missional living: "They began to imitate the way of life of the apostles and of the primitive church. They were constantly engaged in prayers, in vigils and fasts; they preached the word of life to as many as they could; they despised all worldly things as foreign to them; they accepted only the necessaries of life from those whom they taught; in all things they practiced what they preached."[41]

A vital part of their strategy was making contact with King Ethelbert of Kent (ca. 560–ca. 616), who apparently embraced Christianity and allowed the monks to proclaim the gospel freely and establish churches. Ethelbert was surely influenced on matters of faith by his wife Bertha, a princess from Gaul from a Christian background.[42] In the first year of their work, Augustine and his monks reported that 10,000 Angles had been baptized. Bede added that the English were receptive to the monks' message because they were "attracted by the pure life of the saints and by their most precious promises, whose truth they confirmed by performing many miracles."[43] As the English church quickly expanded, Augustine was consecrated as bishop of Canterbury and continued in that role until his death.[44]

Columban

Columban's (543–615) story represents a different trajectory of mission— that is, Christian ministry that originated from the outside or fringes of the Roman Empire in Ireland to within the empire. In 590, Columban left the monastery in Bangor and established a community of monks at Luxeuil, France where he served for twenty years. Though he initially found favor with the king of Burgundy and was given the freedom to preach, he was later expelled by the monarch for preaching against his immorality. After leaving Luxeuil, Columban and his monks continued evangelizing other parts of France and Northern Italy.[45] Hence, Columban's mission involved

---

41. Bede, *HE gent. Angl.* 1.26 (all translations are from McLure and Collins, *Ecclesiastical History*).

42. Sterk, "Mission from Below," 11.

43. Bede, *HE gent. Angl.* 1.26.

44. Neill, *History of Christian Missions*, 58–59; also Irvin and Sundquist, *History of the World Christian Movement*, 327–39.

45. Neill, *History of Christian Missions*, 62–63; Dunaetz, *Early Religious History of France*, 76.

a community of monks, deliberate engagement with political leaders, and proclamation.

In many ways, Columban's actions represented some observed values of the Celtic monastic missions movement that functioned largely on the fringes of the empire in the sixth and seventh centuries. Around 633, Oswald emerged victorious in battle and gained control of the throne of Northumbria (modern England). Previously, he had lived in political exile and found himself on the island of Iona, which had been established as a monastic mission center by Columba (521–597) around 565.[46] Having been converted at Iona, one of Oswald's first actions in consolidating power in Northumbria was to invite Celtic monks from Iona to teach his new subjects. The response from Iona was to send Columba's disciple Aiden (d. 651) who settled on the nearby island of Lindisfarne, which became a base for monastic living, evangelism, and teaching.[47] Eventually, following the Council of Whitby in 663–64, the Northumbrian church would become aligned with Rome.[48]

Aiden's ability to interact with political leaders was surely a skill that he acquired from Columba. The Celtic missionary abbot seemed comfortable relating to political leaders because of his own noble background in Ireland. In addition to evangelizing the Pictish people of the Scottish highlands through first engaging King Bridius [Brute], Adomnan recorded Columba praying for the coronation of a monarch named Aiden, and generally staying abreast of Irish political developments even while living in the isolated island monastery at Iona.[49]

In summary, the Celtic monks following in Columba's footsteps were quite adept at relating to political leaders and their engagement of tribal leaders and monarchs was a vital part of their strategy both on the fringes of the Roman Empire and within the empire. The monks aimed to convert these leaders and then obtain their favor in order to build monasteries, preach, teach, and establish churches.[50]

46. Bede, *HE gent. Angl.* 3.4.

47. Bede, *HE gent. Angl.* 3.3; Adomnan, *VCol.* 1.1.

48. Neill, *History of Christian Missions*, 61.

49. Bede, *HE gent. Angl.* 3.4; Adomnan, *VCol.* 1.8; 3.5.

50. Though space does not allow for it in this essay, these qualities of Columban and Columba can also be observed in Patrick's mission to the Irish.

Imperial Mission to Nubia

For a final example of mission within Christendom, let us consider the narrative of the presbyter Julian who was sent outside of the Roman Empire to Nubia (modern southern Egypt, northern Sudan) in the sixth century. This account has a colorful backstory in that the imperial couple—Justinian and Theodora—were at odds over Christology as the emperor supported the Chalcedonian party, while his wife supported those that rejected the Christological formula. According to John of Ephesus, the aging presbyter Julian, who had been burdened for some time about the evangelization of the Nubians, approached the queen with his vision. She responded by blessing the mission and then told her husband about it, who then retaliated by sending his own missionaries to the region.[51]

With the political jockeying acknowledged, MacMullen actually argues that this account is a missional anomaly during the reign of Justinian. That is, most of his efforts to Christianize Rome came through the typical methods of Christendom, particularly anti-pagan legislation.[52] If we believe John of Ephesus, it appears that Julian's approach in Nubia was quite missional. He began by approaching the Nubian king who received Julian and allowed him to preach. Enduring the heat for at least two years, Julian's work included preaching, catechism, and baptism. According to John, the king, his nobles, and many of his subjects were baptized and, as a result, the king of neighboring Alodia wrote to the Nubian king inquiring about the Christian faith. The Nubian king responded by dispatching the missionary bishop Longinus to evangelize the Alodian people.[53] In short, while a number of monarchs were involved in the Nubian mission, both in sending and receiving, the nature of the work seems more characteristic of Christian mission than Christendom expansion.

CONCLUSION

In this article, I have argued that the rise of Constantine and the emergence of Christendom over the first millennium did not signal a death blow to authentic Christian mission. Though the narrative does get quite confusing

51. Coakley and Sterk, *Readings in World Christianity,* 188–92.

52. MacMullen, *Christianity and Paganism,* 30.

53. Coakley and Sterk, *Readings in World Christianity,* 190–91; also Sterk, "Captive Women and Heretical Monks," 22.

at points regarding the agents of mission, mission strategies, and the motives for conversion, we do not see mission as defined at the outset of the essay disappearing. Rather, we have observed ambiguous accounts of mission—stories of those like Basil, Augustine, and Boniface who apparently had access to the benefits of Christendom, but did not always use it. Mostly, it has been argued that many missionaries, including monks, accepted the Christendom paradigm as a reality and they labored to evangelize, teach, baptize, and establish churches within it. Others approached mission in full view of political authorities. In short, mission from the margins—that which avoids contact with political leaders—cannot adequately describe the mission of the church in this period.[54]

This study raises a couple of important questions for further study for evangelicals contemplating mission today. First, for modern evangelicals—especially those in the Anabaptist, free church tradition—reflecting on this period of church history can be troubling as it challenges some deep presuppositions about the nature of the church, the state, and how the gospel spreads. Should we be disturbed by accounts of political leaders being converted or even national conversions? Perhaps this historical reflection will challenge us to read with fresh eyes the Old Testament canonical book of Jonah in which a king's conversion and a nation's repentance figure prominently:

> The word reached the king of Nineveh, and he arose from his throne, removed his robe, covered himself with sackcloth, and sat in ashes. And he issued a proclamation and published through Nineveh, "By the decree of the king and his nobles: Let neither man nor beast, herd nor flock, taste anything. Let them not feed or drink water, but let man and beast be covered with sackcloth, and let them call out mightily to God. Let everyone turn from his evil way and from the violence that is in his hands. Who knows? God may turn and relent and turn from his fierce anger, so that we may not perish." When God saw what they did, how they turned from their evil way, God relented of the disaster that he had said he would do to them, and he did not do it. (Jonah 3:6–10 ESV)

Second, this essay raises the critical question, is imperial Christianity incompatible with a biblical theology of mission? Though a number of missionaries in this period seemed to co-exist with and work within the

---

54. To the contrary, Sterk "Captive Women and Heretical Monks," 21–23) has made a helpful case for the work of captured Christian women outside of Rome—in Armenia and Georgia—who functioned as missionaries.

Christendom paradigm, there are certainly some non-negotiable distinctives of authentic mission. First, the agent of Christian mission is always the church and never the state. Second, the activities of mission must include kerygmatic proclamation and the related ministries of teaching, baptism, establishing churches, and caring for real human needs. These values seem evident in the ministry of Basil—a bishop who preached, taught, baptized, and cared for the poor under the administration of an Arian emperor who clearly fell outside the bounds of Christian orthodoxy. On the contrary, the violent and coercive actions of Charlemagne toward the Saxons cannot be deemed as missional.

In summary, as Scripture is read with a hermeneutic of mission, there is also much value in reading and evaluating Christian history missiologically.[55] While this study has certainly revealed the messiness of Christian and missions history, it has also shown that the essence and activities of mission have endured in a Christendom and now post-Christendom period.[56]

---

55. This was the contribution of Bosch in his seminal work *Transforming Mission*.

56. I am grateful for the feedback on this essay not only from the other authors in the volume but also from my Columbia International University colleagues David Cashin, Christopher Little, and Mike Barnett. Also, I am thankful for my dialogue with Peter Leithart at the eastern regional Evangelical Theological Society meeting (March 2, 2012 in Lancaster, PA), which helped to clarify my thought on the subject.

Epilogue

Bryan M. Litfin

MOST OF US AT one time or another have watched a caricature artist ply his trade along a busy street where tourists gather. The subject sits primly on a stool, a little embarrassed at the attention, while a crowd of onlookers tries to decide whether the portrait is accurate. Oblivious to the impromptu art critics, the artist's swift pencil captures the sitter's features stroke by stroke. At last, the cartoonist removes the sketch from his easel and hands over a memento whose exaggerations aren't nearly as obvious to the sitter as they are to everyone else.

Unfortunately, the historian of antiquity is like a caricature artist with no one seated on the stool. Yet the absence of a live sitter has never stopped the historian from putting pencil to paper and proceeding to draw. Soon a comical figure begins to emerge: a bulbous nose, a jutting chin, a bristly pair of eyebrows. We expect the portrait to resemble the ostensible sitter, and perhaps it does to some degree. Yet like any caricature, it lacks the crisp fidelity a camera could provide. You can't take a picture of a person who isn't there.

Emperor Constantine is one of the most frequently drawn caricatures from the historical past. Confronted with such a wide array of sketches, the emperor would probably chuckle, scratch his head, and perhaps even grumble at some of his recent portrayals. Since the world scarcely needs another charcoal drawing to flutter down onto the already-thick pile, the present volume takes a different approach. The judicious use of an eraser—correcting a flaw here, an embellishment there—helps us imagine the first Christian emperor in a more accurate way. While Constantine might have been able to laugh at his exaggerated features in a caricature, we moderns are better served by hanging a more realistic portrait in the gilded gallery of professional history.

Glen Thompson's introductory chapter began our task of erasure by dismantling the binary set of options facing scholars who study Constantine's conversion to Christianity. For too long, historians have been forced into the straitjacket of an either/or dilemma. Constantine's demonstrations of piety were adduced as evidence of genuine conversion to the faith, or else his unjust actions and remnants of paganism cast him as an impostor whose Christian devotion was nothing but pretense. The emperor had to fall in one or the other of these fixed categories. In contrast to this dualistic approach, Thompson borrowed from his Lutheran heritage to reveal a man who is, like every other Christian, *simul justus et peccator*. Constantine's spirituality is allowed to evolve as he makes a series of progressive moves— sometimes with halting steps followed by severe regression—toward authentic worship of Jesus Christ.

In chapter two, Brian Shelton helped us rethink Constantine by scrubbing away the myth that the first Christian emperor became a religious enforcer who perpetrated reverse persecution against the pagans. Though scholars are aware that Serapis was toppled in the acrimonious age of Theodosius, not Constantine, even so the *Zeitgeist* of the late fourth century is often read back into earlier decades. But by peering through the Lactantian window that Shelton opened up, we discovered an emperor whose cultural outlook did not yet exemplify the more dogmatic days to come. With Lactantius as an irenic voice whispering in the ear of Constantine, Shelton helped us reconstruct an imperial religious policy in the wake of the Milvian Bridge that was far more tolerant and liberal than might first be imagined.

David Alexander's third chapter extended the theme of Constantinian gradualism by pointing out how the Donatist crisis initiated the political and theological trajectories for which the emperor later became famous. Superficial caricatures of Constantine tend to jump from the shining cross in the sky to the Council of Nicaea, with little historical stage-setting in the intervening years. But the purple-robed Constantine who presided over the archetypal Christian council in 325 did not suddenly appear with a *homoousian* Christology and a fully-formed policy of catholic unity. Both his theological method and his approach to ecclesial diplomacy were forged in the crucible of an African church schism that looked far more daunting than the philosophical hair-splitting Arius later introduced. David Alexander's chapter took a comprehensive look at how the Donatist schism forced Constantine to negotiate the treacherous waters of episcopal wrangling (such as at Arles in 314) long before his more famous efforts at Nicaea. Thus, a greater degree of nuance makes its way into our contemporary portrait of the emperor.

In chapter four, the erudition behind Jonathan Armstrong's recent translation of the Isaiah commentary of Eusebius brought groundbreaking scholarship to bear on the question of Constantine's role at Nicaea. Fresh insights about Eusebius' staunch orthodoxy served to validate his historical reliability on other matters as well—namely, the emperor's involvement at the momentous council of 325. The traditional picture of Constantine's vital role in establishing Nicene trinitarianism came to be redrawn by scholars who began to doubt any report from the pen of Eusebius. Now, Armstrong marshals new evidence to erase those hesitant lines and return to the traditional view with bold and confident strokes. Having restored Eusebius as a reliable historical source, Armstrong invites us to imagine Constantine again in ways that earlier, less skeptical scholarship was inclined to do.

Paul Hartog used chapter five to undermine a depiction of Constantine whose history runs deep in the free church tradition: the supposed "Constantinian fall" from an originally pristine gospel to a corrupt, politicized, institutional pseudo-Christianity. Hartog focused on the particular issue of Sabbath worship, demonstrating that here, at least, modern Baptists and other Evangelicals owe a debt to a figure they often disdain. Yet Constantine wasn't the inventor of Sunday worship. As Hartog pointed out, the emperor was only writing into civil law a practice already established among Christians. Very soon the mandate to worship on Sunday turned it into a day of rest as well—a decision appreciated by later generations of believers. In pointing out these positive fourth-century developments, Hartog erased a bit of the caricature that depicts Constantine as Christianity's greatest enemy who plunged the church into ruin.

Edward Smither's final chapter confronted the accusation that Constantine brought an end to Christian mission. Though many Christians today consider the development of a state-church paradigm to have sounded the death knell of missionary work, Smither dragged a wide net through the waters of church history and turned up many examples that contradict such a gloomy assessment. Of course, as "Christendom" came to be conceived, articulated, and implemented in the fourth century and beyond, the specific nature of missional activity took a decided turn. Yet this is quite different than saying Christian mission disappeared altogether. Smither appropriately closed out the present volume by correcting a misrepresentation, not just of Constantine, but of his enduring legacy.

And so, with our portrait of the first Christian emperor touched up and redrawn, a way has been opened for scholars and laymen alike to envision more accurately the man whose conversion set in motion cultural forces that are still with us today. As Constantinian studies continue to evolve, and as the emperor sits, perhaps unwillingly, to have his image sketched anew, we will do well to insist that certain caricatures must disappear from the sketch pad. The authors of the present volume hope they have corrected some misconceptions that will no longer make their way into the imperial portraiture of Constantine the Great.

Bibliography

Adomnan of Iona. *Vita Columbae*. Corpus of Electronic Texts Edition. Online: http://www.ucc.ie/celt/published/L201040/index.html (accessed January 27, 2013).

Agathangelos. "History of the Armenians." In *Readings in World Christian History*, edited by John W. Coakley and Andrea Sterk, 122–30. Maryknoll, NY: Orbis, 2004.

Alexander, David C., and Edward L. Smither. "Bauer's Forgotten Region: North African Christianity." In *Orthodoxy and Heresy in Early Christian Contexts*, edited by Paul Hartog. Eugene, OR: Pickwick, forthcoming.

Alföldi, Andreas. *The Conversion of Constantine and Pagan Rome*. Oxford: Clarendon, 1948.

Ammianus Marcelinus. *Rerum gestarum libri qui supersunt*. Edited by W. Seyfarth. 2 vols. Leipzig: Teubner, 1978.

Anastasius of Sinai. *Questiones et Responsiones* (Appendices). Edited by J. A. Munitiz and M. Richard. *CCSG* 59. Turnholt: Brepols, 2006.

Anatolios, Khaled. *Retrieving Nicaea: The Development and Meaning of Trinitarian Doctrine*. Grand Rapids: Baker Academic, 2011.

Andrews, John Nevins. *The Complete Testimony of the Fathers of the First Three Centuries Concerning the Sabbath and First Day*. Battle Creek, MI: Steam, 1873.

Andrews, John Nevins, and Ludwig Richard Conradi. *History of the Sabbath and the First Day of the Week*. 4th ed. Washington, DC: Review and Herald, 1912.

Apostolic Constitutions. Edited by James Donaldson. In *ANF*, edited by Alexander Roberts et al., 7:391–505. Peabody, MA: Hendrickson, 1999.

Arand, Charles P. "Response to Craig L. Blomberg." In *Perspectives on the Sabbath: Four Views*, edited by Christopher John Donato, 387–96. Nashville: B. & H. Academic, 2011.

Augustine. *De Haeresibus*. In *S. Aurelii Augustini Opera Omnia*. PL 42. Online: http://www.augustinus.it/latino/eresie/index.htm.

Ayres, Lewis. *Nicaea and Its Legacy: An Approach to Fourth-Century Trinitarian Theology*. Oxford: University Press, 2004.

Baab, Lynne M. *Sabbath Keeping: Finding Freedom in the Rhythms of Rest*. Downers Grove, IL: InterVarsity, 2005.

Bacchiocchi, Samuele. *Anti-Judaism and the Origin of Sunday*. Rome: Pontifical Gregorian University Press, 1975.

———. *Divine Rest for Human Restlessness: A Theological Study of the Good News of the Sabbath for Today*. Rome: Pontifical Gregorian University Press, 1980.

———. *From Sabbath to Sunday: A Historical Investigation of the Rise of Sunday Observance in Early Christianity*. Rome: Pontifical Gregorian University, 1977.

Bibliography

————. "The Rise of Sunday Observance in Early Christianity." In *The Sabbath in Scripture and History*, edited by Kenneth A. Strand 132–50. Washington, DC: Review and Herald, 1982.

————. "Rome and the Origin of Sunday Observance." *The Ministry* 50 (1977) 16–19.

Barclay, William. *The Ten Commandments for Today*. New York: Harper & Row, 1973.

Bardill, Jonathan. *Constantine, Divine Emperor of the Christian Golden Age*. Cambridge: Cambridge University Press, 2012.

Ballenger, A. F. "Protestantism True and False." *Religious Liberty Library* 19 (1894) 3–23.

Barnes, Timothy. "The Beginnings of Donatism." *Journal of Theological Studies* 26 (1975) 13–22.

————. "Constantine and Christianity: Ancient and Modern Interpretations." *Zeitschrift für antikes Christentum* 2 (1998) 274–94.

————. *Constantine and Eusebius*. Cambridge MA: Harvard University Press, 1981.

————. *Constantine: Dynasty, Religion and Power in the Later Roman Empire*. Oxford: Wiley-Blackwell, 2011.

————. *From Eusebius to Augustine: Selected Papers, 1982–1993*. Aldershot: Variorum, 1994.

————. "Lactantius and Constantine." *The Journal of Roman Studies* 63 (1973) 29–46.

————. *The New Empire of Diocletian and Constantine*. Cambridge MA: Harvard University Press, 1982.

————. "Was There a Constantinian Revolution?" *Journal of Late Antiquity* 2, no. 2 (2009) 374–84.

Basil of Caesarea. *Epistulae*. Edited by B. Coulie and B. Kindt. *CCTPG* 17. Turnhout, Belgium: Brepols, 2002.

Bassett, Sarah. *The Urban Image of Late Antique Constantinople*. Cambridge: Cambridge University Press, 2004.

Bauckham, Richard J. "The Lord's Day." In *From Sabbath to the Lord's Day: A Biblical, Historical, and Theological Investigation*, edited by D. A. Carson, 221–250. Grand Rapids: Zondervan, 1982.

————. "Mission as Hermeneutic for Scriptural Interpretation." Online: http://richardbauckham.co.uk/uploads/Accessible/Mission%20as%20Hermeneutic.pdf.

————. "Sabbath and Sunday in the Post-Apostolic Church." In *From Sabbath to the Lord's Day: A Biblical, Historical, and Theological Investigation*, edited by D. A. Carson, 251–298. Grand Rapids: Zondervan, 1982.

Bauder, Kevin T. "Shall We Keep Sabbath?" Online: http://sharperiron.org/2008/04/15/shall-we-keep-sabbath.

Baus, Karl. *Handbook of Christian History, Volume 1: From the Apostolic Community to Constantine*. New York: Herder & Herder, 1965.

Baynes, Norman. *Constantine the Great and the Christian Church*. Oxford: Oxford University Press, 1972.

Beckwith, Roger T. "The Daily and Weekly Worship of the Primitive Church." *Evangelical Quarterly* 56 (1984) 65–80, 139–158.

Beckwith, Roger T., and Wilfrid Scott. *This Is the Day: The Biblical Doctrine of the Christian Sabbath in its Jewish and Early Christian Setting*. London: Marshall, Morgan & Scott, 1978.

Bede. *The Ecclesiastical History of the English People; The Greater Chronicle; Bede's Letter to Egbert*. Translated by Judith McClure and Roger Collins. Oxford World's Classics. New York: Oxford University Press, 2009.

———. *Historiam Ecclesiasticam Gentis Anglorum.* The Latin Library. Online: http://www.thelatinlibrary.com/bede.html.

Birley, A. R. "Some Notes on the Donatist Schism." *Libyan Studies* 18 (1987) 29–41.

Bleckmann, Bruno. *Konstantin der Grosse.* Reinbek: Rowohlt, 1996.

Bleicken, Jochen. *Constantin der Grosse und die Christen: Überlegungen zur Konstantinischen Wende.* Münich: Oldenbourg, 1992.

Bosch, David. *Transforming Mission: Paradigm Shift in Theology of Mission.* Maryknoll, NY: Orbis, 1991.

Bowlin, John R. "Tolerance among the Fathers." *Journal of the Society of Christian Ethics* 26 (2006) 3–36.

Bradshaw, Paul F., and Maxwell E. Johnson. *The Origins of Feasts, Fasts, and Seasons in Early Christianity.* Collegeville, MN: Liturgical, 2011.

Brinsmead, Robert D. "A Digest of the Sabbath Question." *Verdict* 1 (1982) 1–21. Online: http://www.lifeassuranceministries.com/pdf%20files/A%20DIGEST%20OF%20THE%20SABBATH%20QUESTION%20.pdf.

———. *Sabbatarianism Re-Examined.* Fallbrook, CA: Verdict, 1981.

Bringmann, Klaus. "Die Konstantinische Wende: Zum Verhältnis von politischer und religiöser Motivation." *Historische Zeitschrift* 260 (1995) 21–47.

Brown, Peter. *The Rise of Western Christendom: Triumph and Diversity, A.D. 200–1000.* West Sussex, UK: Wiley-Blackwell, 2003.

Bruun, Patrick. *The Constantinian Coinage of Arelate.* Suomen muinaismuistoyhdistyksen Aikakauskirja 52/2. Helsinki, 1953.

———. "The Disappearance of Sol from the Coins of Constantine." *Arctos,* N.S. 2 (1958) 15–37.

———. *The Roman Imperial Coinage.* Vol. 7, *Constantine and Licinius A.D. 313–337.* London: Spink, 1966.

Buchanan, Mark. *The Rest of God: Restoring Your Soul by Restoring Sabbath.* Nashville: Thomas Nelson, 2007.

Burckhardt, Jacob. *The Age of Constantine the Great.* Translated by Moses Hadas. London: Broadway House, 1949.

Burns, J. Patout. *Cyprian the Bishop.* New York: Routledge, 2002.

Cairns, Earle. *Christianity through the Centuries: A History of the Christian Church.* Grand Rapids: Zondervan, 1996.

Cairus, Aecio E. "Clement of Alexandria and the Lord's Day." *Andrews University Seminary Studies* 40 (2002) 273–76.

California Institute for Ancient Studies. "A Brief History of the Sabbath between the 2nd and 4th Century A.D." Online: http://www.specialtyinterests.net/lords_day_history.html#itn.

Cameron, Alan. *The Last Pagans of Rome.* Oxford: Oxford University Press, 2011.

Cameron, Averil. "Constantine and the 'peace of the church.'" In *The Cambridge Companion to the Age of Constantine,* edited by Noel Lenski, 538–51. Cambridge: Cambridge University Press, 2006.

Cardman, Francine. "The Emperor's New Clothes: Christ and Constantine." In *Above Every Name: The Lordship of Christ and Social Systems,* edited by Thomas E. Clarke, 191–210. Ramsey, NJ: Paulist, 1980.

Carson, D. A. *From Sabbath to the Lord's Day: A Biblical, Historical, and Theological Investigation.* Grand Rapids: Zondervan, 1982.

Chadwick, Henry. *The Early Church.* New York: Penguin, 1993.

Bibliography

Chantry, Walter J. *Call the Sabbath a Delight.* Carlisle, PA: Banner of Truth, 1991.

Christian Biblical Church of God. "Rome's Challenge: Why Do Protestants Keep Sunday?" Online: http://cbcg.org/romes_challenge.htm.

Coakley, John W. and Andrea Sterk, editors. *Readings in World Christian History.* Maryknoll, NY: Orbis, 2004.

Coleman, L. "Historical Sketch of the Christian Sabbath," *Bibliotheca Sacra* 1 (1844) 526–51.

Collingwood, R. G. *The Idea of History.* New York: Oxford University Press, 1975.

Colot, Blandine. "Historiographie Chrétienne et Romanesque: Le *De Mortibus Persecutorum* de Lactante (250–325 AP. J.C.)." *Vigiliae Christianae* 59 (2005) 135–51.

"Constantine Changes the Sabbath Day to Sunday 321." Online: http://propheticnews fortheendtimes.lefora.com/2012/04/29/constantine-changes-the-sabbath-day-to-sunday-321-/.

Corcoran, Simon. "Diocletian." In *Lives of the Caesars,* edited by A.A. Barrett, 228–254. Oxford: Blackwell, 2008.

Cotton, Paul. *From Sabbath to Sunday: A Study in Early Christianity.* Bethlehem, PA: Times, 1933.

Cox, Robert. *Sabbaths: An Inquiry into the Origin of Septenary Institutions and the Authority for a Sabbatical Observance of the Modern Sunday.* London: Waterlow & Sons, 1850.

Crews, Joe. "How the Sabbath Was Changed." SabbathTruth.com, 2010. Online: http://www.sabbathtruth.com/sabbath-history/how-the-sabbath-was-changed.aspx.

Curran, John R. *Pagan City and Christian Capital: Rome in the Fourth Century.* Oxford: Clarendon, 2000.

Dagron, Gilbert. *Emperor and Priest: The Imperial Office in Byzantium.* Translated by Jean Birrell. Cambridge: Cambridge University Press, 2003.

Dassmann, Ernst. *Konstantinische Wende und spätantike Reichskirche.* Stuttgart: Kohlhammer, 1996.

Dawn, Marva J. *Keeping the Sabbath Wholly: Ceasing, Resting, Embracing, Feasting.* Grand Rapids: Eerdmans, 1989.

Dearn, Alan. "The Abitinian Martyrs and the Outbreak of the Donatist Schism." *Journal of Ecclesiastical History* 55, no. 1 (2004) 1–18.

Deck, Norman C. *The Lord's Day or the Sabbath: A Reply to Seventh-Day Adventists.* London: Pickering & Inglis, 1950.

Decret, François. *Early Christianity in North Africa.* Translated by Edward L. Smither. Eugene, OR: Cascade, 2009.

Didascalia Apostolorum. Translated by Hugh R. Connolly. Oxford: Clarendon, 1929.

Digeser, Elizabeth DePalma. "Lactantius and Constantine's Letter to Arles: Dating the Divine Institutes." *Journal of Early Christian Studies* 2 (1994) 33–52.

———. "Lactantius, Eusebius, and Arnobius: Evidence for the Causes of the Great Persecution." *Studia Patristica* 39 (2006) 33–46.

———. *The Making of a Christian Empire: Lactantius and Rome.* Ithaca, NY: Cornell University Press, 2000.

Donato, Christopher John. *Perspectives on the Sabbath: Four Views.* Nashville: B. & H. Academic, 2011.

Dörries, Hermann. *Constantine and Religious Liberty.* Translated by R. H. Bainton. New Haven: Yale University Press, 1960.

———. *Das Selbstzeugnis Kaiser Konstantins.* Göttingen: Vandenhoeck & Ruprecht, 1954.

Drake, H. A. *Constantine and the Bishops: The Politics of Intolerance.* Baltimore: Johns Hopkins University Press, 2000.

———. "Constantine and Consensus," *Church History* 64, no. 1 (1995) 1–15.

———. "The Impact of Constantine on Christianity." In *The Cambridge Companion to the Age of Constantine,* edited by Noel Lenski, 111–36. Cambridge: Cambridge University Press, 2006.

———. "Lessons from Diocletian's Persecution." In *The Great Persecution,* edited by D. Vincent Twomey and Mark Humphries, 49–60. Portland, OR: Four Courts, 2009.

Dugmore, C. W. "Lord's Day and Easter." In *Neotestamentica et Patristica,* edited by Oscar Cullmann, 272–81. Leiden: Brill, 1962.

Dunaetz, David R. *The Early Religious History of France.* Claremont, CA: Martel, 2012.

Eadie, John William. *The Conversion of Constantine.* New York: Holt, Rinehart & Winston, 1971.

Eusebius. *Commentary on Isaiah.* Translated by Jonathan J. Armstrong. Ancient Christian Texts. Downers Grove, IL: InterVarsity, 2013.

———. *De laudibus Constantini.* Edited by I. A. Heikel. Eusebius Werke 1. *GCS* 7. Leipzig: Hinrichs, 1902.

———. *Der Jesajakommentar.* Edited by Joseph Ziegler. *GCS* 9. Berlin: Akademie, 1975.

———. *The Ecclesiastical History.* Vol. 1. Translated by Kirsopp Lake. LCL 153. Cambridge, MA: Harvard University Press, 1965.

———. *The Ecclesiastical History in Two Volumes.* Translated by J. E. L. Oulton and H. J. Lawlor. LCL 264–265. Cambridge, MA: Harvard University Press, 2007.

———. *Historia ecclesiastica.* Edited by G. Bardy. 3 vols. *SC* 31, 41, 55. Paris: Éditions du Cerf, 1952, 1955, 1958.

———. *Historia ecclesiastica.* Edited by Eduard Schwartz. Leipzig, n.p., 1908.

———. *Life of Constantine.* Translated by Averil Cameron and S. G. Hall. Oxford: Oxford University Press, 1999.

———. *Vita Constantini.* Edited by F. Winkelmann. *Eusebius Werke* 1.1, *GCS* 7.1. Berlin: Akademie, 1991.

Eutropius. *Breviarium ab urbe condita.* Edited by H. Droysen. *MGH, Auct. Antiqu.* 2. Berlin: Weidmann, 1879.

Evers, A. "A Fine Line?: Catholics and Donatists in Roman North Africa." In *Frontiers in the Roman World: Proceedings of the Ninth Workshop of the International Network Impact of Empire (Durham, 16–19 April 2009),* edited by Ted Kaizer and Olivier Hekster, 175–97. Leiden: Brill, 2011.

Fairbairn, Patrick. *The Typology of Scripture Viewed in Connection with the Whole Series of Divine Dispensations.* New York: Funk & Wagnalls, 1900.

Faulkner, John Alfred. "The First Great Christian Creed." *The American Journal of Theology* 14 (1910) 47–61.

Ferguson, Everett. *Early Christians Speak: Faith and Life in the First Three Centuries.* Vol. 1. Abilene, TX: ACU, 1999.

———. "Sabbath: Saturday or Sunday? A Review Article." *Restoration Quarterly* 23 (1980) 172–81.

Fisher, William Logan, and Edward M. Davis. *The Sunday Question: Sabbath of the Jews, Sunday of Constantine.* Philadelphia: n.p., 1855.

Foerster, Werner. *Palestinian Judaism in New Testament Times.* Translated by Gordon E. Harris. Edinburgh: Oliver & Boyd, 1964.

Bibliography

Freeman, Charles. *A.D. 381: Heretics, Pagans, and the Christian State*. Woodstock, NY: Overlook, 2009.

Frend, W. H. C. "Donatism." In *Encyclopedia of Early Christianity*, edited by Everett Ferguson et al. London: Routledge Religion Online, 1998. Online: http://www .routledgeonline.com.ezproxy.liberty.edu:2048/religion/Book.aspx?id=wo18_e360.

―――. *The Donatist Church: A Movement of Protest in Roman North Africa*. Oxford: Oxford University Press, 1952, 1985.

―――. *The Rise of Christianity*. Philadelphia: Fortress, 1984.

Frend, W. H. C., and K. Clancy. "When Did the Donatist Schism Begin?" *Journal of Theological Studies* 23 (1977) 104–9.

Freund, Stefan. "Christian Use and Valuation of Theological Oracles: The Case of Lactantius' Divine Institutes." *Vigiliae Christianae* 60 (2006) 269–84.

Gaffin, Richard. *Calvin and the Sabbath: The Controversy of Applying the Fourth Commandment*. Fearn: Mentor, 1997.

Gane, Erwin R. "The Significance of the Apostolic Constitutions and Its Sources for the History of the Early Christian Sabbath." MTh thesis, Andrews University, Seventh-Day Adventist Theological Seminary, 1968.

Gaudemet, Jean, "La législation religieuse de Constantin." *Revue d'histoire de l'Église de France* 33 (1947) 25–61.

Geiermann, Peter. *The Convert's Catechism of Catholic Doctrine*. St. Louis: Herder, 1913.

Geraty, Lawerence T. "The Pascha and the Origin of Sunday Observance." *Andrews University Seminary Studies* 3 (1965) 85–96.

Girardet, Klaus Martin. "Die Konstantinische Wende und ihre Bedeutung für das Reich: Althistorische Überlegungen zu den geistigen Grundlagen der Religionspolitik Konstantins d. Gr." In *Die Konstantinische Wende*, edited by Ekkehard Mühlenberg, 9–122. Gütersloh: Kaiser, 1998.

―――. *Die Konstantinische Wende: Voraussetzungen und geistige Grundlagen der Religionspolitik Konstantins des Grossen*. Darmstadt: Wissenschaftliche Buchgesellschaft, 2006.

―――. "Vom Sonnen-Tag zum Sonntag. Der dies solis in Gesetzgebung und Politik Konstantins d. Gr." *Zeitschrift für antikes Christentum* 11 (2007) 279–310.

Grant, Michael. *Constantine the Great: The Man and his Times*. New York: Scribner's, 1994.

Grant, Robert M. *Augustus to Constantine: The Rise and Triumph of Christianity in the Roman World*. New York: History Book Club, 1993.

―――. "Religion and Politics at the Council of Nicaea." *Journal of Religion* 55 (1975) 1–12.

Gregory of Nazianzus. *Oratio 43*. Edited by Jean Bernardi. SC 384. Paris: Éditions du Cerf, 1992.

―――. *Oration 43*. In *NPNF* 2/7. Online: http://www.ccel.org/ccel/schaff/npnf207.iii. xxvi.html.

Green, Bernard. *Christianity in Ancient Rome*. London: T. & T. Clark, 2010.

Green, Joseph L. *The Power of the Original Church: Turning the World Upside Down*. Shippensburg, PA: Destiny Image, 2011.

Greenslade, S. L. *Church and State from Constantine to Theodosius*. London: Camelot, 1954.

Gross-Albenhausen, Kirsten. "Zur christlichen Selbstdarstellung Konstantins." *Klio* 78 (1996) 171–85.

Gruenewald, Thomas. *Constantinus Maximus Augustus: Herrschaftspropaganda in der zeitgenössischen Überlieferung.* Historia, Einzelschriften 64. Stuttgart: Steiner, 1990.

Guder, Darrell. "Defining and Describing 'Mission.'" In *MissionShift: Global Mission Issues in the Third Millenium,* edited by David J. Hesselgrave and Ed Stetzer, 51–61. Nashville: B. & H. Academic, 2010.

Gurgel, Richard L. "In the Cross Hairs: The Sabbath Day." *WELS, Forward in Christ* 90, no. 6 (2003). Online: http://www.wels.net/news-events/forward-in-christ/june-2003/in-cross-hairs-sabbath-day.

Guy, Fritz. "The Lord's Day in the Letter of Ignatius to the Magnesians." *Andrews University Seminary Studies* 2 (1964) 1–17.

Gwynn, David M. *The Eusebians: The Polemic of Athanasius of Alexandria and the Construction of the "Arian Controversy."* Oxford: Oxford University Press, 2007.

Habicht, Christian. "Zur Geschichte des Kaisers Konstantin." *Hermes* 86, no. 3 (1958) 360–78.

Hall, Stuart, G. "Ecclesiology forged in the wake of persecution." In *The Cambridge History of Christianity,* edited by Margaret M. Mitchell and Frances M. Young, 1:470–83. Cambridge: Cambridge University Press, 2006.

Hanson, R. P. C. *The Search for the Christian Doctrine of God: The Arian Controversy, 318–81.* London: T. & T. Clark, 1988.

Harrison, Evelyn B. "The Constantinian Portrait." *Dumbarton Oaks Papers* 21 (1967) 79–96.

Hartog, Paul. "The Complexity and Variety of Contemporary Church—Early Church Engagements." In *The Contemporary Church and the Early Church: Case Studies in Ressourcement,* edited by Paul A. Hartog, 1–26. Eugene, OR: Pickwick, 2010.

———. "Religious Liberty and the Early Church." *Detroit Baptist Seminary Journal* 17 (2012) 63–77.

Hausammann, Susanne. *Alte Kirche.* Vol. 2, *Verfolgungs- und Wendezeit der Kirche: Gemeindeleben in der Zeit der Christenverfolgungen und Konstantinische Wende.* Neukirchen-Vluyn: Neukirchener, 2001.

Hefele, Charles Joseph. *Histoire des conciles d'après les documents originaux.* Translated by H. Leclercq. Paris: Letouzey et Ané, 1907–1952.

Heschel, Abraham Joshua. *The Sabbath: Its Meaning for Modern Man.* New York: Farrar, Straus & Young, 1951.

"Historians and Church Authorities Tell Us Where Sunday Sacredness Came From." The Seventh-Day Sabbath, n.d. Online: http://www.seventh-day.org/historians.htm.

Hollerich, Michael J. *Eusebius of Caesarea's Commentary on Isaiah.* Oxford: Clarendon, 1999.

Holloway, R. Ross. *Constantine and Rome.* New Haven: Yale University Press, 2004.

Holman, Susan. *The Hungry are Dying: Beggars and Bishops in Roman Cappadocia.* Oxford: Oxford University Press, 2001.

Hough, J. N. *Who Changed the Sabbath? The Pope, Constantine, or God?* Colton, CA: published by the author, [1993?].

Hullquist, C. Gary. *Sabbath Diagnosis: A Diagnostic History and Physical Examination of the Biblical Day of Rest.* Brushton, NY: Teach Services, 2004.

Humphries, Mark. "From Usurper to Emperor: The Politics of Legitimation in the Age of Constantine." *Journal of Late Antiquity* 1, no. 1 (2008) 82–100.

Irvin, Dale T., and Scott W. Sunquist. *History of the World Christian Movement: Earliest Christianity to 1453.* Maryknoll, NY: Orbis, 2001.

Bibliography

Jackson-McCabe, Matt A., editor. *Jewish Christianity Reconsidered: Rethinking Ancient Groups and Texts.* Minneapolis: Fortress, 2007.

Jerome. *De Viris illustribus liber.* Edited by Ernest Cushing Richardson. *TU* 14, Leipzig, n.p., 1896.

Jewett, Paul King. *The Lord's Day: A Theological Guide to the Christian Day of Worship.* Grand Rapids: Eerdmans, 1971.

John Chrysostom. *Contra Judaeos et gentiles quod Christus sit deus. PG* 48. Paris, 1862: 813–43.

———. *In epistulam ii ad Corinthios (homiliae 1–30). PG* 61:381–610. Paris, 1862.

Jones, A. H. M. *Constantine and the Conversion of Europe.* London: English Universities Press, 1948.

Jones, A. H. M., and T. C. Skeat. "Notes on the Genuineness of the Constantinian Documents in Eusebius' Life of Constantine." *Journal of Ecclesiastical History* 5 (1954) 196–200.

Kahlos, Maijastina. "The Rhetoric of Tolerance and Intolerance: from Lactantius to Firmicus Maternus." In *Continuity and Discontinuity in Early Christian Apologetics,* edited by Jörg Ulrich, Anders-Christian Jacobsen, and Maijastina Kahlos, 79–96. New York: Lang, 2009.

Kaufman, Peter I. "Donatism Revisited: Moderates and Militants in Late Antique North Africa." *Journal of Late Antiquity* 2, no. 1 (2009) 131–42.

Kendeffy, Gábor. "Lactantius on the Function of the Two Ways." *Studia Patristica* 46 (2010) 39–44.

Kent, Keri Wyatt. *Rest: Living in Sabbath Simplicity.* Grand Rapids: Zondervan, 2008.

Kersten, Nicholas. "Seventh Day Baptists Occupy Unique Part of Baptist Tradition." *Baptist World* 59 (2012) 29.

Kraft, Robert A. "Some Notes on Sabbath Observance in Early Christianity." *Andrews University Seminary Studies* 3 (1965) 18–33.

Krautheimer, Richard. "The Ecclesiastical Building Policy of Constantine." In *Costantino Il Grande: dall'antichità all'umanesimo,* edited by G. Bonamente and F. Fusco, 509–52. Rome: E. G. L. E., 1993.

Kreider, Alan. *The Change of Conversion and the Origin of Christendom.* Eugene, OR: Wipf & Stock, 2007.

Kreider, Alan, and Eleanor Kreider. *Worship and Mission After Christendom.* Scottdale, PA: Herald, 2011.

Kriegbaum, Bernhard. *Kirche der Traditoren oder Kirche der Martyrer.* Innsbruck, Austria: Tyrolia, 1986.

Lactantius. *De mortibus persecutorum.* Edited and translated by J. L. Creed. Oxford Early Christian Studies. Oxford: Oxford University Press, 1984.

———. *De mortibus persecutorum.* Edited by Samuel Brandt and Georg Laubmann. *CSEL* 27. 1890–1897. Reprint, New York: Tempsky, 1965.

———. *Divinae institutiones.* Edited by Samuel Brandt and Georg Laubmann. *CSEL* 19. 1890–1897. Reprint, New York: Tempsky, 1965.

———. *On the Manner in which the Persecutors Died* and *Divine Institutes.* Translated by William Fletcher. In *ANF* 7, edited by Robert Alexander et al., 301–22; 9–223. Peabody, MA: Hendrickson, 1999.

———. *The Minor Works.* Translated by Mary Francis McDonald. *FC* 54 Washington, DC: Catholic University Press of America, 1965.

Lancel, Serge. "Les débuts du Donatisme: la date du 'protocole de Cirta' et de l'élection episcopale de Silvanus." *Revue des etudes augustiniennes* 25 (1979) 217–29.

Lee, Francis Nigel. *The Covenantal Sabbath*. London: Lord's Day Observance Society, 1974. Online: http://www.dr-fnlee.org/docs3/covsab/Covsab_TOC.html.

Leeb, Rudolf. *Konstantin und Christus: Die Verchristlichung der imperialen Repräsentation unter Konstantin dem Grossen als Spiegel siener Kirchenpolitik und seines Selbstverständnisses als christlicher Kaiser.* Berlin: de Gruyter, 1992.

Leithart, Peter. *Defending Constantine*. Downers Grove, IL: InterVarsity, 2010.

Lenski, Noel. "The Reign of Constantine." In *The Cambridge Companion to the Age of Constantine*, edited by Noel Lenski, 59–90. Cambridge: Cambridge University Press, 2006.

Leontius of Neapolis. *Vita Joannis Eleemosynarii episcopi Alexandrini*. Edited by A.-J. Festugière and L. Rydén. Bibliothèque archéologique et historique 95. Paris: Geuthner, 1974.

Lewis, Abram Herbert. *Paganism Surviving in Christianity*. New York: Putnam's Sons, 1892.

Lewis, Richard B. "Ignatius and the 'Lord's Day.'" *Andrews University Seminary Studies* 6 (1968) 49–59.

———. *The Protestant Dilemma: How to Achieve Unity in a Completed Reformation.* Mountain View, CA: Pacific, 1961.

Lienhard, Joseph T. *Contra Marcellum: Marcellus of Ancyra and Fourth-Century Theology.* Washington, DC: Catholic University of America Press, 1999.

Lieu, Samuel N. C., and Dominic Montserrat, editors. *Constantine: History, Historiography, and Legend.* London: Routledge, 2002.

Liftin, Bryan M. "Eusebius on Constantine: Truth and Hagiography at the Milvian Bridge." *Journal of the Evangelical Theological Society* 55, no. 4 (2012) 773–92.

Llewelyn, S. R. "The Use of Sunday for Meetings of Believers in the New Testament,. *Novum Testamentum* 43 (2001) 205–223.

Lohse, Eduard. "Sabbath." In *Theological Dictionary of the New Testament*, edited by Gerhard Kittel et al., 7:9. Grand Rapids: Eerdmans, 1964.

Luther, Martin. *Der Brief an die Römer. D. Martin Luthers Werke. Kritische Gesamtausgabe* 56. Weimar: Böhlaus, 1938.

MacCarty, Skip. "The Seventh-Day Sabbath." In *Perspectives on the Sabbath: Four Views*, edited by Christopher John Donato, 9–72. Nashville: B. & H. Academic, 2011.

MacMullen, Ramsay. *Christianity and Paganism in the Fourth to Eighth Centuries*. New Haven: Yale University Press, 1999.

———. *Christianizing the Roman Empire (A.D. 100–400)*. New Haven: Yale University Press, 1984.

———. *Constantine*. New York: Dial, 1969.

Markus, R. A. *Christianity in the Roman World*. New York: Scribner's 1974.

Maxwell, C. Mervyn. "Early Sabbath-Sunday History." In *Sourcebook for the History of Sabbath and Sunday*, edited by C. Mervyn Maxwell and P. Gerard Damsteegt, 136–161. Berrien Springs, MI: Seventh-Day Adventist Theological Seminary, 1992.

Maxwell, Stanley M. "From Sabbath to Sunday: The Explosive Reawakening of Sabbath Worship in Reformation England that Spread World-Wide." MDiv thesis, Andrews University, Seventh-Day Adventist Theological Seminary, 2001.

————. "Sabbath and Sunday: Views, Attitudes, and Practices in the Early Church." Unpublished paper, Andrews University, Seventh-Day Adventist Theological Seminary, 2001.

McKay, Heather A. *Sabbath and Synagogue: The Question of Sabbath Worship in Ancient Judaism.* Leiden: Brill, 1994.

McQuilkin, Robertson. *An Introduction to Biblical Ethics.* Wheaton, IL: Tyndale, 1995.

Modéran, Yves. "La conversion de Constantin et la christianisation de l'empire romain." In *Conférence pour la Régionale de l'APHG en juin 2001.* Online : http://aphgcaen.free.fr/conferences/moderan.htm.

Moffet, Samuel. *A History of Christianity in Asia: Beginnings to 1500.* Maryknoll, NY: Orbis, 1998.

Moreau, Jacques, editor. *Lactance: De la mort des persécuteurs.* 2 vols. *Sources chrétiennes* 39. Paris: Cerf, 1954.

Moreau, A. Scott, et al. *Introducing World Missions: A Biblical, Historical, and Practical Survey.* Grand Rapids: Baker Academic, 2004.

Morgan-Cole, Trudy J. "Christ or Constantine: Whom Will You Join?" *Adventist Review* (2003) 12.

Morrison, Michael. "Sabbath and Sunday in Early Christianity." Online: http://www.gci.org/law/sabbath/history1.

————. *Sabbath, Circumcision, and Tithing: Which Old Testament Laws Apply to Christians?* Lincoln, NE: iUniverse, 2002.

Moule, C. F. D. *The Birth of the New Testament.* San Francisco: Harper & Row, 1982.

Muller, Wayne. *Sabbath: Finding Rest, Renewal, and Delight in our Busy Lives.* New York: Bantam, 2000.

Naylor, C. W. *Did Constantine Change the Sabbath?* Anderson, IN: Gospel Trumpet Company, n.d.

Neill, Stephen. *A History of Christian Missions.* London: Penguin, 1991.

Neumann, Michael D. "Enjoy Your Sabbath Rest (Mark 2:23–28)." St. Paul's Lutheran Church (WELS), 2013. Online: http://www.stpaulalex.com/vsItemDisplay.dsp&objectID=BC117B16-75FC-402E-B971A7202E6B38A6&method=display.

Newbigin, Leslie. *The Open Secret: An Introduction to the Theology of Mission.* Grand Rapids: Eerdmans, 1995.

Nicholson, Oliver. "Preparation for Martyrdom in the Early Church." In *The Great Persecution,* edited by D. Vincent Twomey and Mark Humphries, 61–90. Portland: Four Courts, 2009.

Nixon, C. E. V., and Barbara Saylor Rodgers. *In Praise of Later Roman Emperors: The Panegyrici Latini.* Berkeley: University of California Press, 1994.

Noll, Mark A. *Turning Points: Decisive Moments in the History of Christianity.* 3rd ed. Grand Rapids: Baker, 2012.

O'Brien, John A. *The Faith of Millions: The Credentials of the Catholic Religion.* Huntington, IN: Our Sunday Visitor, 1974.

Odahl, Charles M. *Constantine and the Christian Empire.* 2nd ed. London: Routledge, 2010.

Oden, Thomas C. *Early Libyan Christianity: Uncovering a North African Tradition.* Downers Grove, IL: InterVarsity, 2011.

Odom, Robert L. "Pagan Sunday Observance." *The Ministry* 23 (1950) 18–19. Online: https://www.ministrymagazine.org/archive/1950/May/pagan-sunday-observance.

————. *Sabbath and Sunday in Early Christianity*. Washington, DC: Review & Herald, 1977.

Optatus of Milevis. *Against the Donatists* (with Appendices). Translated by O.R. Vassall-Phillips. London: Longmans, 1917. Online: http://tertullian.org/fathers/index. htm#Against_the_Donatists.

"Palladus." In *Anthologia Graeca*. Edited by H. Beckby. 4 vols. 2nd ed. Munich: Heimeran, 1965–1968.

Philostorgius. *Historia ecclesiastica*. Edited by F. Winkelmann. 3rd ed. *GCS* 21. Berlin: Akademie, 1981.

Pipa, Joseph A. "The Christian Sabbath." In *Perspectives on the Sabbath: Four Views*, edited by Christopher John Donato, 119–271. Nashville: B. & H. Academic, 2011.

————. *The Lord's Day*. Fearn: Christian Focus, 1997.

————. "Response to Craig L. Blomberg." In *Perspectives on the Sabbath: Four Views*, edited by Christopher John Donato, 374–87. Nashville: B. & H. Academic, 2011.

Pohlsander, Hans A. *The Emperor Constantine*. London: Routledge, 2004.

Porvaznik, Philip. "Emperor Constantine: Pagan, Christian, or First Pope?" Online: http://www.philvaz.com/apologetics/ConstantinePaganChristian.htm.

Potter, David S. *Constantine the Emperor*. New York: Oxford University Press, 2013.

Rapp, Claudia. "Imperial Ideology in the Making: Eusebius of Caesarea on Constantine as 'Bishop.'" *Journal of Theological Studies* 49, no. 2 (1998) 685–95.

Ray, Bruce A. *Celebrating the Sabbath: Finding Rest in a Restless World*. Phillipsburg, NJ: Protestant & Reformed, 2000.

Rebenich, Stefan. "Vom dreizehnten Gott zum dreizehnten Apostel? Der tote Kaiser in der Spätantike." *Zeitschrift für antikes Christentum* 4 (2000) 300–324.

Reimer, James A. "Constantine: From Religious Pluralism to Christian Hegemony." In *Future of Religion*, edited by Michael R. Ott, 69–90. Leiden: Brill, 2007.

Ricciltti, Giuseppe. *The Age of the Martyrs: Christianity from Diocletian to Constantine*. Milwaukee: Bruce, 1959.

Riggle, H. M. *The Sabbath and the Lord's Day*. Anderson, IN: Gospel Trumpet, 1928.

Ritter, Adolf Martin. "Constantin und die Christen." *Zeitschrift für die neutestamentliche Wissenschaft und die Kunde der älteren Kirche* 87 (1996) 251–68.

Robert, Dana. *Christian Mission: How Christianity Became a World Religion*. West Sussex, UK: Wiley-Blackwell, 2009.

Roldanus, Johannes. *The Church in the Age of Constantine: The Theological Challenges*. London: Routledge, 2006.

Roll, Susan K. "The Origins of Christmas: The State of the Question." In *Between Memory and Hope: Readings on the Liturgical Year*, edited by Maxwell E. Johnson, 273–290. Collegeville, MN: Liturgical, 2000.

Rordorf, Willy. *Sunday: The History of the Day of Rest and Worship in the Earliest Centuries of the Christian Church*. Translated by A. A. K. Graham. Philadelphia: Westminster, 1968.

Rousseau, Philip. *Basil of Caesarea*. Berkley: University of California Press, 1998.

Rouwhorst, Gerard. "Jewish Liturgical Traditions in Early Syriac Christianity." *Vigiliae Christianae* 51 (1997) 72–93.

————. "The Reception of the Jewish Sabbath in Early Christianity." In *Christian Feast and Festival: The Dynamics of Western Liturgy and Culture*, edited by Paulus Gijsbertus Johannes Post et al., 223–66. Leuven: Peeters, 2001.

Bibliography

Rufinus. *Apologia contra Ieronymum.* Edited by P. Lardet. *CCSL* 79. Turnholt: Brepols, 1982.

———. *The Church History of Rufinus of Aquileia.* Translated by Philip R. Amidon. Oxford: University Press, 1997.

Ruhbach, Gerhard. *Die Kirche angesichts der Konstantinischen Wende.* Wege der Forschung 306. Darmstadt: Wissenschaftliche Buchgesellschaft, 1976.

Rusch, William G., editor. *The Trinitarian Controversy.* Philadelphia: Fortress, 1980.

Sanford, Robert. "Constantine's Council of Nicea and the Effect It Had on the Ten Commandments." Online: http://bobsstudies.tripod.com/constanstine/.

"Saturday (Sabbath) or First Day?" Online: http://www.bible.ca/H-sunday.htm.

Saunders, Herbert E. *The Sabbath: Symbol of Creation and Re-Creation.* Plainfield, NJ: American Sabbath Tract Society, 1970.

Schaff, Philip. *History of the Christian Church.* New York: Scribner's, 1910.

Schreven, Leo Anthony. *Now That's Clear: Prophetic Truth Made Simple.* College Place, WA: Color, 1997.

Schwartz, Eduard. *Zur Geschichte des Athanasius. Gesammelte Schriften.* Vol. 3. Berlin: de Gruyter, 1959.

Searle, Mark. "Sunday: The Heart of the Liturgical Year." In *Between Memory and Hope: Readings on the Liturgical Year*, edited by Maxwell E. Johnson, 59–76. Collegeville, MN: Liturgical, 2000.

Shelton, W. Brian. Review of *The Making of a Christian Empire: Lactantius and Rome*, by Elizabeth DePalma Digeser. *Journal of Greco-Roman Christianity and Judaism* 8 (2012) 164–67.

Shepherd, Massey H. "Liturgical Expressions of the Constantinian Triumph." *Dumbarton Oaks Papers* 21 (1967) 57–78.

Shigley, Gordon. "Historical Review of Sabbath Keeping among Early Christians," Online: http://www.sduame.com/Sabbath/SabbathHistory.htm.

Silli, Paolo. *Testi costantiniani nelle fonti letterarie. Materiali per una palingenesi delle costituzioni tardo-imperiali* 3. Milano: Giuffrè, 1987.

Simonetti, Manlio. *La Crisi Ariana nel IV Secolo.* Rome: Institutum Patristicum Augustinianum, 1975.

Smith, Andrew. "Philosophical Objections to Christianity on the Eve of the Great Persecution." In *The Great Persecution*, edited by D. Vincent Twomey and Mark Humphries, 33–48. Portland: Four Courts, 2009.

Smither, Edward L. "Augustine, a Missionary to Heretics? An Appraisal of Augustine's Missional Engagement with the Donatists." In *In Africa There Are Dissensions*, edited by Matthew Gaumer and Anthony DuPont. Leuven: Peeters (forthcoming).

———. "Basil of Caesarea: An Early Christian Model of Urban Mission." In *Reaching the City: Reflections on Urban Mission for the Twenty-first Century*, edited by Gary Fujino et al., 77–95. Pasadena, CA: William Carey Library, 2012.

Socrates. *Historia ecclesiastica.* Edited by P. Maraval and P. Périchon. *SC* 477. Paris: Cerf, 2004.

Socrates, Sozomenus: Church Histories. In *NPNF* 2/2, edited by Phillip Schaff and Henry Wace. New York: Christian Literature, 1890.

Staehelin, Felix. "Constantin der Grosse und das Christentum." *Zeitschrift für schweizerische Geschichte* 17 (1937) 385–417.

Stephenson, Paul. *Constantine: Roman Emperor, Christian Victor.* New York: Overlook, 2010.

Stead, G. C. "Eusebius and the Council of Nicaea." *Journal of Theological Studies* 24 (1973) 85–100.

Sterk, Andrea. "Captive Women and Heretical Monks: Reassessing Christianization on the East Roman Frontiers." *Historically Speaking* 8, no. 5 (2007) 21–23.

———. "Mission from Below: Captive Women and Conversion on the Eastern Frontiers." *Church History* 79, no. 1 (2010) 1–39.

———. *Renouncing the World Yet Leading the Church: The Monk-Bishop in Late Antiquity.* Cambridge, MA: Harvard University Press, 2004.

———. "'Representing' Mission from Below: Historians as Interpreters and Agents of Christianization." *Church History* 79, no. 2 (2010) 271–304.

Stewart-Sykes, Alistair. "The Seating of Polycarp at *Vita Polycarpi*: A Liturgy of Scholastic Christianity in the Third Century," *Studia Patristica* 35 (2001) 323–29.

Strand, Kenneth A. "From Sabbath to Sunday in the Early Christian Church: A Review of Some Recent Literature, Part I: Willy Rordorf's Reconstruction." *Andrews University Seminary Studies* 16 (1978) 333–42.

———. "From Sabbath to Sunday in the Early Christian Church: A Review of Some Recent Literature, Part II: Samuele Bacchiocchi's Reconstruction." *Andrews University Seminary Studies* 17 (1979) 85–104.

———. "The Sabbath and Sunday from the Second through Fifth Centuries." In *The Sabbath in Scripture and History*, edited by Kenneth A. Strand, 323–32. Washington, DC: Review & Herald, 1982.

———. "Some Notes on the Sabbath Fast in Early Christianity." *Andrews University Seminary Studies* 3 (1965) 167–74.

———. "Sunday in the Early Church." *The Ministry* 50 (1977) 11–15. Online: https://www.ministrymagazine.org/archive/1977/January/sabbath-and-sunday-observance-in-the-early-church.

———. "Tertullian and the Sabbath." *Andrews University Seminary Studies* 9 (1971) 129–46.

Strand, Kenneth A., editor. *The Sabbath in Scripture and History.* Washington, DC: Review & Herald, 1982.

Straub, Johannes. "Constantine as ΚΟΙΝΟΣ ΕΠΙΣΚΟΠΟΣ: Tradition and Innovation in the Representation of the First Christian Emperor's Majesty." *Dumbarton Oaks Papers* 21 (1967) 37–55.

———. "Konstantins Verzicht auf den Gang zum Kapitol." *Historia: Zeitschrift für alte Geschichte* 4 (1955) 297–313.

Strutwolf, Holger. *Die Trinitätstheologie und Christologie des Euseb von Caesarea: Eine Dogmengeschichte Untersuchung seiner Platonismusrezeption und Wirkungsgeschichte.* Göttingen: Vandenhoeck & Ruprecht, 1999.

"Sunday—The Perfect Deception." *The Sunday Deception.* Online: http://www.markofbeast.net/sunday-deception.html.

Swartley, Willard M. *Sabbath, Slavery, War and Women: Case Studies in Biblical Interpretation.* Scottsdale, PA: Herald, 1983.

Tanner, Norman P., editor. *Decrees of the Ecumenical Councils.* 2 vols. London: Sheed & Ward, 1990.

Talley, Thomas J. "Constantine and Christmas." In *In Between Memory and Hope: Readings on the Liturgical Year*, edited by Maxwell E. Johnson, 265–72. Collegeville, MN: Liturgical, 2000.

Tennent, Timothy. *Invitation to World Missions: A Trinitarian Missiology for the Twenty-first Century.* Grand Rapids: Kregel Academic, 2010.

Bibliography

Tertullian. *On Prayer.* In *ANF* 3, edited by Robert Alexander et al. Peabody, MA: Hendrickson, 1999.

The Testament of our Lord. Translated by James Cooper and Arthur John Maclean. Edinburgh: T. & T. Clark, 1902.

Theodoret. *Historia ecclesiastica.* Edited by F. Scheidweiler. 2nd ed. *GCS* 44. Berlin: Akademie, 1954.

Theodoret, Jerome, Gennadius, Rufinus: Historical Writings, etc. In *NPNF* 2/3, edited by Phillip Schaff and Henry Wace. New York: Christian Literature Publishing Company, 1892.

Tilley, Maureen A. *The Bible in Christian North Africa: The Donatist World.* Minneapolis: Fortress 1997.

———. *Donatist Martyr Stories: The Church in Conflict in North Africa.* Liverpool: Liverpool University Press, 1996.

———. "North Africa." In *The Cambridge History of Christianity*, edited by Margaret M. Mitchell and Frances M. Young, 1:381–96. Cambridge: Cambridge University Press, 2006.

———. "When Schism Becomes Heresy." *Journal of Early Christian Studies* 15, no. 1 (2007) 1–21.

Triglot Concordia: The Symbolical Books of the Evangelical Lutheran Church: German-Latin-English. St. Louis: Concordia, 1921.

Ulrich, Jörg, et al. *Continuity and Discontinuity in Early Christian Apologetics.* New York: Lang, 2009.

Van Dam, Raymond. *Remembering Constantine at the Milvian Bridge.* Cambridge: Cambridge University Press, 2011.

———. *The Roman Revolution of Constantine.* Cambridge, New York: Cambridge University Press, 2007.

Vanderark, August Morrow. "Constantine's Edict of Milan and its Influence upon the Christianity of its Day." BDiv thesis, Northern Baptist Theological Seminary, 1952.

Veith, Walter J. "Constantine and the Sabbath Change." Amazing Discoveries, April 23, 2010. Online: http://amazingdiscoveries.org/S-deception-Sabbath_change_Constantine.

Veyne, Paul. *When Our World Became Christian, 312–394.* Translated by Janet Lloyd. Cambridge, Malden, MA: Polity, 2010.

Walker, Peter W. L. *Holy City, Holy Places? Christian Attitudes to Jerusalem and the Holy Land in the Fourth Century.* Oxford: Clarendon, 1990.

Wallace-Hadrill, D. S. *Eusebius of Caesarea.* London: Mowbray, 1960.

Wallraff, Martin. "Constantine's Devotion to the Sun after 324." *Studia Patristica* 34 (2001) 256–69.

Wardner, Nathan. *Constantine and the Sunday.* Alfred Centre, NY: American Sabbath Tract Society, n.d.

———. *The Lord's Day, or, Christian Sabbath.* Glasgow: n.p., 1877.

Weiss, Herold. "The Sabbath in the Writings of Josephus." *Journal for the Study of Judaism* 29 (1998) 363–90.

Weiss, Peter. "Die Vision Constantins." In *Colloquium aus Anlass des 80. Geburtstages von Alfred Heuss*, edited by Jochen Bleicken, 143–69. Kalmünz: Lassleben, 1993.

White, Ellen G. *The Great Controversy Between Christ and Satan During the Christian Dispensation.* Oakland: Pacific, 1888.

———. *The Spirit of Prophecy.* Oakland: Pacific, 1885.

Wilken, Robert Louis. "In Defense of Constantine." *First Things* 112 (2001) 36–40.

———. *The Spirit of Early Christian Thought: Seeking the Face of God.* New Haven: Yale University Press, 2003.

Wilkinson, Kevin W. "Palladas and the Age of Constantine." *Journal of Roman Studies* 99 (2009) 36–60.

Williams, Rowan. *Arius: Heresy and Tradition.* Grand Rapids: Eerdmans, 2002.

Wilson, Nate. "Principles for Observing Sabbath as Christians." Sermon, Christ the Redeemer Church, Manhattan, KS, 13 May 2012. Online: http://www.natewilsonfamily.net/sabbath2.htm.

Winkelmann, Friedhelm. "Die 'Konstantinische Wende' und ihre Bedeutung für die Kirche." In *Die Konstantinische Wende*, edited by Ekkehard Mühlenbergm, 123–43. Gütersloh: Kaiser, 1998.

———. *Die Textbezeugung der Vita Constantini des Eusebius von Caesarea.* Texte und Unterzuchungen zur Geschichte der altchristlichen Literatur 84. Berlin: Akademie, 1962.

———. "Zur Geschichte des Authentizitäts problems der Vita Konstantini." *Klio* 40 (1962) 187–243.

Woolf, Sarah. "Seeing Apollo in Roman Gaul and Germany." In *Roman Imperialism and Provincial Art*, edited by Sarah Scott and Jane Webster, 139–152. Cambridge: Cambridge University Press, 2003.

Wortley, John. "The 'Sacred Remains' of Constantine and Helena." In "Byzantine Narrative: Papers in Honour of Roger Scott," edited by J. Burke, special issue, *Byzantina Australiensia* 16 (2006)351–67.

Wright, Christopher. *The Mission of God: Unlocking the Bible's Grand Narrative.* Downers Grove, IL: InterVarsity, 2006.

Wynne, Kerry. "Lying for God." 2010. Online: http://www.bible.ca/7-lying-for-god-Kerry-Wynne.htm.

Wyss, Johann David. *The Swiss Family Robinson.* Translated by William H. G. Kingston. LaVergne, TN: Simon & Brown, 2012.

Young, N. H. "The Use of Sunday for Meetings of Believers in the New Testament: A Response." *Novum Testamentum* 45 (2003) 111–22.

XII Panegyrici latini. Edited by R. A. B. Mynors. Oxford: Clarendon, 1964.

Index